D0742155

More Kinds of Being

E. J. LOWE

MORE KINDS OF BEING

A Further Study of
Individuation,
Identity, and the
Logic of Sortal Terms

WILEY-BLACKWELL

A John Wiley & Sons, Ltd., Publication

This second edition first published 2009

© 2009 E. J. Lowe

Edition history: Basil Blackwell Ltd (1e, *Kinds of Being*, 1989)

Blackwell Publishing was acquired by John Wiley & Sons in February 2007. Blackwell's publishing program has been merged with Wiley's global Scientific, Technical, and Medical business to form Wiley-Blackwell.

Registered Office
John Wiley & Sons Ltd, The Atrium, Southern Gate, Chichester, West Sussex, PO19 8SQ, United Kingdom

Editorial Offices
350 Main Street, Malden, MA 02148-5020, USA

9600 Garsington Road, Oxford, OX4 2DQ, UK

The Atrium, Southern Gate, Chichester, West Sussex, PO19 8SQ, UK

For details of our global editorial offices, for customer services, and for information about how to apply for permission to reuse the copyright material in this book please see our website at www.wiley.com/wiley-blackwell.

The right of E. J. Lowe to be identified as the author of this work has been asserted in accordance with the Copyright, Designs and Patents Act 1988.

Library of Congress Cataloging-in-Publication Data

Lowe, E. J. (E. Jonathan)
  More kinds of being : a further study of individuation, identity, and the logic of sortal terms / E. J. Lowe. -- [New, expanded ed.].
    p. cm.
  Includes bibliographical references and index.
  ISBN 978-1-4051-8256-0 (hardcover : alk. paper)   1. Identity (Philosophical concept)
2. Individuation (Philosophy)   3. Mind and body.   4. Logic.   5. Language and languages–Philosophy.   I. Title.
BC199.I4L69 2009
126–dc22

                                                                    2009020889

A catalogue record for this book is available from the British Library.

Set in 10/12pt Plantin by Graphicraft Limited, Hong Kong
Printed and bound in Malaysia by Vivar Printing Sdn Bhd

1   2009

Contents

Preface

In 1989, my book *Kinds of Being: A Study of Individuation, Identity, and the Logic of Sortal Terms* was published by Blackwell in the Aristotelian Society monograph series. The book received quite favourable reviews, including one by Peter Simons in *Mind* and another by Harold Noonan in *Philosophy*, and it has subsequently been referred to by numerous other authors in books and journals. In the latter part of the 1990s the book went out of print and copies of it have been increasingly difficult to obtain, even though the frequency of references to it has not diminished. For this reason alone, a case could be made out for bringing out a second edition. However, it would have been a missed opportunity to let such a second edition of the book differ from the first only in respect of a few minor revisions to the text and an updating of references. Apart from anything else, my views on a number of topics dealt with in the book have developed in quite major ways since 1989, some of these developments being reflected in various later articles and books of mine, but especially in my *The Possibility of Metaphysics: Substance, Identity, and Time* (Oxford: Clarendon Press, 1998) and *The Four-Category Ontology: A Metaphysical Foundation for Natural Science* (Oxford: Clarendon Press, 2006). See also my chapter 'Individuation', in M. J. Loux and D. W. Zimmerman (eds), *The Oxford Handbook of Metaphysics* (Oxford: Clarendon Press, 2003).

Perhaps the most important of these developments was my conversion to what I call 'the four-category ontology', a metaphysical system that draws its inspiration from Aristotle and maintains that there are four fundamental ontological categories – (1) substantial individuals, (2) substantial universals or 'kinds', (3) attributive universals, and (4) particularized properties or 'modes'. In effect, the first edition of *Kinds of Being* was explicitly committed only to the first and second of these categories and implicitly to the third. It recognized no place for what I call *modes* and other philosophers nowadays commonly call 'tropes' – that is, properties conceived as particulars rather than universals, such as the individual whiteness of a particular piece of white marble. There is very little in the first edition of *Kinds of Being* that I now consider to be positively *mistaken*, but there is a good deal that warranted careful reworking to bring it into line with my current metaphysical opinions and to make it a more useful resource for readers of my later books, especially *The Four-Category Ontology*. For example, in *The Four-Category Ontology* I do not devote much discussion to what I call 'sortal logic' (only part of Chapter 4), crucial though this is for a proper understanding of my account of natural laws and dispositions. Rather, I refer the reader to my extensive treatment of this topic in *Kinds of Being*. However, because the ontology of *Kinds of Being* is not the fully fledged four-category ontology of my later work, readers who do turn to it for this purpose are in danger of being confused.

Kinds of Being merited not only extensive reworking, but also some expansion. In particular, there are two closely related topics that are underdeveloped in the first edition of the book but which deserve fuller treatment, in line with later work of mine on these topics. The topics in question are those of *number* and *plurality* (including plural quantification). In a paper published in 1991, 'Noun Phrases, Quantifiers, and Generic Names', *Philosophical Quarterly* 41, pp. 287–300, I offer reasons for thinking that the apparent reference of sortal terms to *kinds* cannot be explained away in terms of plural quantification over individuals, thereby filling a gap in my argument, in *Kinds of Being*, in favour of such reference being genuine. In another paper published in 2003, 'Identity, Individuality, and Unity', *Philosophy* 78, pp. 321–36, I compare Locke's view of number with Frege's, coming down more in favour of the former than of the latter. Since issues concerning number and issues concerning identity are intimately related, and Locke's and Frege's positions concerning the latter are extensively discussed in the first edition of *Kinds of Being*, it was appropriate to augment the book with a chapter on the topic of number, since there is no extended treatment of this in the first edition. Thus the revised version of the book contains twelve chapters instead of just ten, the two new chapters drawing on and further developing the ideas first presented in the articles just mentioned. Here I should also remark that, while I do discuss number in both *The Possibility of Metaphysics* and *The Four-Category Ontology*, I have significantly new things to say on the topic in the additional chapter concerning it.

Another, albeit lesser, change to the book concerns its discussion of *criteria of identity*. In the same year in which *Kinds of Being* was published, 1989, a paper of mine entitled 'What is a Criterion of Identity?' appeared in *Philosophical Quarterly* 39, pp. 1–21. This paper, which has frequently been cited, contains a much fuller discussion of certain issues that were touched upon only briefly in the relevant parts of *Kinds of Being*, and since 1989 I have had extensive further thoughts concerning these important issues: see, especially, my 'Objects and Criteria of Identity', in Bob Hale and Crispin Wright (eds), *A Companion to the Philosophy of Language* (Oxford: Blackwell, 1997). It was clearly appropriate to mention some of my latest thinking on these matters in the new version of the book. Although the foregoing is a particularly noteworthy example, there are many other issues discussed in *Kinds of Being* whose treatment was clearly capable of improvement by a substantial reworking in the light of more recent thoughts of mine on the subjects in question, such as the notion of *material constitution* – the relationship that I take to hold between, for instance, a bronze statue and the lump of bronze from which it is fashioned.

There are some distinguished recent precedents for a project of the kind that I have now undertaken – that is, a thorough reworking and expansion of a book, going beyond what is normal for a 'second edition'. I have in mind, in particular, David Wiggins's *Sameness and Substance Renewed* (Cambridge: Cambridge University Press, 2001), his reworking of *Sameness and Substance* (Oxford: Blackwell, 1980), and D. H. Mellor's *Real Time II* (London and New York: Routledge, 1998), his replacement for *Real Time* (Cambridge: Cambridge University Press, 1981). In each case, the gap between the two versions was in the region of twenty years, which is the same in the case of *Kinds of Being* and *More Kinds of Being*. Since Wiggins and Mellor are amongst the philosophers whose work in metaphysics I have always admired the most, I am more than happy to follow their example in this regard. Just as they did, I have retained an echo of the title of the original book in the title of the new version. I thought it particularly appropriate to call the new version *More Kinds of Being*, not only because this version expands upon the work of *Kinds of Being*, but also because it reflects my new commitment to the existence of a kind – in the sense of *category* – of being not recognized in the earlier work, namely, the category of *modes* or tropes. Perhaps, in this regard, I could justly say to my earlier self what Hamlet said to his friend Horatio, 'There are more things in heaven and earth, Horatio, than are dreamt of in [y]our philosophy' (*Hamlet*, act 1, scene 5).

In order to gain a clearer view of the extent of the changes made to *Kinds of Being*, it may be helpful for the reader to compare the original table of contents of *Kinds of Being* with that of *More Kinds of Being*. In the latter, I have marked with an asterisk additional chapters or chapter-sections, as well as the new Preface and Bibliography. Note that Chapter 12 in *More Kinds of Being* covers much the same territory as does the corresponding Chapter 10 of *Kinds of Being*, but has been given a more perspicuous title and is subdivided into two sections. Note also that the new fourth section of the introductory Chapter 1 explains more fully to the reader how and why the new version of the book differs from the old and how the new version relates to other recent work of mine, especially my *The Four-Category Ontology*.

Acknowledgements

In the course of this study I have drawn on material contained in the following previously published articles of mine, and I am grateful to the editors and publishers of the journals and book in which they appeared for permission to re-use this material. Chapter 2 draws partly on my chapter 'Substance' in G. H. R. Parkinson (ed.), *An Encyclopaedia of Philosophy* (London: Routledge, 1988). Chapters 3, 5 and 6 are based partly on 'Instantiation, Identity, and Constitution', *Philosophical Studies* 44 (1983), pp. 45–59, published by D. Reidel Publishing Company, and partly on 'Sortal Terms and Absolute Identity', *Australasian Journal of Philosophy* 64 (1986), pp. 64–71. In addition, some parts of Chapter 6 are drawn from 'The Paradox of the 1,001 Cats', *Analysis* 42 (1982), pp. 27–30, 'Reply to Geach', *Analysis* 42 (1982), p. 31, and 'On Being a Cat', *Analysis* 42 (1982), pp. 174–4. Chapter 4 – which is new to this version of the book – is based on 'Identity, Individuality, and Unity', *Philosophy* 78 (2003), pp. 321–36. Chapter 9 is based on 'Sortal Terms and Natural Laws', *American Philosophical Quarterly* 17 (1980), pp. 253–60, and Chapter 11 on 'Laws, Dispositions, and Sortal Logic', *American Philosophical Quarterly* 19 (1982), pp. 41–50. Chapter 10 – which is again new to this version of the book – is based on 'Noun Phrases, Quantifiers, and Generic Names', *Philosophical Quarterly* 41 (1991), pp. 287–300.

I should like to repeat my thanks to all those who read the manuscript of *Kinds of Being* at various stages of its composition and whose comments and criticisms contributed so greatly to its improvement – above all Jennifer Hornsby, in her role as a member of the Aristotelian Society Monographs Committee. I am also very grateful to the readers who, on behalf of Wiley–Blackwell, commented so helpfully on my proposal to rework the book in its present form. Some of these readers remain anonymous, but I must record a particular debt of gratitude to John Heil, who commented in detail not only on the proposal but also on the penultimate draft. There are in addition many more people than I could hope to list here individually to whom I owe intellectual debts for ideas developed in the course of the book, in both of its versions. Many of these are referred to in the book and cited in the Bibliography. Last but not least, I should mention that the manuscript of this book was completed with support from the Arts and Humanities Research Council's Research Grant AH/F009615/1, 'The New Ontology of the Mental Causation Debate'.

1

Introduction

My aim in this study is to examine a cluster of interrelated issues in metaphysics, logic, and the philosophy of language, a common factor being the importance that I attach to *sortal* concepts in my treatment of these issues.[1] A sortal concept is a concept of a distinct *sort* or *kind* of individuals. Individuals may be either *concrete* (like chairs and people) or *abstract* (like propositions and sets), but my concern in what follows will mostly be with concrete individuals and the kinds to which they belong.[2] Where concrete individuals are concerned, kinds may be *natural* (horses, trees, electrons, and so on) or they may be *artefactual* (tables, books, computers, cities, and so on), although in the present study I place much more emphasis on the former. This stress on the concrete and the natural is motivated by the conviction that entities in this class must enjoy some sort of ontological priority over both abstract and artefactual objects – although the defence of this conviction is not something that I undertake in the ensuing pages.

Sortal concepts are characteristically governed by *criteria of individuation and identity* – metaphysically grounded semantic principles which determine what are to count as individual instances of the sorts or kinds in question and the conditions for their identity or diversity at a time and (where this is appropriate) over time. Criteria of identity may be the same for many closely related sortal concepts – for example, for the concepts of various different kinds of animals – but differ radically for sortal concepts relating to different ontological categories: for instance, for *geological* as opposed

---

[1] The term 'sortal' itself we owe to John Locke: see his *An Essay Concerning Human Understanding*, ed. P. H. Nidditch (Oxford: Clarendon Press, 1975), III, III, 15.

[2] For more on the abstract/concrete distinction, see my 'The Metaphysics of Abstract Objects', *Journal of Philosophy* 92 (1995), pp. 509–24.

to *biological* sortal concepts.[3] Thus I take it to be evident that *mountains* are not governed by the same identity criterion as *mice*. Where two sortal concepts are governed by different criteria of identity, it simply makes no sense to identify an individual falling under one of these concepts with an individual falling under the other.

This is one of the principal claims that I advance in this study, and I defend it in depth against a rival position advocated by adherents of the relativist conception of identity – a conception most famously championed by P. T. Geach.[4] The implications of this claim for metaphysics are profound, especially insofar as it provides a means to block various reductivist strategies, and I shall devote a substantial part of this study to illustrating this in connection with the issues of personal identity and the mind/body problem. I argue that *persons* constitute a distinct sort or kind of entity and are not to be identified with the biological entities in which they are embodied. The position that I defend is not, however, to be confused with any version of Cartesian dualism.[5]

In the final third of the book I examine in detail the semantics and logic of sortal terms in natural language, although inextricably intertwined with this discussion is an account of the place of sortal concepts in the formulation and empirical confirmation of scientific laws and theories. Amongst other things, I maintain that the most satisfactory approach to the semantics of sortal terms (or, at least, of natural kind terms) is to accord them a genuinely referential or name-like role, regarding their referents (sorts or kinds) as *universals* conceived in the manner of 'Aristotelian' or 'immanent' realism. I also urge that scientific law-statements are best interpreted precisely as expressing propositions purporting to concern such 'real' sorts or kinds, and predicating of them properties and relations which attach only derivatively to their individual exemplars or instances. The approach that I recommend in this study is shown to have considerable advantages over more orthodox nominalist and inductivist accounts of scientific laws and scientific method.[6]

[3]   For more on the notion of an ontological category, see my *The Four-Category Ontology: A Metaphysical Foundation for Natural Science* (Oxford: Clarendon Press, 2006), especially Part I.

[4]   See P. T. Geach, *Reference and Generality*, 3rd edn (Ithaca, NY: Cornell University Press, 1980).

[5]   My fullest defences of the position that I now call *non-Cartesian substance dualism* may be found in my *Subjects of Experience* (Cambridge: Cambridge University Press, 1996) and my *Personal Agency: The Metaphysics of Mind and Action* (Oxford: Oxford University Press, 2008).

[6]   Some of these advantages are explained more extensively in my *The Four-Category Ontology*, Part III. However, the logical aspects of my position are developed most fully in the present study, which for that reason alone constitutes an indispensable adjunct to *The Four-Category Ontology*.

Finally, I argue that when it comes to the question of precisely which sorts of things exist, our inquiries must be guided by a judicious mixture of *a priori* metaphysical principle and *a posteriori* scientific theory-construction.[7] Such an approach, I maintain, will entitle us to claim to be 'carving nature at the joints' without pretending to unwarrantable infallibility in such matters.

In most of what remains of this introduction, I shall focus on certain important topics which crop up repeatedly throughout the study, and which accordingly find no concentrated and exhaustive treatment in any one place. Two of these topics are associated with alternative readings of the deliberately ambiguous title of the first version of this book, *Kinds of Being*. On one reading of that phrase, it is intended to convey my wish to defend the thesis that the verb 'to be' has a variety of uses, or may play a variety of different logical roles. On the other reading, it is intended to highlight two other pivotal contentions of this study. The first of these is that particular objects are individuable and identifiable only as particulars of this or that *sort* or *kind* – there are no 'bare particulars'.[8] The second is that the notions of 'individual' and 'kind' are mutually dependent, with neither being in any sense more fundamental than the other – a corollary of which I take to be that individuals and kinds are ontologically on an equal footing, at least in the sense that neither may be reduced to the other, even though their manners of existing may obviously differ.

The Varieties of 'Is'

I distinguish between the following four uses of 'is' as a copula. (1) The 'is' of *attribution*, as in 'Socrates *is* wise' and 'Grass *is* green'. (2) The 'is' of *identity*, as in 'Napoleon *is* Bonaparte' and 'Water *is* H_2O' (at least on one common reading of the latter). (3) The 'is' of *instantiation*, as in 'Mars *is* a planet' and 'A horse *is* a mammal'. And (4) the 'is' of *constitution*, as in 'This ring *is* gold' and 'A human body *is* a collection of cells'. I do not, however, claim that all of these uses of 'is' are equally fundamental from a logical point of view. I regard the 'is' of attribution as being logically

---

[7] This kind of relationship between metaphysics and empirical science is something that I recommend and defend more generally in my *The Possibility of Metaphysics: Substance, Identity, and Time* (Oxford: Clarendon Press, 1998), Chapter 1.

[8] The *Oxford English Dictionary* does not have an entry for 'individuable', nor indeed for the uglier 'individuatable', but such a word is clearly needed. I form the adjective 'individuable' from the verb 'individuate', by analogy with the formation of the adjective 'separable' from the verb 'separate', and from the adjective 'individuable' I form the noun 'individuability'.

redundant, a relatively superficial feature of the English language. As for the 'is' of constitution, I suspect that it, too, is not logically irreducible, although I shall commit myself to no definitive analysis of constitution statements in this study. But the other two uses of 'is' so far mentioned I do consider to be logically primitive, even if for some purposes the 'is' of identity may effectively be defined in terms of the 'is' of instantiation.

Now, this still leaves one other important use of 'is' to which I have not yet alluded: the 'is' of *existence*, as in 'The Dodo *is* no more'. I take this use of 'is' also to be logically primitive, but I do not follow current orthodoxy in identifying its role with that played in symbolic logic by the so-called (but in my view misnamed) existential quantifier, '∃'.[9] That is to say, I do not regard 'is', in the sense of 'exists', as being a *second-level* predicate, although relatively little in this study depends crucially on my taking it to be a first-level one. One thing that I should especially stress in this connection, however, is that I most emphatically do *not* wish the title of this study to convey the impression that I postulate different *kinds of existence*, as opposed merely to different *kinds of thing that exist*. 'Exist' is univocal. This, it should be noted, is not inconsistent with my acceptance, a few moments ago, that individuals and kinds may enjoy different *manners* of existing, for this was not intended to imply any ambiguity in the term 'existence'. Rather, what I intended to accede to was such relatively uncontroversial claims as that concrete individuals exist at specific times and places, whereas kinds, being universals, are not spatiotemporally localized in their existence.

Individuals, Kinds, and Realism

As I have just said, I hold that there are no 'bare' particulars, only individual instances or exemplars of certain sorts or kinds – *tokens* of certain *types*, in another terminology. No doubt lip service is customarily paid to this thesis by many if not most modern philosophers, but I do not think that its far-reaching implications are even yet sufficiently appreciated by more than a few. I also hold, as a corollary of this thesis, that the notions of an 'individual' and of a 'sort' or 'kind' are opposite sides of a single conceptual coin: each is understandable only in terms of the other. Individuals are necessarily individuals *of a kind*, and kinds are necessarily kinds *of individuals*. In consequence, I maintain that realism with regard to individuals, or particular objects – the belief, in my opinion correct, that they may exist independently of the human or indeed any other mind – implies

[9] This is a point on which I have changed my mind since the publication of *Kinds of Being* in 1989. I explain why in Chapter 4 below.

realism with regard to sorts or kinds. I cannot, then, accept John Locke's famous contention that 'All Things, that exist, [are] Particulars' and that '*General and Universal*, belong not to the real existence of Things; but *are the Inventions and Creatures of the Understanding*'.[10]

Realism with regard to sorts need not, however, be unqualified. Perhaps only *natural* kinds need to be accorded a wholly mind-independent ontological status – although this, of course, raises the thorny problem of precisely how we are to draw an objective distinction between natural and non-natural kinds. I shall come to this in a moment. Observe, however, that even granting the general connection between individual and sortal realism, to deny the reality of non-natural kinds (such as artefactual kinds) does not entail denying the reality of individuals instantiating those kinds, so long as the individuals in question can be regarded as also instantiating one or other real, natural kind. Thus, even if *tables* do not constitute a real kind, an individual table might still be acknowledged to be a real particular if it could be identified as, say, a tabular-shaped collection of pieces of wood. My own view is that such an identification would be incorrect, however. If this means that my kitchen table does not really exist, then so be it! Perhaps indeed it is a sort of fiction.[11] But whether artefactual kinds are in fact unreal is, I should stress, an issue on which I remain agnostic in this study, although I shall commonly talk *as if* they are real.

With regard to the distinction between natural and non-natural kinds, my own view is that the crucial distinguishing feature of natural kinds is that they are subjects of *natural law*. Laws of nature, I contend, are expressed by statements concerning sorts or kinds, although derivatively they also concern particulars inasmuch as the latter instantiate one or another sort or kind.[12] And the kinds that they concern are, precisely in virtue of that concern, *natural* kinds. Thus *gold* qualifies as a natural kind because there are laws governing its form and behaviour – such as that it is weighty, ductile, malleable, soluble in aqua regia, and so forth. Similarly, *mammals* constitute a natural kind, in virtue of there being such distinctively mammalian laws as that mammals are warm-blooded and that they suckle their

---

[10] See Locke, *An Essay Concerning Human Understanding*, III, III, 1, and III, III, 11.

[11] This seems to be the position of Peter van Inwagen in his *Material Beings* (Ithaca, NY: Cornell University Press, 1990). For an interesting alternative approach, which retains realism concerning artefacts, see John Heil, *From an Ontological Point of View* (Oxford: Clarendon Press, 2003), Chapter 16.

[12] In *Kinds of Being*, I said at this point that laws of nature are *propositions* concerning sorts or kinds. Now, however, I would prefer to say that laws are the *truthmakers* of natural law statements. I say much more about truthmakers and truthmaking in my *The Four-Category Ontology*, especially Part IV.

young. From these examples, incidentally, it will be apparent that I see a close connection between laws and the *dispositional* features of things – a connection that is explored extensively in Chapters 9 and 11 below. By contrast with the case of these natural kinds, there are no natural laws about tables or books or other such artefactual kinds.

Semantics, Metaphysics, and Necessity

At many points in this study, I make claims to the effect that certain propositions variously constitute *semantic* truths, *conceptual* truths, *metaphysical* truths, *necessary* truths, or *a priori* truths. Something therefore needs to be said about how I understand the status of and relationships between these ways of characterizing propositions. The fact is that I have no fully worked-out theory of such matters, although I do have views concerning some of the implications that any such theory should have. My realist predilections in metaphysics persuade me to regard metaphysical truths as revealing fundamental, and often necessary, features of a largely mind-independent reality. At the same time, I am uneasy with, because more than a little mystified by, the idea of metaphysical necessities that are not ultimately *a priori* in character. This is despite the fact that at some places in this study I do not challenge the currently popular notion of *a posteriori* metaphysical necessity.[13] *Natural* or *physical* necessity is another matter, I believe, and I am content to explicate this in terms of *a posteriori* natural law.

Such a position inevitably raises profound questions concerning the very possibility of metaphysical knowledge and its relationship with empirical scientific inquiry and theory-construction – questions which, for the most part, I do not directly tackle in the chapters that follow.[14] It also raises questions concerning concept-formation and the connection between metaphysics and the semantics of natural language. With regard to these latter

---

[13]   The modern notion of *a posteriori* metaphysical necessity is, of course, due in large measure to the work of Saul A. Kripke: see his *Naming and Necessity* (Oxford: Blackwell, 1980). I discuss it critically in a number of places, including my 'On the Alleged Necessity of True Identity Statements', *Mind* 91 (1982), pp. 579–84, my 'Identity, Vagueness, and Modality', in José L. Bermúdez (ed.), *Thought, Reference, and Experience: Themes from the Philosophy of Gareth Evans* (Oxford: Oxford University Press, 2005), pp. 290–310, and my 'A Problem for A Posteriori Essentialism Concerning Natural Kinds', *Analysis* 67 (2007), pp. 286–92.

[14]   However, my current views about such matters are most fully set out in my *The Possibility of Metaphysics*, Chapter 1, and my *The Four-Category Ontology*, Parts I and III.

questions, one thing that I would wish to emphasize is that conceptual truths, and their embodiment in the semantic structures of our native tongues, are not just for us to make up as we will. They are not for the most part merely the expression of more or less arbitrary stipulative definitions or culture-bound conventions. How we do and should conceptualize the world is substantially constrained by the way the world is, quite independently of our values and interests. And hence to the extent that metaphysics deals in conceptual truths it may at once claim to be addressing the nature of reality and profitably utilize the method of linguistic analysis – although I by no means subscribe to the view that the analysis of 'ordinary language' exhausts the business of philosophical investigation and readily concede that the structure of language is, on its own, a very uncertain guide to the structure of reality.

However, we must surely also concede that if our conceptual scheme is moulded by the way the world is, then this can ultimately only be because it reflects our experience of the world – or, if not always just our own experience, then perhaps also that of our evolutionary forebears. And this brings us again to the question of the relationship between metaphysics and empirical science. Here I should say that I see the proper relationship between scientific and metaphysical thinking as being one of complementarity and cooperation, rather than one of opposition and rivalry. Both have as their ultimate aim a closer coincidence between the way we think of the world and the way the world is: in short, both are concerned with the pursuit of objective truth. But, as I see it, metaphysics and empirical science differ crucially in their attitudes towards the content of experience. For the scientist, experience is a source of evidential support for speculative explanatory hypotheses, and as such its content is accepted relatively uncritically, even if it is often at least partially interpreted in the light of prevailing scientific theory. For the metaphysician, by contrast, the content of experience – and, more especially, the categories and relations that serve to structure that content – are themselves the target of critical inquiry and systematic explication. In taking this stance, I align myself in some respects with a Kantian view of the aim and scope of metaphysical thinking, although many of the metaphysical theses advanced in the following chapters are much more Aristotelian than Kantian in character and spirit.[15]

To conclude, then: because of their quite different attitudes towards the content of experience, metaphysics can help both to underwrite some of

---

[15] As I explain in my *The Possibility of Metaphysics*, Chapter 1, I disagree fundamentally with the transcendental idealism of Kant and wholeheartedly endorse Aristotle's metaphysical realism. What is needed for progress in metaphysics, I believe, is a judicious mixture of the insights of Kant and Aristotle.

the theories of empirical science and yet also to curb the wilder specula-
tions of scientists and the ambitions of some of them to claim a monopoly
of truth and understanding. Metaphysicians cannot afford to ignore
developments in scientific theory, but they only promise to render themselves foolish in the eyes of posterity by slavishly accepting current scientific
orthodoxy.

New Developments

In preceding sections of this introduction, I have said much about the
distinction between 'individuals' and 'sorts' or 'kinds'. I have also made
it clear that I regard sorts or kinds as being *universals*, whereas the individuals of which I have spoken are *particular objects* that are instances of
– that *instantiate* – such sorts or kinds. However, since writing *Kinds of
Being*, I have come round to the view that not all particulars are particular *objects* – that is, items that, in an older terminology, might be described
as being *individual substances*. I now believe that we have to include in
our ontology the items that many contemporary philosophers call *tropes*,
but which I prefer to call – in deference to an older tradition – *modes*.[16]
Another traditional term for such items is 'individual accident', and some
modern philosophers call them 'particularized properties' or 'property
instances'. Calling them property *instances* implies – correctly, as I believe
– that they are instances of property *universals*, with the further implication that these universals are to be distinguished from those that are
instantiated by particular *objects*, that is, from *sorts* or *kinds* as I understand
the latter.

What we have in place now, then, is nothing other than the *four-
category ontology* to which I have alluded in earlier pages, my conversion
to which is the most significant change in my metaphysical thinking since
I wrote *Kinds of Being*.[17] This is the ontology that we find briefly sketched
in the opening passages of Aristotle's *Categories*, the foundational text for

[16]   For an important modern account, see Keith Campbell, *Abstract Particulars*
(Oxford: Blackwell, 1990). The term 'trope' we owe to D. C. Williams. I do
not favour the term 'abstract particular', because one prevalent philosophical
use of the adjective 'abstract' has the implication that the items that it describes
– for example, *numbers* – do not exist in space and time, whereas tropes are
typically not thought of in this way. For further discussion, see again my 'The
Metaphysics of Abstract Objects'.

[17]   I first explicitly announced my allegiance to this ontology in my *The Possibility
of Metaphysics*, pp. 203–4. The ontology is, of course, the subject of my later
book, *The Four-Category Ontology*.

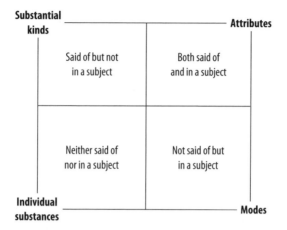

Figure 1   The Aristotelian Ontological Square, version I

all subsequent systems of categorial ontology.[18] It may be most perspicuously represented by a version of the diagram that is known as 'the Ontological Square', shown below in Figure 1.[19] The terms designating the corners of the Square in Figure 1 are not translations of Aristotle's own terms for the items in question in the *Categories*, but are nonetheless traditional ones. In particular, Aristotle spoke of 'primary' and 'secondary' substances in the *Categories*, where I have used the terms 'individual substance' and 'substantial kind' respectively. But he makes it perfectly clear that what he regards as being 'secondary' substances are precisely the *species* and *genera* (that is, the *sorts* or *kinds*) of 'primary' substances, and that the latter are particular *objects*, such as a particular horse or a particular table.

As will be seen from Figure 1, Aristotle considers that substantial kinds or species are 'said of but not in a subject', that attributes are 'both said of and in a subject', that modes are 'not said of but in a subject', and that individual substances are 'neither said of nor in a subject'. I confess that I am not myself entirely happy with this way of explicating the relevant differences between entities belonging to the four different categories, partly because 'said of' ostensibly expresses a *linguistic* rather than a metaphysical

---

18   See Aristotle, *Categories and De Interpretatione*, trans. J. L. Ackrill (Oxford: Clarendon Press, 1963).

19   We owe this name for the diagram to Ignacio Angelelli: see his *Studies on Frege and Traditional Philosophy* (Dordrecht: Kluwer, 1967), pp. 12–15.

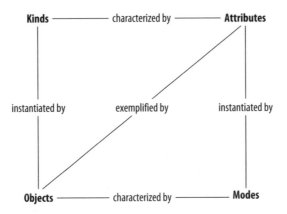

Figure 2 The Ontological Square, version II

relation and partly because the meaning of 'in a subject' is somewhat obscure, being suggestive of a *spatial* relation which seems inappropriate in at least some cases. Anyway, whatever may be the virtues or drawbacks of Aristotle's version of the Ontological Square, my own preferred version is somewhat different and is displayed in Figure 2.

It may be observed that in Figure 2 I have abbreviated 'substantial kinds' to 'kinds' and have replaced the somewhat archaic 'individual substances' by 'objects'. These are merely terminological niceties and nothing much hinges on the choice of labels for the four corners of the Square. What is more significant is that the key relationships between entities belonging to the different categories are differently expressed in my version of the Square – and are expressed there purely in terms of two fundamental *metaphysical* relations, *instantiation* and *characterization*. Kinds are characterized by attributes and instantiated by objects, attributes characterize kinds and are instantiated by modes, modes characterize objects and instantiate attributes, and objects are characterized by modes and instantiate kinds.

It will be noticed that my version of the Square also includes a 'diagonal' relationship between objects and attributes: the former, I say, *exemplify* the latter. However, I do not regard exemplification as being a *fundamental* or *primitive* metaphysical relation, like instantiation or characterization, since I regard it as coming in two different varieties – 'dispositional' and 'occurrent' – each of which is a different 'resultant' of instantiation and characterization, the difference consisting in the *order* in which it is 'composed' out of these two relations. To be more explicit: an object *O* exemplifies an attribute *A dispositionally* when *O* instantiates some kind, *K*, that is characterized by *A*; and an object *O* exemplifies an attribute *A occurrently* when O is characterized by some mode, M, that instantiates A.[20] The two types of exemplification can thus be represented in terms of two different 'routes' that can taken around the Square from the bottom left-hand corner to the top right-hand corner.

This conception of the dispositional/occurrent distinction, although it invokes the four-category ontology, is not fundamentally at odds with the way in which I understood that distinction in *Kinds of Being*. Hence, the chapters dealing with dispositions in that book have not required very extensive revision in the present one. This will become more apparent when we come to them. But whereas, in *Kinds of Being*, I had to regard the distinction between occurrent and dispositional predication as basic and irreducible, with the four-category ontology at my disposal this is no longer so. However, the system of *sortal logic* developed in Chapter 11, which remains unchanged from that presented in Chapter 9 of *Kinds of Being*, does not exploit in full the ontological resources of the four-category ontology. It would be perfectly possible to extend that logic so as to do this, but I deemed it unnecessary for the purposes of this book. For these purposes, it suffices to deploy a logic which quantifies only over items on the *left-hand* side of the Ontological Square – that is, only over particular objects and the kinds that they instantiate.

The upshot of these new developments is, then, that although the four-category ontology provides, I believe, a deeper and more illuminating metaphysical foundation for many of the logical and ontological claims that I advanced in *Kinds of Being*, it does not stand in any kind of tension with those claims, which I am consequently happy to advocate even more confidently in this version of the book.

---

[20] Not everyone will like my choice of the word 'occurrent' to contrast with 'dispositional', but I greatly prefer it to the more common 'categorical' and regard the occurrent/dispositional distinction as a modern counterpart of the Aristotelian distinction between the *actual* and the *potential*, differing from the latter perhaps only verbally. Here I should emphasize, however, that this Aristotelian distinction, as I understand it, should not be confused with the modern metaphysical distinction between the 'actual' and the (merely) 'possible'. In particular, I have no desire whatever to imply that dispositions are *non*-actual in the latter sense – that is, that to ascribe a disposition to an actually existing object is merely to say something about how that object is in some 'possible world' distinct from the 'actual world'. Indeed, I have no sympathy at all for the metaphysics of possible worlds quite generally.

2

Sortal Terms and Criteria of Identity

It is a plausible contention – although one that I shall seek to qualify shortly – that for any given *sort* of individuals there is a *criterion of identity* for individuals of that sort.[1] Linguistically, the point is reflected in a distinction emphasized by P. T. Geach between those general terms that are and those that are not 'substantival'. For Geach, the mark of a substantival general term is precisely that it has associated with its use – as indeed a component of its very sense – a criterion of identity for instances falling under it. By such a criterion, Geach means 'that in accordance with which we judge whether identity holds' in assessing the truth or falsehood of an identity statement concerning individuals.[2] So, for instance, 'man' and 'gold' are by this account substantival general terms – or, as I prefer to call them,

[1] P. F. Strawson, despite earlier work cited in the next footnote, puts some pressure both on this assumption and on the very notion of a criterion of identity in his 'Entity and Identity', in H. D. Lewis (ed.), *Contemporary British Philosophy, Fourth Series* (London: George Allen and Unwin, 1976), reprinted in P. F. Strawson, *Entity and Identity and Other Essays* (Oxford: Clarendon Press, 1997). I hope that what I have to say in the present chapter will help to alleviate such doubts, which Strawson is far from being alone in having expressed.

[2] See P. T. Geach, *Reference and Generality*, 3rd edn (Ithaca, NY: Cornell University Press, 1980), pp. 63ff. Geach – who cites Aquinas as his model – calls those general terms that are not substantival 'adjectival'. In similar vein, P. F. Strawson distinguishes between what he calls *sortal* and *characterizing* universals, remarking that 'A sortal universal supplies a principle for distinguishing and counting individual particulars which it collects': see his *Individuals: An Essay in Descriptive Metaphysics* (London: Methuen, 1959), p. 168. In modern times, the first sustained examination of the notion of a criterion of identity seems to have been by Gottlob Frege, in his *Die Grundlagen*

in deference to John Locke, *sortal* terms – because it seems that there are, at least in principle, ways of determining whether, if *x* and *y* are men or quantities of gold, they are the *same* man or the *same* gold. But a general term like 'red thing' is not for Geach substantival, precisely because it has no such criterion of identity associated with its use.

A sufficient, but not necessary, condition for a general term's being a sortal is that there should exist some principle for *counting* or *enumerating* individual instances falling under it. Thus, there are ways of counting the number of *men* or *tables* or *books* in a given room, but no way of counting the number of *red things* that there are. And this is not because there *is* such a number, but one beyond our powers of determining – as in the case of the number of *atoms* in the room – but rather because it apparently does not even make sense to speak of such a number until the *sort* or *sorts* of red thing that one is to count have been specified. Suppose, for example, that the room contained a red table: then that, it might be urged, is clearly *one* red thing. But what about its red top and its red legs, or the red knob on one of its red drawers? Are *these* to be counted as different 'red things' in the room *in addition to* the red table itself? And what about, say, the red paint covering one of the table's legs: is *that* also to count as a distinct 'red thing' in its own right? It rapidly becomes apparent that there is no principled way of deciding these matters, until we are told what *sorts* of red thing we are supposed to be counting.

Suppose, however, that we were instructed to count *every* sort of red thing in the room: would *that* in principle lead us to a determinate maximal number of red things in the room – perhaps, indeed, an *infinite* number, but still determinate? One problem arising here is that of providing criteria for the identity and diversity of *sorts*. Another is that of providing criteria for determining when two distinct sorts are *disjoint*, since one must avoid counting the same individual twice because, say, it is both a red φ and a red χ. A still more fundamental problem arises, however, once we acknowledge quantities or portions of red *stuffs* (such as portions of red ink) to qualify as red things in the room, as I believe we should. For there is clearly *no* principled way of determining how many such portions there are in a given place, in view of the indeterminate extent to which any such portion is divisible into further portions.[3]

---

der Arithmetik (1884), translated by J. L. Austin as *The Foundations of Arithmetic* (Oxford: Blackwell, 1953): see §§ 62ff. For further discussion of both Frege's and Geach's positions, see Michael Dummett, *Frege: Philosophy of Language*, 2nd edn (London: Duckworth, 1981), Chapter 16. I examine both Frege's view and Dummett's in my 'What Is a Criterion of Identity?', *Philosophical Quarterly* 39 (1989), pp. 1–21.
[3] For further discussion of the some of the issues, see Dummett, *Frege*, pp. 565ff.

For the foregoing reason, general terms such as 'man', 'table', and 'book' (but *not* 'thing') have the logical – and not just the grammatical – status of *count nouns*, and they form, as I say, a subset of sortal terms. But, to repeat, the countability of instances falling under it is not a necessary condition for a general term's being a sortal, since so-called *mass nouns* like 'gold' and 'water' apparently have criteria of identity associated with their use, despite the fact that it makes no sense to ask *how many* instances of gold or water exist in a certain place. Significantly, though, it *does* make sense to ask *how much* gold or water exists in a given place.

The general tenor of my remarks is not without venerable historical precedent. If we were to ask what it is that sortal terms denote, a plausible answer would seem to be that they denote what Aristotle in the *Categories* called *secondary substances*: that is, species and genera – or, in other words, *sorts* or *kinds*. Correspondingly, what Aristotle called *primary substances* we may refer to as the *individuals* or *particulars* instantiating such sorts or kinds. But an important point to appreciate here is that the notions of *individual* (or particular) and *sort* (or kind) are, very arguably, interdependent and mutually irreducible. Individuals are recognizable only as *individuals of a sort*, while sorts are intelligible only as *sorts of individuals*.

When I say that individuals are recognizable only as individuals *of a sort*, I am challenging a notion that has wreaked much havoc in the history of philosophy: the notion of a 'bare particular'. This is the – to my mind – entirely bogus notion of something that is individual or particular *tout court*, quite independently of its falling under any specifiable sortal distinction. In short, it is the purported idea of a mere individual 'thing'. The reason why this is a bogus notion is implicit in some of the observations that I have already made. The point, to put it briefly, is that the noun 'thing' – although superficially a count noun in that it admits of a plural form, 'things' – has no criterion of identity associated with it, is not a genuine sortal, and consequently cannot be used unambiguously to pick out some identifiable individual either as an object of thought or as an object of reference. Thus, if I point in the direction of my desk and say, with referential intent, 'That *thing* is brown', I shall by no means have expressed a proposition with determinate sense – even though my intended audience may well be able to *gather* what I meant. And this is because my words have left it quite indeterminate what *sort* of thing I am supposedly referring to – a *desk*, a *portion of wood*, a *surface*, or what not, all of which sorts of things carry different criteria of identity.

Here it might be objected that this contention fails to accommodate the fact that a question such as 'What is that large brown *thing* over there in the corner of the room?' – a question which, it seems, precisely exhibits ignorance of the *sort* of thing being referred to – nonetheless has perfectly determinate sense. One possible response is to say that, despite superficial appearances, in such a question determinate reference is *not* in fact being made and that, while the question does indeed have determinate sense, this is only because it effectively means something like this: 'There is something large and brown over there in the corner of the room: *what is it?*', in which 'it' plays the role of a variable of quantification, rather than a genuinely referential role.[4] Another possible response is to say that, when asking a question like this, the speaker may well be intentionally picking out a certain *piece of matter* and is merely expressing ignorance as to what sort of thing, if any, it might *constitute* – for example, whether it constitutes some kind of artefact, such as a chair, or some kind of natural object, such as the stump of a tree. In fact, it seems to me, each of these responses may be appropriate in different cases and, certainly, I don't think that the intelligibility of such questions puts any real pressure on my stated reasons for rejecting as bogus the notion of a 'bare particular'.[5]

Locke, as I implied in the Introduction, was one philosopher who was evidently beguiled by the notion of bare particulars.[6] But again I would urge that realism with regard to individuals is just not compatible with a conventionalism as apparently extreme as his with regard to sorts or kinds. We cannot, with Locke, simply suppose that the mind somehow constructs certain 'abstract general ideas' from its experience of concrete particulars and then proceeds to classify all such particulars by reference to these ideas alone: for particulars cannot even be experienced as *being particulars*,

---

[4]   Support for such a view may be extracted from Dummett, *Frege*, p. 577; see also Michael Dummett, *The Interpretation of Frege's Philosophy* (London: Duckworth, 1981), p. 217. Here he argues that not all uses of demonstratives serve to perform acts of singular reference to particular objects.

[5]   I discuss these issues more fully in my 'What Is a Criterion of Identity?' and, more recently, in my 'Sortals and the Individuation of Objects', *Mind and Language* 22 (2007), pp. 514–33. In the latter, I make it clear that, in order for a thinker to pick out a particular object as a determinate object of thought, it may not be necessary for that thinker to be able to classify the object in question as falling under some *specific* sortal concept, so long as he or she can recognize it as belonging to some more general *category* all the individual members of which share the same criterion of identity – such as the category *material artefact* or, indeed, the category *piece of matter*. Note, in this connection, that a *piece* of matter is by no means the same as a mere *portion* or *quantity* of matter, and pieces of matter are certainly *countable*.

[6]   I examine and criticize his reasons for countenancing them in my 'Locke, Martin, and Substance', *Philosophical Quarterly* 50 (2000), pp. 499–514.

without being experienced as particulars *of some sort* – a fact which argues for the innateness of at least some of our sortal distinctions.[7]

The other side of the coin is that sorts, equally, are not intelligible in abstraction from the individuals which instantiate them. A doctrine of Platonic 'Forms' as being the referents of sortal terms is untenable for reasons that Aristotle himself made plain long ago. To go further into this issue now would involve us too deeply for present purposes in the so-called problem of universals, but I shall return to the matter in later chapters.

Now, as I have already implied, *different* sorts of things very often have different criteria of identity – although often, too, they do not: for instance, lions and tigers do not, surprising though this might seem *prima facie*. But the *general* form that a criterion of identity will take is just this:[8]

If x and y are φs, then x is identical with y if and only if x and y satisfy condition C_φ

where, for the reason just stated, the relevant criterial condition, C_φ, may be different for different sorts φ. Clearly, the criterion which determines whether or not a certain *body or quantity of water* encountered on one occasion is *the same* as a body or quantity of water encountered on a previous occasion is different from the criterion which determines whether or not a certain *river* encountered on one occasion is *the same* as a river encountered on a previous occasion. As the water in a river flows down to the sea it is replaced by more and different water, but the river remains the same. Hence – or so I shall argue in due course, since the point is by no means entirely

---

[7]   This may seem to be at odds with what I say in 'Sortals and the Individuation of Objects', where I allow that animals – and so, *a fortiori*, human beings – can *perceive* objects in their environment without necessarily conceiving of them as falling under sortal distinctions. But to experience something *as* a particular, it is not sufficient simply to perceive it: one must also be able to *think* of it as being a particular – and this, I maintain, requires one to think of it as being a particular *of some sort*, not a 'bare' particular.

[8]   For fuller discussion concerning the logical forms that identity criteria may take, and in particular the distinction between 'one-level' and 'two-level' identity criteria, see my 'What Is a Criterion of Identity?' and my 'Objects and Criteria of Identity', in Bob Hale and Crispin Wright (eds), *A Companion to the Philosophy of Language* (Oxford: Blackwell, 1997), a revised version of the latter appearing in my *The Possibility of Metaphysics: Substance, Identity, and Time* (Oxford: Clarendon Press, 1998), Chapter 2. For present purposes, I am concerned solely with 'one-level' identity criteria, whose general form is displayed in the main text above.

uncontroversial – a river is certainly not to be *identified* with the water which, at any given time, 'constitutes' it.

Locke, as it happens, was probably the first philosopher to recognize explicitly the sortal relativity of criteria of identity, exploiting it extensively in his discussion of personal identity in *An Essay Concerning Human Understanding*, where he makes much of the fact that the sortal terms 'man' and 'person' apparently carry different criteria of identity (not that Locke himself uses the *term* 'criterion of identity', which is of much more recent coinage). I shall myself be examining some of the issues that this raises later on, in Chapter 8.

One thing that emerges from the example just mentioned of the river and its water is that different sorts of things may have different *persistence conditions*, these being determined precisely by their respective criteria of identity.[9] Thus, a body or quantity of water ceases to exist if all or part of it undergoes molecular dissociation into its constituent oxygen and hydrogen, whereas a river may very arguably continue to exist even if it has temporarily run dry. An individual x of a sort φ, existing at a time t_1, still exists at a later time, t_2, just in case there exists at t_2 a unique individual y of a sort χ such that, according to the common criterion of identity governing the sorts φ and χ, x may be identified with y. Or so, at least, I wish to maintain. Observe that I am prepared to allow that an individual may be able to change from being an individual of sort φ to being one of a *different* sort, χ. Otherwise, indeed, I would be unable to accommodate the phenomenon of *metamorphosis* – although we shall see in due course that transformations most commonly described in these terms, such as that of a tadpole into a frog, are doubtfully genuine instances of the phenomenon. However, a logical constraint that I would wish to place on any such transformation is that the relevant sorts φ and χ should share *the same criterion of identity*. And that is why, for instance, I believe that Lot's wife in the biblical story cannot literally have 'become' a pillar of salt, if by this it is suggested that she *continued to exist* under this new form.[10] These considerations, of course, lend support to the Aristotelian distinction between 'qualitative' and 'substantial' change, and consequently also to the correlative Aristotelian distinction between 'essence' and 'accident'.

[9] In my *The Possibility of Metaphysics*, pp. 55–6, I distinguish between persistence conditions in the present sense and what I there call *sortal* persistence conditions, these being the conditions necessary and sufficient for an individual to persist as an individual *of the same sort*. Clearly, this is a more restrictive notion of persistence conditions than the one that I am presently concerned with in the main text.

[10] Compare David Wiggins, *Sameness and Substance* (Oxford: Blackwell, 1980), pp. 60ff., or his *Sameness and Substance Renewed* (Cambridge: Cambridge University Press, 2001), pp. 64ff.

While on the subject of persistence, I should remark that, of course, by no means all modern philosophers would wholeheartedly endorse the neo-Aristotelian picture that I have just been sketching. There is a particular school of thought – of which W. V. Quine was perhaps the foremost exponent – according to which all of our common-sense talk of persisting objects, conceived as 'continuants' undergoing qualitative change without loss of identity, would be replaced in a more 'scientific' description of reality by talk in terms of uninterrupted temporal sequences of instantaneous or momentary objects.[11] On this view, what we call a *river*, for instance, is really very much like a *process in time*, a four-dimensional 'spacetime worm' whose temporal parts are the momentary three-dimensional 'time-slices' of that 'worm' – a view of reality which obviously draws its inspiration from the work of twentieth-century physicists such as Einstein and Minkowski.

I must confess that I have grave doubts about the ultimate coherence of this view of things, suspecting that what superficial plausibility it possesses is parasitic upon our prior grasp of the very neo-Aristotelian or 'common-sense' conception which it seeks to challenge. Some of my doubts on this score stem from what I take to be the implications of the work of P. F. Strawson, in particular his arguments to the effect that material objects (conceived as what I have just termed 'continuants') necessarily constitute 'basic' particulars in our conceptual scheme.[12] However, these and related matters will receive a more extensive airing in later chapters, so I shall dwell on them no further at present.

Let me now turn to some more general considerations concerning identity and criteria of identity. One thing that I should emphasize is that a 'criterion of identity', as I am now using the expression, is not to be conceived of as a merely *heuristic* or *evidential* or in any other sense purely *epistemic* principle, but rather as a *metaphysical-cum-semantic* one – although, obviously, questions of knowledge and meaning cannot be wholly separated.[13] That is to say, it is not a requirement of a criterion of identity in

---

[11] See W. V. Quine, 'Identity, Ostension, and Hypostasis', in his *From a Logical Point of View*, 2nd edn (Cambridge, MA: Harvard University Press, 1961) and, for a more recent example, Theodore Sider, *Four-Dimensionalism: An Ontology of Persistence and Time* (Oxford: Clarendon Press, 2001) – although Sider's 'stage-theoretic' version of four-dimensionalism differs subtly from Quine's in ways that need not presently concern us.

[12] See P. F. Strawson, *Individuals: An Essay in Descriptive Metaphysics* (London: Methuen, 1959), Part I.

[13] Compare Anil Gupta, *The Logic of Common Nouns* (New Haven, CT: Yale University Press, 1980), pp. 2 and 22. Gupta uses the expression 'principle of identity' to mean more or less what I mean by 'criterion of identity'.

my sense that it should necessarily provide us with an effective means of coming to *know* whether or not a given identity statement, '*a* is identical with *b*', is true: rather, it should tell us, so to speak, *what it takes* for *a* and *b* to be the same or different – or, in terminology drawn from Locke, 'wherein their identity or diversity consists'.[14] In other words, it should specify – *in an informative way*, be it added – the *truth*-conditions of the statement '*a* is identical with *b*', rather than, say, its *assertability*-conditions. Naturally, *anti-realists* in matters of semantic theory will want to question this distinction but, being no such anti-realist myself, I shall here simply take it for granted. Now, I shall try to indicate, shortly, what exactly I mean by stipulating that such a criterion should specify truth-conditions 'in an informative way'. Meanwhile, as a further *caveat*, I should perhaps just mention that my present use of the term 'criterion' has rather little connection with the way in which this expression is typically used in works of Wittgensteinian exegesis.

Perhaps a very straightforward example of a criterion of identity will be helpful at this point. This and the next example that I shall invoke are, it is true, ones which involve *abstract* individuals rather than the *concrete* individuals that are the primary concern of this study. But this is partly why the examples are relatively simple ones and thus useful for purposes of illustration. Consider, then, the criterion of identity for *sets*. A set is a collection of things, each of which 'belongs to' or 'is a member of' that set. Examples would be the set of the first three odd numbers, {1, 3, 5}, and the set of the intra-Jovian planets of the sun, {Mercury, Venus, Earth, Mars}. And the criterion of identity for sets, based on the Axiom of Extensionality of set theory, is quite simply the following:

If *x* and *y* are *sets*, then *x* is identical with *y* if and only if *x* and *y* *have the same members*.

Thus, the sets {1, 3, 5} and {3, 5, 1} are by this criterion the *same*. However, it is instructive here to compare this criterion of identity for sets with the criterion of identity for *ordered* sets, namely:

If *x* and *y* are *ordered sets*, then *x* is identical with *y* if and only if *x* and *y* *have the same members in the same order*.

For this makes it clear that while the sets {1, 3, 5} and {3, 5, 1} are the same *set*, the ordered sets ⟨1, 3, 5⟩ and ⟨3, 5, 1⟩ are *not* the same *ordered set*, even though the same three numbers are involved in each case.

[14] See John Locke, *An Essay Concerning Human Understanding*, ed. P. H. Nidditch (Oxford: Clarendon Press, 1975), II, XXVII, 9.

Now, a question that arises here – and which will arise again later in other forms – is this. Granted that the ordered sets ⟨1, 3, 5⟩ and ⟨3, 5, 1⟩ are not the same *ordered set*, may it nonetheless be said that they are the same *set* – and thus that they are both identical with the set {1, 3, 5}, the set of the first three odd numbers? The obvious answer, which I would urge is also the right answer, is 'No'. For, in the first place, ordered sets are not *sets* at all, in the sense in which this term was understood when the criterion of identity for sets was stated earlier. And in due course we shall see that the criterion of identity for any given sort of things, φ, is partly constitutive of the *meaning* of the sortal term 'φ'. No ordered set can be *identical* with any 'mere' or 'plain' set, as we might call it, since ordered sets and 'plain' sets are quite *different sorts of things* – although I shall shortly consider a possible challenge to this claim. Now, strictly, of course, just because *x* belongs to a sort φ while *y* belongs to a different sort χ, we cannot automatically infer that *x* and *y* are not identical – although if they *are* indentical, then each must obviously belong to *both* sorts. However, where such an identity does obtain – or so I shall argue – the sorts in question must have the *same* criterion of identity. This will in particular be the case if φ and χ are related as *species* to *genus*, as *horse* is to *mammal*. But *ordered set* and *set* are *not* so related, despite what might be suggested by the *grammatical* relations of these sortal terms.

What *can* be said, of course, is that is that an ordered set and 'plain' set may *have the same members*: but *that* does not make them the same set, or indeed the same *anything* – certainly not by the criterion of identity for sets, since that only has implications for *sets*. That criterion explicitly states that *if x and y are sets*, then they are identical if and only if they have the same members – not, say, that *x* is the same set as *y* if and only if they have the same members, which *would* make the ordered sets ⟨1, 3, 5⟩ and ⟨3, 5, 1⟩ the same set. Of course, this latter point is not decisive in itself, since it is perhaps open to an opponent to challenge my assumptions about the form that a criterion of identity should take.

Another reason, however, for denying that the ordered sets ⟨1, 3, 5⟩ and ⟨3, 5, 1⟩ can be the same set but different ordered sets is that this seemingly flies in the face of the laws of identity – in particular, the law that things that are identical with a third thing are identical with each other. The only way of evading this would be to attempt to *relativize* the notion of identity, admitting only *sortally relativized* identity relations – such as *being the same set as* and *being the same ordered set as* – and not classical 'absolute' identity, that is, just *being the same as*. This strategy, which is more or less followed by Geach, is a subject to which I shall return in due course.[15] The point, however, is that, on the classical view, if *x* and *y* are

---

[15]   Geach develops this view in his *Reference and Generality*. Other important developments of relativism may be found in Nicholas Griffin, *Relative Identity*

the same set, then they are identical *tout court*, while if they are different ordered sets they are *non*-identical *tout court*. Our alternatives to contradiction are thus *either* to abandon classical absolute identity *or* – as I would urge – to insist that no individual can instantiate *both* of two sorts φ and χ if φ and χ have *different* criteria of identity associated with them: that, for instance, nothing can be *both* a 'plain' set *and* an ordered set. Later I shall argue that we are, in any case, bound on pain of absurdity to insist on the latter point and consequently that there can be no reason for abandoning classical absolute identity.

At this point, I must return to some unfinished business, concerning my earlier claim that ordered sets and 'plain' sets are *different sorts of things*. This remark might strike many set theorists as unjustifiably overlooking important work by Wiener and Kuratowski on 'reducing' ordered pairs to sets. On Kuratowski's definition, the ordered pair $\langle x, y \rangle$ is 'defined' as the set $\{\{x\}, \{x, y\}\}$.[16] However, in the first place, it is not apparent to me how this can strictly and literally be understood as a *definition* – because, for instance, the ordered pair $\langle x, y \rangle$ contains x and y as members but the set $\{\{x\}, \{x, y\}\}$ does not. Rather, what the 'definition' effectively does is to identify, for any ordered pair, a unique set which can, for certain logico-mathematical purposes, be regarded as its surrogate or representative. But, furthermore, it is in any case clear that this sort of 'reduction' provides no prospect of legitimizing the suggestion that different *ordered sets* might be the same *set*. For if, say, the different ordered pairs $\langle x, y \rangle$ and $\langle y, x \rangle$ are defined as proposed, they will of course turn out to be *different* sets by virtue of having *different* members – although again I would urge that for this very reason the 'definition' cannot be taken as such seriously, since these ordered pairs surely *do* in fact have the same members, at least on any natural understanding of what it is for something to be a member of an ordered pair. It is hardly plausible to suggest that, on this natural understanding, x is a 'member' of the ordered pair $\langle x, y \rangle$ in virtue of its unit set being a member of the set $\{\{x\}, \{x, y\}\}$, and hence that 'membership' is quite naturally understood in a special way as applied to ordered pairs. In short, I would contend that we have a primitive conception of *ordered pair* certain features of which are simply not retained by the proposed reduction. At the same time, it must be stressed that I have invoked this example of 'plain' sets and ordered sets only for purposes of illustration, so that nothing crucial to my general position turns on the merits or deficiencies of the Wiener-Kuratowski approach.

(Oxford: Clarendon Press, 1977) and Harold W. Noonan, *Objects and Identity* (The Hague: Martinus Nijhoff, 1980).
[16]   See, for example, Patrick Suppes, *Axiomatic Set Theory* (New York: Dover, 1972), p. 32.

Notice this about the criteria of identity cited so far: they do not avoid use of the notion of *identity* itself in stating a necessary and sufficient condition for the identity of things of a given sort φ. And this, I suspect, is no merely parochial feature of the examples that I have selected. Thus the criterion of identity for sets speaks of *same members* and that for ordered sets of *same members* and *same order*. From this it should first of all be clear that a criterion of identity is not to be thought of as being a *definition* of identity – not even as being a definition of identity *for a given sort of things*, since identity is univocal, as I shall stress below. It cannot be a definition of *identity*, of course, simply because a definition should not contain the *definiendum* in the *definiens*.

Another point which emerges here, however, is that where a criterion of identity for a given sort φ *does* make use of the notion of identity itself, it can apparently do so *informatively* only by alluding to the identity of things of *another* sort or sorts. Thus, the criterion of identity for *sets* is stated in terms of the identity of their *members*. And, while it is true that sets may *themselves* be members of sets, it seems crucial to the viability of the criterion of identity for sets just stated that, by means of it, questions concerning set-identity can in principle ultimately be settled – if need be through repeated applications of the criterion – by reference to the identity of set-members that are *not* themselves sets. Obviously, though, there is no *single* criterion of identity that is applicable to all set-members: 'set-member' is not, that is to say, a genuine sortal term. What criterion of identity is applicable to any given set-member will simply depend on what *sort* of thing that set-member is – for example, *planet*, *number* or indeed *set*.

However, what I have just said needs to be qualified in an important way, in the light of the existence of 'pure' set theory of the Zermelo-Fraenkel type, in which all sets save empty sets have only *sets* as their members. Now, in that case, the criterion of identity for sets just stated serves to guarantee that there is just *one* empty set, by reference to which questions concerning the identity of all other sets may ultimately be settled.[17] Why? Simply because sets that have *no* members – empty sets – quite trivially have *the same* members, so that there cannot be two *distinct* sets both of which have no members. What this shows, interestingly enough, is that there need be no vicious circularity involved in supposing that a criterion of identity for φs can enable all questions of φ-identity to be settled without reference to the identity or diversity of anything other than φs, *provided that* the criterion itself serves to individuate a unique φ by reference

---

[17] In Chapter 4 below, I shall express some scepticism about the existence of the 'empty' set, but for present purposes I set aside such doubts.

to which all other questions of φ-identity can ultimately be settled.[18] But, clearly, criteria of identity with this very special property should be regarded as a rare exception rather than as the norm. And, indeed, our stated criterion of identity for sets has this feature only on the highly contentious assumption that there are no sets with *non*-sets as members.

Now if it is a fact, as I suspect it may be, that in general – and setting aside special cases of the kind just discussed – a criterion of identity for things of a given sort φ can be informatively stated only in terms that presuppose the identity of things of *another* sort or sorts, then the implication would appear to be that there must, on pain of an infinite regress, be *some* 'basic' sorts for which we can provide *no* informative criteria of identity.[19] (Obviously, if there *are* such 'basic' sorts, then it cannot after all be a *necessary* condition of a general term's being a sortal that it should have such a criterion of identity associated with it – although we might still hold that it is necessary condition of a general term's being a sortal that *either* it should have an informative criterion of identity associated with it *or else* it should denote a 'basic' sort.) Whether this is so, and if so what such 'basic' sorts might be, and what the truth of identity statements concerning individuals of these sorts could be grounded in – all of these are deep and difficult questions which I cannot undertake to answer at present, although I may as well declare forthwith a leaning towards the view that *person* is a 'basic' sort.

For the time being, however, I want only to emphasize the requirement that has emerged regarding the *informativeness* of a criterion of identity, as an amplification of my earlier stipulation that criteria of identity should specify the truth-conditions of identity statements 'in an informative way'. The crucial point is that – setting aside special cases of the kind discussed a moment ago – in an *informative* criterion of identity for φs, an appeal to φ-identity will not itself figure, either explicitly or implicitly, in the statement of the relevant criterial condition C_φ. A *non*-informative way of specifying such truth-conditions, in the case of sets, would of course simply be to say this:

If *x* and *y* are *sets*, then *x* is identical with *y* if and only if *x* and *y* *include exactly the same sets.*

This statement is *true* – recall that every set includes itself and that mutually inclusive sets are identical[20] – but quite vacuous *as a criterion of identity for*

---

[18]   I discuss this point more fully in my 'Impredicative Identity Criteria and Davidson's Criterion of Event Identity', *Analysis* 49 (1989), pp. 178–81, and in my *A Survey of Metaphysics* (Oxford: Oxford University Press, 2002), pp. 226–8.

[19]   Compare Strawson, 'Entity and Identity'.

[20]   See, for example, Suppes, *Axiomatic Set Theory*, p. 22. The set-*inclusion* relation should not, of course, be confused with the set-*membership* relation.

sets. Its vacuousness for this purpose does not arise, however, from the fact that it makes use of the notion of *identity* in stating the truth-conditions of identity statements concerning sets – for, as we have seen, the accepted criterion stated earlier does this too – nor even because in doing so it makes use of the very notion of a *set*, but rather from the fact that it already pre-supposes an account of the *identity-conditions* of sets.[21]

As I indicated a moment ago, a criterion of identity, in telling us 'wherein identity and diversity consists' for a given sort of things, should *not* be thought of as telling us the *meaning* of the word 'identity', as applied to things of that sort. For 'identity' does not mean anything different when applied to one sort of thing as opposed to another, even though some philosophers misleadingly speak as if it did.[22] When I say that 9 is *identical* with the sum of 4 and 5, I do not mean anything different by 'identical' from what I mean when I say that Queen Elizabeth II is *identical* with the eldest daughter of King George VI, or that Phosphorus is *identical* with Hesperus, or that this chair is *identical* with the chair that I sat in at this time last week. Identity is *univocal*. There are not different *kinds* of identity for dif-ferent kinds of thing, any more than there are different kinds of *existence* – only different *criteria* of identity. In insisting that identity is univocal I mean also, incidentally, to dismiss as misconceived any suggestion that such distinctions, legitimate in themselves, as those between 'numerical' and 'qualitative' identity and between 'synchronic' and 'diachronic' iden-tity should be seen as distinctions between *kinds of identity*, as opposed to distinctions concerning the ontological status or temporal circumstances of items being identified.

When, then, *is* identity, if it is not defined by any criterion of identity? Well, it is, of course, that unique relation which, of necessity, each thing bears to itself and to no other thing. But, obviously, this will not do as a *definition* of identity, since it makes use of the word 'other' – and 'other than' just means 'diverse from', which is just to say 'not *identical* with'.

---

[21]   I have, then, no objection to the fact that, in the accepted criterion of identity for sets, the variables '*x*' and '*y*' take *sets* as their values. This is a point that I develop at greater length in my 'What Is a Criterion of Identity?'. But this is a quite different matter from the question of whether a putative criterion of set-identity makes illicit appeal to considerations that turn on the *identity* of sets.

[22]   Joseph Butler provides an early example of this error, in his *The Analogy of Religion* [1736], Dissertation I, 'Of Personal Identity', where he says: 'The word *same*, when applied to [vegetables] and to persons, is not only applied to dif-ferent subjects, but it is also used in different senses.' See John Perry (ed.), *Personal Identity* (Berkeley, CA: University of California Press, 1975), p. 100.

Again, one might point out, correctly, that the meaning of the English word 'identical' is such that the sentence '*a* is identical with *b*' has the following truth-condition: it is true if and only if the names '*a*' and '*b*' denote the same object. This is the sort of account of the meaning of the identity sign, '=', that one typically finds in recursive truth-conditional semantics for formalized languages, in which context, no doubt, it may be quite unexceptionable. But construed as an attempt to provide any sort of philosophically illuminating *definition* of identity, this is even more transparently circular than the last one, since the very word 'same' is being used.

Identity, I strongly suspect, cannot be *defined* at all – not even in terms of the principle of the *identity of indiscernibles*, granting for the sake of argument the truth of that contentious principle. The trouble with that principle, conceived as a definition of identity, is that 'indiscernible' just means 'having the same properties', so that the notion of identity is presupposed even here. Understanding the principle requires at least an understanding of what it is to identify and distinguish *properties*, with a view to saying whether or not *x* has some property that is *different* from – in other words, not *identical* with – any property of *y*.

It might, I suppose, be wondered whether this last objection can really be sound, in view of the fact that the principle of the identity of indiscernibles can be expressed formally without explicit use of identity expressions on the *right-hand* side of the main biconditional connective, as in the following formula:

$$x = y \leftrightarrow \forall F(Fx \leftrightarrow Fy)$$

Strictly speaking, of course, this formula combines the principle of the identity of indiscernibles proper (right-to-left) with the principle of the indiscernibility of identicals (left-to-right) – though the latter I am for the moment assuming to be uncontroversial. Obviously, a *bi*conditional is needed for a definition, which is why I have done this. The answer to the query that has just been raised is, however, that a correct interpretation of the right-hand side of this biconditional formula presupposes the convention that where a symbol – in this case, '*F*' – is repeated in a formula, it is to be assigned the *same* interpretation at each of its occurrences. So the notion of identity is still presupposed here, albeit only implicitly rather than explicitly.

Perhaps, then, we should just accept that identity is conceptually primitive – indefinable – and thus that it is pointless to expect an informative answer to the question 'What do we *mean* by *identity*?'. Identity may simply be one of those conceptual primitives – like, perhaps, *existence* – of which it is true to say that if one did not already grasp what it is, it could not be explained to one.

Given, however, that the concept of identity is a primitive one, and that criteria of identity are not to be understood as *definitions* of identity, the following question arises. What semantic information *do* such criteria convey? – for they can tell us nothing about the meaning of 'identity' that we do not already implicitly know. Yet such criteria seem to be, at least partly, *semantic* rules: and so they *are* concerned with *meaning*, albeit not with the meaning of the word 'identity'. The answer, of course, is that they tell us something about the meaning of whatever *sortal term* it is that they are associated with.[23] To give the criterion of identity for φs is – at least partially – to explain what sort of things φs *are*. Thus, when I tell you that a 'set' is something whose identity 'consists in' its having the same members, I inform you in part about the meaning of the word 'set'. And by contrasting the criteria of identity for 'plain' and ordered sets, I help to distinguish the meanings of these two sortal terms. But I should stress that, in saying this, I am by no means denying that criteria of identity are at the same time *metaphysical* principles, informing us not just about the *meanings* of sortal terms but also telling us something about the *natures* of the sorts or kinds of thing that those terms denote. We could sum this up, perhaps, by saying that criteria of identity are *metaphysically grounded semantic rules*.

This, incidentally, helps to explain why it is that the principle of the identity of indiscernibles, quite apart from not providing a *definition* of identity, cannot even qualify as a *criterion* of identity in my sense. The reason is that the principle is not relativized to any specific *sort* of things, but affects to be a quite general law, holding of anything whatever. Accordingly, it is not a *semantic rule* connected with the meaning of any particular sortal term, in the way that every genuine criterion of identity is. To put the point another way: the only *apparently* sortal terms that could be used in expressing the principle, in a sufficiently generalized form, would be ones such as 'thing' and 'object' – which, however, are not genuine but only so-called 'dummy' sortals. Their status as such is revealed by the point made earlier that, although 'thing' and 'object' are *grammatically* count nouns, one cannot intelligibly undertake to count how many *things* or *objects* there are in a given room, in the way that one can attempt to count how many *books* or *chairs* or *persons* there are.

I conclude, then, that one only *fully* grasps the nature of a given sort or kind of thing, and hence the meaning of sortal terms designating it, when one grasps the criterion of identity associated therewith – assuming, of course, that there *is* one, because the sort in question is not 'basic'. And so, for example, grasping the respective criteria of identity for, say, *lumps of matter*,

---

[23] In taking this stance, I am directly opposed to the views advanced by Baruch A. Brody in his *Identity and Essence* (Princeton, NJ: Princeton University Press, 1980).

living organisms and perhaps *persons* will be partly constitutive of having an adequate understanding of what it is for something to *be* a lump of matter, living organism or person. (I say only *perhaps* persons because, for reasons that will emerge in Chapter 8, I suspect that persons do in fact constitute a 'basic' sort.) One would expect, then, that developing a grasp of such criteria is one of the primary learning tasks of human infants, although indeed it may well be that an implicit grasp of at least *some* criteria of identity is and has to be *innate* in human beings, perhaps playing a vital role in enabling the infant to pick out certain perceptual invariants amidst the flux of sensory stimulation.[24]

Of course, manifesting a *practical* grasp of a particular criterion of identity, in displaying an ability to re-identify an object of a certain sort correctly as 'the same one again', does not entail possessing a capacity to *articulate* or *excogitate* such a criterion – so that attributing such a grasp to infants is not necessarily over-intellectualizing their cognitive abilities. Moreover, we need not, and indeed probably should not, suppose that the criteria manifested in the identity judgements of infants are identical with the fully fledged versions employed by adults – not least because at first infants learn only to re-identity objects over comparatively short periods of time or in otherwise restricted sets of circumstances. Thus, an infant may grasp that losing its leaves is not inimical to the identity of a *tree*, while not yet grasping that a mature oak and a young sapling might be one and the same living organism encountered at different times. It should be emphasized, too, that it is not to be supposed that infants have to grasp a distinct new criterion of identity for each new sortal term that they learn, since species falling under the same genera share the same criterion of identity. Thus, there is not a different criterion for oaks and elms, say, both of which conform to the criterion of identity for living organisms in general.

I should perhaps just add, finally, a word about my own conception of the distinctive role of *philosophical* theorizing about criteria of identity. It is not part of that conception that philosophers should see themselves as merely being in the business of revealing what criteria of identity 'ordinary

---

[24] Some of the work of the developmental psychologist Tom Bower on early infant perception and related motor activity certainly seems to support the view that, even from their earliest months, human infants can perceptually individuate discrete objects in their immediate environment. See, for instance, Tom Bower, *The Perceptual World of the Child* (London: Fontana, 1977). For an illuminating discussion of some of the philosophical issues, see Eli Hirsch, *The Concept of Identity* (Oxford: Oxford University Press, 1982), Chapters 8 and 9. For further elaboration of my own views on these matters, see again my 'What Is a Criterion of Identity?' and 'Sortals and the Individuation of Objects'.

folk' implicitly and perhaps quite unreflectively employ in making identity judgements concerning things of this or that familiar sort. Of course philosophical analysis may fruitfully *start* with ordinary linguistic usage: but it need not – and will not, if it is to be of much interest and profit – always *stay* with it. For ordinary linguistic usage is sometimes vague, confused, and unduly limited in its range of application. At times, the task of philosophical analysis is not so much to tell us what we *do* mean, for at times our meaning may be far from clear. Rather, its task may be to offer a coherent and reasoned account of what we *should* mean: to *improve* our concepts, not just to report on them. And since I regard criteria of identity as being, at least in part, semantic principles, I cannot regard them as being entirely resistant to improvement of this kind.

It should also be said, however, that the distinctively philosophical task of articulating and attempting to improve upon the concepts implicit in ordinary linguistic usage should not be confused with – although it may profitably draw upon the results of – the empirical psychological task of examining the cognitive processes underlying an individual's engagement in the linguistic practices which characterize that usage. Philosophers employed in 'conceptual analysis' must constantly be on their guard against the temptation to indulge in psychological speculation. But it would be equally mistaken of psychologists to suppose that this leaves philosophers without any distinctive task of their own to perform.[25]

[25]   Here I refer the reader back to my remarks in the Introduction.

3

Individuals, Sorts, and Instantiation

Two kinds of 'is' which are commonly conflated by philosophers and logicians are the 'is' of *attribution*, figuring in a sentence like 'This pen *is* yellow', and what I call the 'is' of *instantiation*, figuring in sentences like 'Dobbin *is* a horse' and 'A horse *is* a mammal' – that is, sentences of the form 'Such-and-such is (a) φ', where 'φ' is a sortal term and where 'such-and-such' may either be a particular or *individual* term (like the proper name 'Dobbin') or else again a sortal term. Sentences of this form I shall call *instantiation sentences*. Before saying more about the 'is' of instantiation, however, I must say something further about the terms, sortal and individual, which may figure in sentences featuring it.

As we saw in the previous chapter, an important characteristic of sortal terms from a *semantic* point of view is that they typically have associated with them *criteria of identity* – unless, perhaps, they designate what I called 'basic' sorts, if indeed such sorts exist. But I would urge, in agreement with Geach, that *individual* terms – such as proper names – also typically have, as an essential semantic feature, criteria of identity associated with their application.[1] This, it may be observed, runs somewhat counter to the currently popular view that proper names have no Fregean 'sense' and are purely denotative or referential – but not necessarily wholly counter to it.[2] I do not want to suggest that the sense of a proper name is the same as that of some identifying description: that, for example, 'Aristotle' might have the sense of 'the tutor of Alexander the Great' or 'the greatest pupil of Plato', say, nor even that the sense of a proper name involves the senses

---

[1]   See P. T. Geach, *Reference and Generality*, 3rd edn (Ithaca, NY: Cornell University Press, 1980), pp. 67–8.

[2]   I am thinking, primarily, of the view made famous by Saul A. Kripke in his book *Naming and Necessity* (Oxford: Blackwell, 1980).

of a 'cluster' such descriptions, as Searle suggests.[3] What I do hold is that, by whatever means a person may have been introduced to a certain proper name, he has not grasped its correct use unless he has grasped what criterion of identity is associated with it. Thus, for instance, if someone has picked up the name 'Aristotle' from overhearing a conversation amongst philosophers, but does not grasp that it has associated with it the criterion of identity for a *man* (because, say, he thinks that these philosophers are referring to a *book*), then I should say that he fails to refer to *Aristotle* in his subsequent attempts to use the name – indeed, that he fails to refer to *anything*.

This thesis concerning the semantics of proper names is, of course, intimately connected with my contention that individuals must always be thought of as being individuals *of some sort*. The criterion of identity associated with a proper name will just be the one associated with those *sortal terms* that designate the sort(s) or kind(s) which any individual capable of being referred to by that name instantiates. Thus, 'Aristotle', conceived as a name for a *man*, must have associated with it the criterion of identity which is also associated with the sortal term 'man'. So I do not – and certainly need not – insist that the sense of a proper name determines *which individual it refers to*, but at most only what *sort* of individual its referent is: for it is this that determines which criterion of identity is associated with the name.

From these remarks concerning the *semantics* of individual and sortal terms, I want to pass on now to a fuller characterization of their syntax. Typical *individual* terms, apart from *proper names* like 'Dobbin' and 'Scamander', are *demonstrative noun phrases*, such as 'that horse' and 'this river', and *definite descriptions*, such as 'the horse in Farmer Brown's field' and 'the river in which I stepped yesterday'. (It will be noticed that such noun phrases and descriptions, although individual terms, involve sortal terms in their construction. Whether or not such noun phrases and descriptions are to be regarded as genuine *semantic* units in their own right is, however, not an issue that I shall address at present.) Typical *sortal* terms are *count nouns* like 'horse' and 'river' and *mass nouns* like 'water' and 'gold'. But there are also *complex* sortal terms, in which such nouns are qualified by adjectives or adjectival phrases – for example, 'wild horse', 'boiling water', and 'tree which sheds its leaves in winter'. The semantics of complex sortal terms raises special problems which I shall discuss in Chapter 12. For the time being, I shall concentrate on simple sortal terms.

It should be remarked, however, that for semantic purposes the distinction between simple and complex sortal terms cannot be drawn purely

---

[3] See John R. Searle, 'Proper Names', *Mind* 67 (1958), pp. 166–73.

syntactically. 'Ice', for instance, although syntactically simple, very arguably – I don't say *indisputably* – has the same meaning as the syntactically (and semantically) complex sortal term 'frozen water'. By contrast, 'heavy water', although syntactically complex, is plausibly *not* best seen as being semantically determined by the meanings of its syntactic components, 'heavy' and 'water'. Clearly, at least, 'heavy water' does not just mean 'water which is heavy', in the way that 'frozen water' means 'water which is frozen'. (Heavy water is in fact water whose molecules are made of oxygen and *deuterium*, a heavy isotope of hydrogen whose atoms contain not only a proton but also a neutron. So, while we can see that heavy water is *aptly* so-named, it is not apparent that the 'heavy' in 'heavy water' actually contributes to the *meaning* of the term.) To say that a sortal term is *semantically* simple is just to say that it is not *semantically analysable* – in other words, that its meaning is not a compound of the meanings of certain other expressions, such as the meanings of its syntactic components (if it has any), or the meanings of the syntactic components of some syntactically complex sortal term with which it is synonymous.

I would venture to say – although detailed argument in favour of this view will have to wait until later – that a semantically simple sortal term is one which, superficial syntax notwithstanding, has no other semantic function than simply to designate a *distinct sort* of things or stuff. (The question of what *criteria* we do or should employ for determining sortal distinctness is one that I cannot yet address, however.) Thus, one reason why I am persuaded to regard 'heavy water' as being semantically simple is that heavy water is genuinely a distinct kind of substance in its own right: it is, in fact, *a kind of water*. By contrast, 'frozen water' very plausibly does not denote a distinct *kind* of water at all. It should be borne in mind, then, that when I say that I shall for the present concentrate on *simple* sortal terms, I have in mind *semantically* simple ones, even though I am not yet in a position to explain fully what warrants an ascription of semantic simplicity to a sortal term. Fortunately, we can for the time being place some confidence in the probability that natural language is not, in this regard, unduly misleading in its syntax – that cases like that of 'ice' are probably the exception rather than the norm and that, for the most part, syntactic and semantic simplicity or complexity go hand in hand.

A further point about the syntax of sortal terms that I ought to mention is this. The question arises, in the case of a sortal term involving a count noun, whether we should sometimes include the *indefinite article* or a *plural suffix* as part of that term. Consider, for instance, the instantiation sentences cited at the outset of this chapter: 'Dobbin is a horse' and 'A horse is a mammal'. According to what I have said so far, 'horse' and 'mammal' are the two (simple) sortal terms figuring in these sentences.

But it will often be convenient to speak, rather, of *indefinite noun phrases*, such as '*a* horse' and '*a* mammal', as being sortal terms. Again, when we consider that the sentence 'A horse is a mammal' may be paraphrased as 'Horses are mammals', we see that it will often be equally convenient to regard *plural nouns*, such as 'horses' and 'mammals', as sortal terms. The convenience that I allude to here is convenience in respect of *formalization*, or representation by means of symbols for logical purposes. The point is that, for these purposes, I want to represent sentences such as 'Dobbin is a horse' and 'A horse is a mammal' – or the latter's equivalent, 'Horses are mammals' – as being sentences of the forms, respectively, '*a* is φ' and 'φ is χ', where the 'is', of course, is the 'is' of instantiation.

In thus absorbing the indefinite article or a plural suffix into a sortal term, I do not think that I can be accused of ignoring any *logically significant* feature of English grammar – for I agree with Geach's view, that these particles and suffixes are for the most part superficial peculiarities of English syntax that are not encountered in all natural languages. Thus, for example, Geach makes the point that the Latin translation of 'I met a man' has no word for 'a'.[4] This is not, of course, an *instantiation* sentence, but we could equally well point out that the Latin translation of the instantiation sentence 'Caesar is a man' is *Caesar est homo*, while 'A man is an animal' is similarly translated as *Homo est animal*. Interestingly enough, indeed, English itself allows the indefinite article to be dropped in the latter case – 'Man is an animal' – although, curiously, this is not permissible with certain other count nouns, such as 'horse'.

I hasten to add that I by no means deny that the indefinite article or a plural suffix may have logical significance is *some* English sentences, only that they have any such significance in *instantiation* sentences. In some English sentences, of course, these grammatical appendages may play a *quantificational* role, often conveying distinctions of *number*. Thus, there is a clear difference in sense between the sentences 'There is *a horse* in that field' and 'There are *horses* in that field' – by contrast with the already noted synonymy between 'A horse is a mammal' and 'Horses are mammals'.

The foregoing considerations obviously apply only to *count* nouns, as opposed to *mass* nouns like 'water' and 'gold'. But some may question my very lumping together of count and mass nouns within the single category of sortal terms. They might be willing to admit as sortal terms such complex noun phrases as 'drop of water' or 'lump of gold', but not the simple mass nouns 'water' and 'gold' themselves. My own view – which I hope will be seen to be vindicated in the course of this study – is that analogies between the logical behaviour of mass nouns like 'gold' *standing alone* and those undisputed sortal terms involving count nouns, such as 'a

---

[4] See Geach, *Reference and Generality*, p. 8.

horse' or 'horses', are sufficiently pervasive to warrant the assimilation that I make. For example, there is the obvious analogy between 'Horses are mammals' – or 'A horse is a mammal' – and 'Gold is (a) metal'. Again, as we noticed in the previous chapter, we may speak of 'the same gold' exactly as we speak of 'the same man'. Indeed, it is worth remarking that the very *grammar* of mass nouns is in some ways quite similar to that of *plural* count nouns, particularly in constructions involving expressions of *quantity*. For instance, we speak of 'a lot of horses' in very much the same manner in which we speak of 'a lot of wood'.

I shall revisit this issue in due course. Meanwhile, however, I should just remark that I do not want to *deny* the status of *sortal term* to such complex count-noun phrases as 'drop of water', but only want to extend that status to simple mass nouns like 'water' itself, standing alone.

I return now to the distinction between the 'is' of attribution and the 'is' of instantiation. In modern times, at least, these two varieties of 'is' have generally been conflated. But we should observe, first of all, that the 'is' of attribution is, from a logical point of view, really just redundant, whereas the 'is' of instantiation is clearly not. For example, it is merely a relatively parochial feature of English that, instead of saying something like 'This pen *is yellow*', we don't say something like 'This pen *yellows*', utilizing a single verb rather than a copula plus an adjective.[5] Thus, it seems that a predicate like '— is yellow' is, from a logical point of view, a simple semantic unit – is *semantically unanalysable* – in a way in which predicates like '— is a horse' and '— is water' are very plausibly not.[6] (I speak of *predicates* here in a broad sense, in which they are just expressions completable by noun phrases to form sentences.) The reason why the 'is' of instantiation is not redundant – and, hence, one reason why it must be distinguished from the 'is' of attribution – is intimately connected with the fact that sortal terms can figure in sentences in the role of *grammatical subject*. More importantly, it appears that they cannot always be *eliminated* from this role by means of paraphrase – except, perhaps, by paraphrases involving the use of sortal *variables*, or their natural language counterparts, in subject position.

This is, in fact, closely analogous with the reason why the 'is' of *identity* must also be distinguished from the 'is' of attribution, and so it may

---

5   In fact, languages such as Russian and Arabic do, I believe, employ precisely this sort of construction for ascriptions of colour. For some interesting discussion, see N. R. Hanson, *Patterns of Discovery* (Cambridge: Cambridge University Press, 1958), pp. 32–3.

6   Certain considerations mentioned in the Introduction complicate this matter somewhat, but not in any way that need detain us here.

be of some help to expand on the latter point. Suppose that this last distinction were denied and that the 'is' in 'Cicero *is* Tully' were alleged to be the same as that in 'Cicero *is* wise'. This would make the predicate '— is Tully' a simple semantic unit, like '— is wise'. But there would then threaten to be a quite intolerable *systematic ambiguity* between the use of 'Tully' as a grammatical subject, as in 'Tully is wise', and its appearance in its allegedly attributive role in 'Cicero is Tully'. Now, of course, the immediate difficulty here might be circumvented by arguing that 'Tully' can always be removed from subject position by means of paraphrase, so that it need only ever appear in the context '— is Tully'. Just such a programme of systematic removal was in fact notoriously canvassed by Quine, in the context of his defence of a 'descriptive' theory of proper names.[7] However, it is evident that even a descriptive theorist is not, in virtue of this strategy, relieved of the need for a distinction 'is' of identity, so long as he retains at least the use of *individual variables* (or their natural language counterparts) in subject position. For such a theorist will still need to allow such variables to flank *both* sides of an 'is', which in such an occurrence will still therefore have to be recognized as making an independent semantic contribution to the meaning of a sentence, unlike the 'is' of attribution. Thus if, following Quine, 'Tully is wise' is first paraphrased as 'The thing which is Tully is wise', and the definite description here is then eliminated in Russell's way, to give 'For some x, x is Tully and for all y, if y is Tully then y is x, and x is wise', an 'is' of identity now appears in the expression 'y is x'. The claim that I am now defending regarding the non-redundancy of the 'is' of identity and its distinctness from the 'is' of attribution is not, thus, narrowly tied to a particular theory of proper names, but turns rather on general ontological considerations connected with the use of quantifiers with individual variables.

Now, analogously, the need to recognize a distinctive 'is' of *instantiation* is connected with the fact that, just as in the case of individual terms, *sortal* terms too can often figure as grammatical subjects in sentences which cannot be paraphrased by other sentences in which sortal terms, or at least sortal *variables*, no longer appear in subject position. One very important category of such sentences consists of those that are expressive of *natural laws*, or *nomological generalizations*, such as 'Water is translucent'. The sortal term 'water' appears here in subject position and this sentence cannot, I contend, be paraphrased satisfactorily by any other sentence in which 'water' appears only in the predicative context '— is water', with

---

[7]   See W. V. Quine, 'On What There Is', in his *From a Logical Point of View*, 2nd edn (Cambridge, MA: Harvard University Press, 1961), p. 8, where he uses the example of the name 'Pegasus'. I should stress that I am not an advocate of such a theory myself.

the blank being occupied only by an *individual* term or variable. Thus, for instance, 'For all x, if x is water, then x is translucent' will certainly not do as a paraphrase, as I shall argue in detail in Chapter 9. Once more, the crucial point is that in order to cope with the *logic* of nomological sentences we shall have to allow an 'is' to be flanked on *both* sides at least by sortal *variables*, and hence to concede that in such an occurrence the 'is' makes an independent semantic contribution to the sentence concerned. This will be a contribution which, moreover, cannot always simply be identified with that of the 'is' of *identity*, since in at least some contexts it will prove not to involve a symmetrical relation. At root, then, the issue is again an ontological one connected with quantification. We need to recognize a distinctive 'is' of instantiation ultimately because we have to admit variables which range over *sorts* or *kinds*. But I shall say much more about this later in the book.

Here a possible query might be raised, as follows. It might be objected that *colour terms* like 'yellow', with which I am presently *contrasting* sortal terms, can also figure as grammatical subjects, in sentences such as 'Yellow is the colour of this pen' and 'Yellow is a colour'. So shouldn't the lesson be that the 'is' of *attribution* is likewise non-redundant? And then how are we to distinguish it from the 'is' of instantiation? Well, in the first place, in order to endorse this line of argument we would need to be sure that suitable eliminative paraphrases of such sentences are not always available. But arguably they *are* – in these cases, in the form of the sentences 'This pen is yellow' and 'Everything that is yellow is coloured'. I concede, however, that the latter paraphrase, at least, is questionable. Now, if colour terms *cannot* always be paraphrased out of subject position in some such fashion, then I suggest that, for that very reason, we should perhaps be willing to countenance them as being *sortal* terms after all, by regarding them – at least in certain of their occurrences – as *mass* terms.[8] Clearly, however, there is no real prospect at all of regarding adjectives like 'long' or 'wise' or 'heavy' in this way – and this shows that the distinction that I am trying to draw is a genuine one, even if there may be some disagreement as to where exactly the boundary lies as far as ordinary English sentences are concerned.

I have, of course, been assuming that, just as it would be undesirable to be forced to acknowledge a systematic ambiguity between certain uses of a proper name like 'Tully', so it would with regard to uses of a sortal term like 'water'. However, Geach, it may be remarked, *is* prepared to allow just such a systematic ambiguity.[9] This is because he countenances a sense

8   Compare W. V. Quine, *Word and Object* (Cambridge, MA: MIT Press, 1960), pp. 91ff. And, indeed, we do quite often talk of colours as if they were kinds of *stuff*, when we speak, for instance, of 'a bit of yellow' or 'a lot of red'.
9   See Geach, *Reference and Generality*, p. 172.

in which sortal terms – or substantival general terms, as he calls them – occur in *semantically simple* (that is, unanalysable) identity predicates of the form '— is the same φ as . . .', as well as a sense in which they occur as grammatical subjects. The supposed semantic simplicity of these predicates on Geach's view is connected, of course, with his *relativist* position concerning the nature of identity, which I shall examine more fully in a later chapter. Here I shall remark only that, in my view, a commitment to systematic ambiguity of the kind described is something to be avoided if at all possible. In Chapter 5, I shall try to show that Geach, at least, provides no good reason for thinking such avoidance to be *im*possible.

As I understand it, a sentence of the form 'Such-and-such is (a) φ' standardly affirms that such-and-such is an *instance of the sort or kind* φ. (I say 'standardly' because I acknowledge that sentences involving a distinctive 'is' of *constitution* may also take this form, although I believe that they may always be paraphrased so as to eliminate the ambiguity. I shall say more about the 'is' of constitution in Chapter 6.) Thus, 'Dobbin is a horse' affirms that Dobbin is an individual instance of the kind *horse*; and 'This portion of metal is gold' affirms that this portion of metal is an individual instance or sample of the kind *gold*. 'A horse is an animal' and 'Gold is (a) metal' are analogous, in that they affirm one sort or kind to be a *species* of another – and for present purposes, at least, I take the species–genus relation to be the same as the relation between an individual and any sort or kind that it instantiates. Thus, any *dis*analogy between 'Dobbin is a horse' and 'A horse is an animal' seems to me to reside not so much in the sense of 'is' figuring in each, which I take to be univocal, as in the mere fact that 'Dobbin' denotes an *individual* whereas '(a) horse' denotes a *sort* or *kind*.

I readily acknowledge that this assimilation of the species–genus 'is' to the 'is' of instantiation is not entirely uncontroversial, but in its favour is the consideration that we should not multiply the different senses of 'is' beyond necessity and – as we shall see in due course – the logical properties of the relations in question are very plausibly the same. Hence, on grounds of economy alone the assumption seems to be a reasonable one, in the absence of countervailing evidence. But I shall not undertake any more detailed defence of it at present.

Returning for a moment to the issue of whether mass nouns may be regarded as sortal terms – as I think they may – I should say that it seems to me that individual bodies or portions of water stand in the same relationship to the sort or kind *water* as individual horses do to the sort of kind *horse* – namely, as individual *instances*, *samples*, or *exemplars*. I would certainly want to resist any tendency to see a mass noun like 'water' as denoting a 'scattered' *individual*, the mereological sum of all the various individual bodies or portions of water in the world.[10] 'Water', it seems to me, is in *no* sense an individual term, comparable with 'Dobbin'. For one thing, there are different *kinds* of water – for instance, so-called *heavy* water – but no kinds of *Dobbin*. (It is, I believe, no use saying that 'heavy water' just denotes a *part* of the world's sum total of water – namely, that part of it whose molecules contain deuterium instead of ordinary hydrogen.) But, given that 'water' is indeed a sortal term, there seems to be little alternative but to regard as its referent's individual instances all the various individual bodies or portions of water that there are, such as the portion of water poured from a certain bottle during the last three seconds, or the body of water filling the Scamander's river-bed on a certain day.[11]

Given, however, that both individuals and sorts stand in the instantiation relation to sorts, the following question arises: what, then, *is* an 'individual', and how is it to be distinguished from a 'sort'? I don't think that *spatiotemporal* considerations are of much use for elucidating this distinction, firstly, because I suspect that spatiotemporal relationships already presuppose an ontology of identifiable particulars or individuals, and, secondly, because the notion of an individual which is *not* spatiotemporally located certainly does not appear to be incoherent. I have already discussed, in the previous chapter, *abstract* individuals such as *sets*, which do not appear to be in any sense spatiotemporally located – not, at least, unless all of their *members* are, which certainly does not always seem to be the case.[12] But even if we limit ourselves to *concrete* individuals, there is the *prima facie* coherent hypothesis of Cartesian *souls* or *egos*, which are clearly conceived of as not

---

[10]   For such a view, see Quine, *Word and Object*, pp. 97ff.

[11]   Here I deliberately use the disjunctive expression 'body or portion' in order to allow for the possibility that particular instances of the kind *water* are or include *quantities* of water, in Helen M. Cartwright's sense of that term: see her 'Quantities', *Philosophical Review* 79 (1970), pp. 25–42. The point is that 'body' suggests a connected mass of matter, all contained within a certain surface or boundary, whereas 'portions' of matter of any kind may, it seems, be scattered without limit, or mixed with other portions of different kinds of material stuff. I shall say more about quantities of matter and their ontological status in the next chapter, where we shall see that it is in fact problematic to regard them as *individuals*. That being so, we should strictly say only that they are *particular*, not *individual*, instances of kinds of material stuff. But this complication need not detain us at present.

[12]   I make this qualification in order to accommodate Penelope Maddy's view that sets all of whose members are *concrete* things are in fact themselves concrete and located where their members are: see her *Realism in Mathematics* (Oxford: Clarendon Press, 1990), pp. 50ff. I have no sympathy for the view myself.

being *spatially* locatable, at least. I hasten to add that I don't want to suggest that I endorse this hypothesis myself, only that it seems *coherent*.

My own answer – although only a tentative one – would be roughly along the following lines. *A* is an *individual* if and only if *A* is an instance of something, *B*, other than itself, and *A* itself has no instances, other than itself. And *A* is a *sort* if and only if there is something, *B*, such that *B* is an instance of *A* and *B* is distinct from *A*. More formally, the proposal is to adopt the following definitional equivalences, where the slash sign, '/', is used to signify instantiation:

A is an individual $=_{df} \exists B(A/B \ \& \ B \neq A) \ \& \ \sim\exists B(B/A \ \& \ B \neq A)$
A is a sort $=_{df} \exists B(B/A \ \& \ B \neq A)$

In this way, the distinction between individuals and sorts is defined by means of the instantiation relation itself. Moreover, it follows from the definitions, as it presumably should, that the distinction between individuals and sorts is mutually exclusive: nothing can be *both* an individual *and* a sort.

Notice that I do not insist that sorts always instantiate 'higher' sorts: for there may presumably be 'highest' sorts of which this is not true. Individuals, by contrast, must always instantiate sorts, for reasons already discussed earlier – there are no 'bare' particulars. Hence the asymmetry between the two definitions. Notice too that, in the proposed definitions, the variables '*A*' and '*B*' must obviously not be viewed as being specifically either *individual* or *sortal* variables, but rather as being quite 'neutral' in this regard.[13] I propose to call them, quite simply, *objectual* variables. The distinction between individual and sortal variables then has to be introduced sub-sequently, precisely on the basis of the proposed definitions – provided, of course, that they are accepted. I myself follow the practice of using the lower-case Roman letters '*x*', '*y*', '*z*', and so on as *individual* variables and the lower-case Greek letters '*φ*', '*χ*', '*ψ*', and so on as *sortal* variables.

It will be observed that the foregoing definitions make use not only of the 'is' of instantiation but also of the 'is' of *identity*. A further economy

---

[13] However, as I shall explain in Chapter 11 below, it is in fact questionable whether it ultimately makes sense to work with a system of logic containing such supposedly 'neutral' variables, at least if this is taken to imply that the domain of quantification is not already *essentially divided* into entities belonging to two fundamentally different ontological categories, *individuals* and *sorts*. Hence, the 'definitions' of *individual* and *sort* just proposed are probably best seen merely as providing *elucidations* of those notions, rather than *reductive analyses* of them.

might therefore be achieved by defining the latter, *as it is used here*, in terms of the former – specifically, by defining identity here in terms of *mutual instantiation*. In other words, we could adopt additionally the following definitional equivalence:

$$A = B =_{df} A/B \ \& \ B/A$$

Note that this definition would still only define identity for 'objects' – that is, for individuals and sorts – not identity quite generally. But if, as I maintained in Chapter 2, identity is *univocal*, such a restricted 'definition' must be regarded with suspicion, at least if it is taken to imply that 'identity' has a special meaning as applied to *objects*, as opposed, say, to *properties* or *states of affairs*. Analogously, it would be questionable to think of defining identity for *sets* in terms of their mutual inclusion, even though mutual inclusion is logically necessary and sufficient for set-identity. (The analogy is, however, imperfect, because this condition for set-identity is simply derivable from the criterion of identity for sets together with the definition of set-inclusion, whereas no analogous derivation is available in the case now under examination.) Consequently, we would be advised to speak of 'definition' here only in a loose sense. Our proposed 'definition' would, however, certainly preserve the logical characteristics of identity as an *equivalence* relation – a relation that is reflexive, symmetrical, and transitive – on the assumption, at least, that instantiation itself is a *reflexive* relation, which has some plausibility. However, I do not propose to pursue this line of speculation any further in the present study. (Observe, incidentally, that if instantiation is alternatively conceived to be an *irreflexive* relation, then the conjunct '$B \neq A$' may of course be omitted at each of its occurrences in the definitions of *individual* and *sort* proposed earlier.)

According to the definitions of *individual* and *sort* suggested above, what distinguishes the individual *Dobbin* from the species or sort *horse* is that Dobbin has no instances (except, quite possibly, himself) whereas the horse does. That is, 'horse' *divides its reference*, but 'Dobbin' does not. It is indivisibility of *reference* rather than *material* indivisibility that, it seems clear, the notion of 'individuality' implies, when we employ it in speaking of 'individual' as opposed to 'sortal' terms. Dobbin is, of course, not 'indivisible' in the sense that he cannot be cut into pieces, merely in the sense that nothing (apart perhaps from Dobbin himself) – such as any one of these pieces – qualifies as an *instance* of Dobbin. There is no plurality of different *Dobbins*, in the way that there are many different *horses*. (Of course, in *another* way there *are* many different Dobbins, but only in the sense that many different individual horses may be called by the same name, 'Dobbin'. These different individuals are not, however, *instances* of some one individual, Dobbin.) It might be wondered whether these considerations apply equally in the case of an individual such as a lump of gold, since each piece into which it is divided (down to a certain spatial level, at least) is again a lump of gold. But even here it is not the case that each such piece is an *instance* of the original lump, as opposed to a *part* or *portion* of it.

Nonetheless, the definitions just proposed are still arguably not entirely satisfactory, because they apparently fail to take into account the possibility of *infimae species* lacking individual instances. An *infima species*, or lowest species, if there can be such a thing, would be a sort without any distinct sub-sort instantiating it. There are, however, various ways in which one might seek to evade this difficulty. One, which superficially seems quite plausible, would simply be to deny the possibility of *infimae species*, on the grounds that any sortal term 'φ' whatever can be suitably qualified or restricted so as to generate another – albeit complex – sortal term 'χ', such that 'χ is φ' is a true instantiation sentence: for example, 'Boiling water is water', 'A wild horse is a horse', and so on. The trouble with this proposal, however, is that it misconceives the semantics of complex sortal terms – which, as I have said, I shall discuss more fully in a later chapter. Specifically, it makes the mistake of supposing that an expression like 'boiling water' denotes a *kind* of water. Without this supposition the proposal will not work, since it merely appeals to the purely *syntactical* fact that any sortal term, however complex, can in principle be further qualified adjectivally, *ad infinitum*.

Another possibility would simply be to regard individuals precisely *as* lowest species. This suggestion might quite attract some metaphysicians, on account of its economy and simplicity. But it has little *prima facie* plausibility and I shall not pursue it any further.[14]

Yet another possibility would be to employ *modal* expressions in the definitions of 'individual' and 'sort', saying something to the effect that *A* is an individual only if *A cannot* have instances (other than itself). One potential difficulty with this is that there may perhaps be some *sorts* which cannot have individual instances, such as the mythological sorts *centaur*, *mermaid*, and *dragon*, individual instances of which would arguably be at least *physically* impossible objects. However, here I am strongly inclined to retort that, precisely because they have always *actually* lacked individual instances, there cannot really *be* any such sorts as these at all.

---

[14]   However, it is worth comparing it with Leibniz's contention that 'what St Thomas [Aquinas] assures us on this point of angels or intelligences (*quod ibi individuum sit species infima*) is true of all substances': see his *Discourse on Metaphysics*, trans. P. G. Lucas and L. Grant (Manchester: Manchester University Press, 1961), p. 14.

Mythological sortal terms like those just mentioned very arguably *fail of reference*, just as do mythological proper names, such as 'Pegasus' and 'Hercules'.[15] In short, the position that I am inclined to adopt is that there cannot be *infimae species* lacking individual instances, *not* because there cannot be *infimae species*, but rather because there cannot be any species or sorts *at all* that altogether lack individual instances. (There can still be species like the *Dodo*, no individual instances of which *now* exist, but that is a different matter, since for an animal species to lack individual instances *altogether* is for it to lack them at *all* times and places. In other words, the mere fact that the Dodo has become extinct does not make it comparable to a mythological species. Presumably, indeed, it is even possible, in principle, for scientists to recreate individual instances of it, given enough knowledge of its genetic structure.) If all this is correct, then the definitions of *individual* and *sort* proposed earlier may be allowed to stand, without any need to introduce modal expressions into them.

[15] Compare Geach, *Reference and Generality*, p. 217.

4

Number, Unity, and Individuality

In previous chapters, I have had a good deal to say about the notion of *identity* and something, but considerably less, about that of *individuality*. Now I want to say more about how these notions relate to those of *number* and *unity*, while also taking the opportunity to say more about individuality. Much of my discussion will focus on the distinctive contributions of Locke and Frege to our understanding of these matters – my only justification for this being that these are the authors whose work I have found most thought-provoking in this regard.

In distinguishing between the primary and secondary qualities of bodies in the *Essay*, Locke notoriously included *number* amongst the first:[1]

> The *Qualities* then that are in *Bodies* rightly considered, are of *Three Sorts*. *First*, the *Bulk, Figure, Number, Situation*, and *Motion, or Rest* of their solid Parts . . . These I call *primary* Qualities. (II, VIII, 23)

Later in the *Essay*, in the chapter entitled 'Of Number', he goes on to say:

> Amongst all the *Ideas* we have, as there is none suggested to the Mind by more ways, so there is none more simple, than that *of Unity*, or One: . . . every Thought of our Minds brings this *Idea* along with it . . . For Number applies it self to Men, Angels, Actions, Thoughts, every thing that either doth exist, or can be imagined. (II, XVI, 1)

---

[1] See John Locke, *An Essay Concerning Human Understanding*, ed. P. H. Nidditch (Oxford: Clarendon Press, 1975), from which edition all quoted passages are taken.

Just as well-known as Locke's view of number and unity is Berkeley's peremptory repudiation of that view, in his *Principles of Human Knowledge*.[2] There Berkeley asserts, concerning number:

> That number is entirely the creature of the mind . . . will be evident to whoever considers, that the same thing bears a different denomination of number, as the mind views it with different respects. Thus, the same extension is one or three or thirty-six, according as the mind considers it with reference to a yard, a foot, or an inch . . . We say one book, one page, one line; all these are equally units, though some contain several of the others. (Part 1, §12)

And in the next paragraph he continues, concerning unity:

> Unity I know some will have to be a simple or uncompounded idea, accompanying all other ideas into the mind. That I have any such idea answering the word *unity*, I do not find; and if I had, methinks I could not miss finding it; on the contrary it should be the most familiar to my understanding, since it is said to accompany all other ideas. (§13)

In his earlier work, *An Essay towards a New Theory of Vision*, Berkeley expresses similar contempt for Locke's conceptions of number and unity, again making the point that

> [N]umber . . . is entirely the creature of the mind . . . According as the mind variously combines its ideas the unit varies: and as the unit, so the number, which is only a collection of units, doth also vary. We call a window one, a chimney one, and yet a house in which there are many windows and many chimneys hath an equal right to be called one, and many houses go to the making of one city. (§109)

This last passage is quoted, with apparent approval, by Frege in *The Foundations of Arithmetic* – although, of course, Frege should not be taken to concur with Berkeley's suggestion that number is somehow subjective, 'entirely a creature of the mind', in view of Frege's own vehement opposition to psychologism in the philosophy of logic and mathematics.[3]

---

[2]   Quoted passages are taken from George Berkeley, *Philosophical Works*, ed. M. R. Ayers (London: Dent, 1975).

[3]   See Gottlob Frege, *The Foundations of Arithmetic*, trans. J. L. Austin, 2nd edn (Oxford: Blackwell, 1953), p. 33, from which edition all subsequent quoted passages are taken.

Frege's agreement with Berkeley extends only as far as the latter's rejection of the view that, as Frege puts it, 'Number is a property of external things' (p. 27). Frege's own view is that

> [T]he content of a statement of number is an assertion about a concept. This is perhaps clearest with the number 0. If I say 'Venus has 0 moons', there simply does not exist any moon or agglomeration of moons for anything to be asserted of; but what happens is that a property is assigned to the *concept* 'moon of Venus', namely that of including nothing under it. If I say 'the King's carriage is drawn by four horses', then I assign the number four to the concept 'horse that draws the King's carriage'. (p. 59)

Frege himself appeals, on several occasions, to the sort of consideration that Berkeley adduces for rejecting Locke's view of number, namely that

> While looking at one and the same external phenomenon, I can say with equal truth both 'It is a copse' and 'It is five trees', or both 'Here are four companies' and 'Here are 500 men'. (p. 59)

Here is another passage in which he makes the same point:

> I am able to think of the Iliad either as one poem, or as 24 Books, or as some large Number of verses. (p. 28)

And here is a third:

> The Number 1, . . . or 100 or any other Number, cannot be said to belong to [a] pile of playing cards in its own right, but at most to belong to it in view of the way in which we have chosen to regard it. (p. 29)

In this last case, the suggestion is that what is, from one point of view, one pack of cards is, from another point of view, 52 cards, while from yet another it is four suits, and so on. Even so, there is every indication that Frege is ambivalent about endorsing Berkeley in quite these terms – and not just on account of Berkeley's subjectivism concerning number. Rather, the problem is that it is not hard to discern a latent incoherence in this way of putting things. The incoherence is very near the surface in one of the passages from Frege quoted a moment ago, where he says that 'While looking at one and the same external phenomenon, I can say with equal truth "It is a copse" and "It is five trees"'. For how can Frege say that *one and the same* 'external phenomenon' is both one copse and five trees? (Admittedly, the German text reads 'derselben äussern Erscheinung', so that Austin's translation might be criticized for having 'one and the same' instead of just 'the same': but the difficulty is made only marginally less obvious by this amendment.)

What *is* this 'it' that is somehow both a single copse and five different trees? Frege is clearly aware of the difficulty, for in first presenting the example of the pack of cards he remarks:

> [I]f I place a pile of playing cards in [someone's] hands with the words: Find the Number of these, this does not tell him whether I wish to know the number of cards, or of complete packs of cards, or even say of honour cards at skat. To have given him the pile in his hands is not yet to have given him completely the object he is to investigate; I must add some further word – cards, or packs, or honours. (pp. 28–9)

Clearly, Frege does not really want to say, *on his own account*, that one and the same thing can literally be both one and more than one. This is why he admits, later, that

> Several examples given earlier gave the false impression that different numbers may belong to the same thing. This is to be explained by the fact that we were there taking objects to be what has number. As soon as we restore possession to the rightful owner, the concept, numbers reveal themselves as no less mutually exclusive in their own sphere than colours are in theirs. (p. 61)

It would seem, then, that Frege's use of the controversial examples is supposed to contribute towards a *reductio ad absurdum* of the view that numbers are properties of objects. The idea seems to be that *if* we suppose that numbers are properties of objects, then we shall have to say that different numbers may, with equal legitimacy, be assigned to the same object or objects: that, for example, the same thing may be regarded as one pack of cards or as 52 cards. However, the trouble is that, far from creating a difficulty for philosophers like Locke, the argument, thus understood, rebounds against Frege himself. Berkeley, it should be noted, used the contentious examples to try to show that number is not a 'primary quality' of objects, which they possess independently of the mind: it was no part of his purpose to argue that number is not in any sense a property of objects. But Frege clearly recognizes the incoherence of saying that *anything* could be at once one thing and more than one thing and that this incoherence does not go away simply by supposing that number is somehow mind-dependent, or a matter of how we 'view' or 'regard' whatever it is to which we are assigning a number. If this is incoherent, however, then it cannot be something to which any philosopher is committed simply in virtue of supposing that number is a property of objects or things, as opposed to Fregean concepts. Rather, the philosopher who takes the former view must clearly just insist that, for example, one pack of cards cannot be *identified* with 52 different cards, even though it may, of course, *consist* of 52 different cards.

Frege's own contribution to our understanding of identity statements and his introduction of the notion of a criterion of identity, far from making difficulties for Locke's view of number, actually aid the adherent of that view to rebut the sort of objection that Berkeley advances. *Cards* and *packs of cards* are kinds of things that are governed by quite *different* criteria of identity, with the consequence that it makes no sense to say that something could fall under *both* of the sortal concepts *card* and *pack of cards* – a quite general point for which I shall argue more fully in Chapter 5 below. *A fortiori*, then, something cannot intelligibly be assigned the number one inasmuch as it is regarded as falling under the concept *pack of cards* and the number 52 inasmuch as it is regarded as falling under the concept *card*. The upshot of all this is that Frege's frequent appeal to the sort of objection to Locke's view of number that we find in Berkeley is entirely broken-backed.

Frege has related remarks about the notion of *unity* which are equally unsatisfactory, although in this case we may also take issue with what Locke himself says on the matter. Berkeley, as we saw earlier, expresses contempt for Locke's suggestion that the idea of unity accompanies every other idea, saying that he can find no such idea in his own mind. Part of what Locke is suggesting, clearly, is that everything whatever that exists or could exist is 'one' or a 'unit': that simply in virtue of being self-identical and distinct from anything else, everything has 'unity'. But Frege is just as contemptuous as Berkeley about this suggestion. Sarcastically, he comments:

> It must strike us immediately as remarkable that every single thing should possess this property [of being 'one'] . . . It is only in virtue of the possibility of something not being wise that it makes sense to say 'Solon is wise'. The content of a concept diminishes as its extension increases; if its extension becomes all-embracing, its content must vanish altogether. It is not easy to imagine how language could have come to invent a word for a property which could not be of the slightest use for adding to the description of any object whatsoever. (p. 40)

This argument, too, backfires on Frege. In fact, in Austin's translation, the first sentence in the passage just quoted looks manifestly absurd: 'It must strike us immediately as remarkable that every single thing should possess this property [of being "one"]' – for what is a 'single' thing if not, precisely, *one* thing? Singularity and unitariness are, if not identical concepts, at least intimately related. And is the concept of singularity somehow left devoid of content if we suppose that *everything* exhibits singularity? I ask this question without presuming that such a supposition is correct, for in point of fact I think that the supposition can certainly be challenged, for reasons that I shall give later. My point here is merely that one could not legitimately convict a philosopher of incoherence or vacuity for contending that everything that exists is singular in character. However, it would be unfair to press this objection to Frege simply on the strength of Austin's translation, for the translation is misleading at this point. Frege's original words do not contain anything translatable as 'single' or 'singular'. The sentence in question reads, in German, simply as follows: *Auffallend wäre zunächst, dass jedes Ding diese Eigenschaft hätte.* Nonetheless, the general point still stands, that it is a poor argument against a putative concept that those who profess to deploy it suppose it to apply to everything whatever. Most philosophers (and, clearly, even Frege himself) would accept that the concept of *self-identity* applies to everything whatever, but they cannot be convicted on that account of evacuating the concept of all content.

Frege supplements the poor argument that I have just criticized by urging that 'Solon was one' does not make sense in anything like the way that 'Solon was wise' does, because the former is not 'intelligible on its own in isolation' (p. 40). He goes on:

> This is even clearer if we take the plural. Whereas we can combine 'Solon was wise' and 'Thales was wise' into 'Solon and Thales were wise', we cannot say 'Solon and Thales were one'. But it is hard to see why this should be impossible, if 'one' were a property both of Solon and of Thales in the same way that 'wise' is. (pp. 40–1)

However, the natural and correct response to this is to point out that being one is necessarily a property only of *single things*, whereas Solon and Thales are not a single thing: rather, they are two things, whence they possess the property of *being two*. (This will become clearer shortly, when we come to discuss pluralities.) It remains the case that we can still say, quite truly, 'Solon and Thales were *each* one', while also saying, with equal truth, 'Solon and Thales (together) were two'. The fact that Solon and Thales were two, even though Solon was not two and Thales was not two, is no more puzzling than the fact, say, that Smith and Jones moved the piano, even though Smith did not move the piano and Jones did not move the piano (the piano being too heavy for one person to move). Any oddity that attaches to sentences like 'Solon was one' and 'Solon and Thales were two' is, I suggest, purely pragmatic in character, arising from the fact that the applicability of the predicate is already apparent from the grammatical form of the subject, so that such sentences appear to be stating the obvious. However, what is obvious is not precluded from being both meaningful and true.

Even so, the suggestion that everything has the property of being one – that everything is *one* thing – might be questioned on the ground that the numbers, including the number one, are used in *counting* things, but that it makes no sense to count *things* as such, since we can only count things of specifiable sorts or kinds. This, indeed, was the implication of Frege's remarks, quoted earlier, concerning the pile of cards, and the indeterminacy of the instruction to 'Find the Number of these'. One needs to be told whether one is to count the packs, or the cards, or the honour cards, or whatnot. However, while there is something that is right about what Frege says in this connection, there is also something that is wrong or at least misleading. It is wrong, and obviously so, to suppose that one cannot include things of many different kinds in a single count. I could quite coherently ask someone to count the packs *and* the cards, for instance. If there were 52 cards and 4 complete suits, then the answer to the question 'What is the number of packs and cards?' would be 53. This would be an odd question to ask, but not an unintelligible or unanswerable one. Similarly, it would make perfectly good sense to ask how many *children and books* there were in a certain classroom. On the other hand, it is not so easy to make sense of an instruction, say, to count *the cards and the honour cards*, simply because each honour card *is* a card and we presumably ought to avoid double-counting. Even so, given a suitable disambiguation of this instruction, it too could be coherently carried out. Indeed, on the most reasonable interpretation of it, the answer would seem to be, in the case envisaged, 52 – in other words, there are just as many cards and honour cards as there are cards.[4]

Where problems of principle *do* arise in matters of counting is where we are expected, somehow, to include in the count items that do not qualify as *single things*. For many philosophers – including, it would appear, Locke – no such problem can ever arise, precisely because, in their view, everything whatever that exists or could exist is a single thing. However, as I have already indicated, this view can certainly be challenged. And, of course, anyone who does challenge it will not be vulnerable to Frege's objection, for what it is worth, that it is vacuous to attribute 'oneness' to objects because this is a property that everything would have to have.

---

[4]   For a recent repudiation of the thesis that it is somehow incoherent to inquire, *without qualification*, into 'the number of things', see Peter van Inwagen, 'The Number of Things', *Philosophical Issues* 12 (2002), pp. 176–96. My own view about this matter was stated earlier, in Chapter 2 above.

But, it will now be asked, how *can* it make sense to say that something might fail to be one, singular, or unitary – fail to possess oneness, singularity, or unitariness? If the question were how some *thing* could fail to be one, singular, or unitary, then I might indeed be inclined to dismiss as incoherent the thought that there could be any such failure, because the concept of a 'thing' seems already to have the notion of singularity or unitariness built into it. However, while 'Everything is something' is, apparently, a trivial truth of logic, 'Everything is some *thing*' looks like a more substantive metaphysical claim.

One reason for denying that everything is a thing is that the world, as well as containing individual things, contains *pluralities* of things – and a plurality of things is not a single thing. Indeed, if we are to take seriously Locke's suggestion that number is a property of things, then, clearly, the only number that can be assigned to a *single* thing – Berkeley's objection having been repudiated – is *one*. And this means, of course, that numbers other than one can only be assigned to more than one thing – that is, to pluralities of things. We say, for example, and quite properly, that the planets are nine in number, as are the muses. In the sentence 'The planets are nine', the subject term, 'the planets', refers plurally to Mercury, Venus, Mars, Earth, Jupiter, Saturn, Uranus, Neptune, and Pluto, and the predicate attributes the property of being nine to that plurality. We should not be misled here by the fact that the expression 'that plurality' is grammatically singular in form. This is a mere idiosyncrasy of idiom and does not signify that there is some further *thing*, 'the plurality of the planets', in addition to the planets themselves. When I suggest that pluralities provide a plausible exception to the thesis that 'Everything is a thing', I mean just this: pluralities *exist*, and yet, manifestly, are not single things. For instance, *the planets* exist, and yet are not one thing. To the extent, then, that the so-called universal quantifier, expressed in English by means of the word 'everything', ranges at least over what exists, it ranges over pluralities as well as over single things, given that pluralities exist. Hence it is true to say that not everything is a thing.

But this is not the only reason for denying that everything is a thing. Pluralities of individual things can at least be assigned a number. The planets are 9 and the books of the *Iliad* are 24. To avoid potential confusion, let us henceforth use the term 'entity' to denote anything whatever that does or could exist, whether or not it is an individual thing. Then, I want to say, there are or could be entities to which numbers cannot even in principle be assigned. One of the most plausible supporting examples for this thesis is provided by *quantities of matter*, especially if these are conceived of as being homogeneous and infinitely divisible. Such a quantity of matter might seem to be a good candidate for being a plurality – but it cannot, it seems, be a plurality of *individual things*. This is because, although it includes distinct entities, each of the entities that it includes is in turn a (lesser) quantity of matter. If all quantities of matter were ultimately made up of indivisible atoms – which may be something like the truth as far as the actual physical world is concerned – then they would indeed be very good candidates for being pluralities, namely, pluralities of atoms. (Locke himself was sympathetic to atomism, of course.) But it doesn't really make sense, it would seem, to talk of a plurality which is not a plurality of individual things, since the concept of a plurality is tied to that of number and where there are no individual things no number can meaningfully be assigned.

We need, it would seem, a new ontological term to apply to entities such as our hypothetical quantities of homogeneous and infinitely divisible matter. We could call them, perhaps, *dividuals*.[5] Dividuals cannot be assigned numbers – neither the number one nor any greater number. They are not single things, nor are they pluralities. Yet dividuals may be distinguished: the quantity of matter in one bowl may be wholly distinct from the quantity of matter in another bowl. Any proper part of a quantity of matter is a quantity of matter which is distinct from the whole of which it is a part and distinct, too, from other proper parts of that same whole. To avoid any misunderstanding here, it must be emphasized that a quantity of matter is not the same as a *piece* of matter. A piece of matter is an individual thing, composed of matter that is gathered together to make a single connected whole. That same quantity of matter could be divided and separated in infinitely many different ways, without thereby ceasing to exist. It would continue to exist even if it were scattered across the entire universe. A *piece* of matter, on the other hand, continues to exist only so long as the quantity of matter composing it remains gathered together.

I have just said that numbers – and here I mean cardinal numbers, quite generally – cannot be assigned to dividuals. But there is, of course, a perfectly good sense in which numbers *can* be assigned to dividuals, such as quantities of matter. For we can say, concerning a certain quantity of matter, *how much* of it there is and assign a number to this amount, given an appropriate choice of units for the purposes of measurement. (Here we may in principle need recourse not just to integral or rational numbers but to *real* numbers, given the hypothesized infinite divisibility of quantities of matter.) So, for example, if we use kilograms as our units of mass, we may say that there are 2.35 kilograms of matter in the bowl. However, it is important to appreciate that in thus assigning a number to the quantity

---

[5] The *Oxford English Dictionary* includes this word but describes its use as noun as obsolete. I first used it myself in my 'Primitive Substances', *Philosophy and Phenomenological Research* 54 (1994), pp. 531–52. See also my *The Possibility of Metaphysics: Substance, Identity, and Time* (Oxford: Clarendon Press, 1998), p. 161.

of matter in the bowl, we are focusing on just one physical property of the matter, its mass. After all, we might alternatively want to assign a number to the *volume* of the quantity of matter rather than to its mass. So, what we are measuring and thus assigning numbers to is not really the mere quantity of matter as such but, rather, certain of its properties, such as its mass or its volume. It would seem that there are and can be no 'units' for measuring *how much matter*, as such, a quantity of matter is. And, in any case, it is clear that the sense in which we can assign numbers to quantities of matter is completely distinct from that in which we can assign numbers to pluralities of individual things and in no way undermines the ontological distinction that I just have proposed between individuals and dividuals.

So far, I have mainly been concerned to defend the Lockean view that number is a property of objects against Frege's view that number is a property of *concepts*. (Of course, in this connection it is important to appreciate that Frege thinks of concepts as being objective and mind-independent, and hence as being quite distinct from the psychological entities that Locke and Berkeley call 'ideas'.) Even the most ardent supporter of Frege must surely concede that Frege's view on this matter is relatively counter-intuitive – and, after all, he himself implicitly pays tribute to the intuitiveness of the Lockean view by spending so much effort to convince us of its falsehood.

One consideration which, as a passage quoted earlier indicates, seems to have weighed heavily with Frege is the apparent problem confronted by the Lockean view in the case of the number 0. As Frege remarks, 'If I say "Venus has 0 moons", there simply does not exist any moon or agglomeration of moons for anything to be asserted of'. In other words, even if we can maintain that the property of being one is a property that an object can (and indeed must) possess and that numbers greater than one can be possessed by pluralities of objects, it seems that there plainly can't be any object that possesses the property of being zero. By contrast, the concept *moon of Venus* clearly can have assigned to it the property of 'including nothing under it', which is how Frege recommends us to think of something's having the number 0. Moreover, this way of thinking of the bearers of numerical properties famously enables him to forge a link between distinctions of number and quantificational distinctions, as expressed by words like 'all', 'some', and 'none'. This in turn enables him to observe that

> [E]xistence is analogous to number. Affirmation of existence is in fact nothing but denial of the number nought. Because existence is a property of concepts the ontological argument for the existence of God breaks down. (p. 65)

How can an adherent of Locke's view of number respond to these points? Well, first of all, it may be pointed out that, although it comes very naturally to a mathematician to think of 'zero' as denoting a number, most ordinary folk would consider it at best a bad joke to be told that, say, there is a number of pound notes in a sealed envelope that has just been given to them, when in fact the envelope is empty. The response 'Well, I did say *a number* of pound notes, and nought is a number' would do nothing to pacify the irate recipient. The introduction of the zero *symbol* was undoubtedly an important landmark in the history of mathematics, but we should not assume that its utility in calculation is dependent upon its actually denoting some object or expressing some property. In particular, we should not uncritically accept the currently standard view that 'zero' denotes *the empty set*, because it is far from clear that the notion of such a set really makes sense. All that we are ever informed about the empty set is that it is (1) a set, (2) has no members, and (3) is unique amongst sets in having no members. However, there are very many things that 'have no members', in the set-theoretical sense – namely, all non-sets. It is perfectly clear why these things have no members, for they are not sets. What is unclear is how there can be, uniquely amongst sets, a *set* which has no members. We cannot conjure such an entity into existence by mere stipulation – although this is, in effect, what Frege himself does with respect to the number nought.

Frege defines the number nought as follows:

> Since nothing falls under the concept 'not identical with itself', I define nought as follows: 0 is the Number which belongs to the concept 'not identical with itself'. (p. 87)

But what entitles him to suppose that anything exists which satisfies this definition?

Here he can appeal to another definition, namely, his general definition of Number:

> [T]he Number which belongs to the concept F is the extension of the concept 'equal to the concept F' (pp. 79–80),

where, as he has already explained, a concept F is 'equal' to a concept G just in case it is possible to 'correlat[e] one to one the objects which fall under the one concept with those which fall under the other' (p. 79). From this and the previous definition it follows that 0 is the extension of the concept 'equal to the concept "not identical with itself"'. But what entitles Frege to suppose that the 'extension' of this concept *exists*? Well, the notorious Axiom V of Frege's *Grundgesetze der Arithmetik* will give him what he needs, since that axiom says, in effect, that the extension of the concept F is identical with the extension of the concept G if and only if all and only the objects which fall under F also fall under G – and this in turn implies that every concept has an extension. But that, of course, is what brings about the downfall of Axiom V, because it thereby falls victim to Russell's paradox.[6]

However, the so-called 'neo-logicists' think that Frege has the resources with which to proceed in another and more satisfactory way, by appealing not to Axiom V but to his own criterion of identity for cardinal numbers – a criterion which now often goes by the name of 'Hume's principle' and is expressible in the form: 'The number which belongs to the concept F is identical with the number which belongs to the concept G if and only if it is possible to correlate one to one the objects which fall under the concept F with those which fall under the concept G'. Then he can 'prove' the existence of the number nought by taking both 'F' and 'G' in Hume's principle to stand for 'not identical with itself', to give us as a supposedly true equivalence: 'The number which belongs to the concept "not identical with itself" is identical with the number which belongs to the concept "not identical with itself" if and only if there are exactly as many non-self-identical things as there non-self-identical things'. Since what stands on the right-hand side of this equivalence is an analytic and indeed logical truth, what stands on the left is true, given that the equivalence itself is true. But what stands on the left entails 'There is something that is identical with the number which belongs to the concept "not identical with itself"'. However, since Frege has just defined nought as the number which belongs to the concept 'not identical with itself', it follows from this that there is something that is the number nought – in other words, that the number nought exists.[7] What is remarkable is that Frege imagined that he could, one way or another, pull this particular rabbit out of the hat so shortly after having criticized adherents of the ontological argument for doing something very similar in the case of God.

The proper response to all of this, it seems to me, is to deny Hume's principle, at least in its Fregean formulation. I am happy to accept an alternative formulation, to the effect that pluralities whose members are one – one correlatable are equinumerous, or possess the same number. Taking a single object to be the limiting or degenerate case of a plurality, this allows us to say that every single object possesses the number one. But since the notion of a 'null' plurality is a manifest absurdity, we are not committed to

[6] See, for example, Crispin Wright, *Frege's Conception of Numbers as Objects* (Aberdeen: Aberdeen University Press, 1983), p. 155.
[7] Precisely this proof may be found in Wright, *Frege's Conception of Numbers as Objects*, pp. 158–9.

the existence of 'the number nought'. A particularly objectionable feature of Hume's principle in its Fregean formulation, from an ontological point of view, is that it entails (in conjunction with a definition of 'successor') not only the existence of the number nought, as defined by Frege, but the existence of infinitely many cardinal numbers, namely, all the successors of the number nought. Some philosophers clearly think that this is, on the contrary, a great virtue of Frege's version of Hume's principle, since it gives them mathematical objects on the cheap. But in serious ontology there is no such thing as a free lunch.

It should also be remarked that invoking the name of Hume in this connection is highly misleading, in any case, since Hume himself did not appear to have anything like Frege's criterion of identity for cardinal numbers in mind when he wrote the passage cited by Frege, namely, that 'When two numbers are so combined as that the one has always an unit answering to every unit of the other, we pronounce them equal' (p. 73).[8] Hume seems to have in mind, rather, a method for determining, for arbitrarily chosen natural numbers n, n', m, and m', whether or not $(n + n') = (m + m')$ – for example, whether or not $(7 + 5) = (9 + 3)$.

But what are we to say about the linkage, forged by Frege, between numerical notions and the notions of quantification and existence? In particular, if we reject his view of number, should we also reject his view of the meaning of existential statements? According to Frege, existence is a 'second-level' concept. Thus, in 'On Concept and Object' he remarks:[9]

> I have called existence a property of a concept. How I mean this to be taken is best made clear by an example. In the sentence 'there is at least one square root of 4', we have an assertion . . . about a concept, *square root of 4*; viz. that it is not empty. (pp. 48–9)

And a little later:

> I do not want to say it is false to assert about an object what is asserted here about a concept; I want to say it is impossible, senseless, to do so. The sentence 'there is Julius Caesar' is neither true nor false but senseless. (p. 50)

However, 'Julius Caesar exists' seems to make perfectly good sense and is most improbably analysed as meaning anything like, say, 'There is at

---

[8] See David Hume, *A Treatise of Human Nature*, ed. L. A. Selby-Bigge and P. H. Nidditch (Oxford: Clarendon Press, 1978), I, III, §1 (p. 71).

[9] See *Translations from the Philosophical Writings of Gottlob Frege*, 2nd edn, ed. P. T. Geach and M. Black (Oxford: Blackwell, 1960).

least one thing that is identical with Julius Caesar', even if it entails the latter. That is to say, it is most implausible to suggest that in affirming Julius Caesar's existence we mean to affirm, about the concept *identical with Julius Caesar*, that it is 'not empty'. In any case, in what does the 'non-emptiness' of such a concept consist? Surely, simply in the *being* of something which 'falls under it'. But all that can 'fall under it' is an *object* – in this case, Julius Caesar. So the non-emptiness of this particular concept can only consist in the being – the existence – of Julius Caesar. More generally, far from its being the case that existence is to be explained in terms of the 'non-emptiness' of concepts, quite the reverse seems most plausible – that the 'non-emptiness' of concepts, which is a technical rather than a common-sense notion, calls out for explanation in terms of the existence of objects falling under them. The proper conclusion to draw is that existence, like number, is a property of objects. The fact that these properties are very unlike commonplace empirical properties, such as the physical properties of colour and shape, is neither here nor there. The same is true of such 'formal' properties as the property of being self-identical, the property of being an object and, indeed, the property of being a property.

Where now does this leave us with regard to the key ontological notions of identity, individuality and unity? The general position that I wish to recommend may be summarized as follows. Not every particular entity that does or could exist is an individual object of some kind, although every entity is necessarily self-identical. An individual object is an entity which, quite literally, *counts as one* entity of some kind, in order to do which it must possess unity. Only unitary entities can qualify as individual or single objects, capable in principle of being enumerated along with other such objects. There are or could be particular entities which lack unity, which we might call *dividuals*, as opposed to individuals. Putative examples of such entities are quantities of homogeneous and infinitely divisible matter. This distinction between dividuals and individuals is reflected in ordinary language in the distinction between mass nouns and count nouns.

Both dividuals and individuals may have parts, but the parts of dividuals are further dividuals and need not be unified in any way. In contrast, a composite individual – one that has proper parts – must have parts that are integrated according to some principle that is characteristic of individuals of its kind. For example, an animal, such as a tiger, is a composite individual of such a kind that it must have organic parts that are spatially and causally connected so as to enable them to function in the right sort of way to sustain the life of the individual animal that they compose. Typically, the parts of a composite individual of a given kind are individuals of various other kinds – as, for example, the parts of a tiger include such things as its heart, eyes, stomach, legs, and so forth.

Only individuals are countable. Each individual counts as one – that is, as one thing of its kind. No individual can count as more than one. Only pluralities of individuals can count as more than one. Although a composite individual, such as an individual pack of cards, may have many parts, the composite individual itself can still only count as one. What counts as more than one in such a case is not the composite individual but a plurality of its parts. Since the parts of a composite individual may themselves have parts, which are also parts of the composite individual in question (since parthood is transitive), there may be many different pluralities of parts that may be said to compose the same individual. Thus, for example, an individual tiger is composed by its various organs and limbs, but is also composed by a plurality of atomic and sub-atomic particles. The different pluralities composing the same composite individual may very well have different numbers assignable to them. But, once more, the composite individual itself may only be assigned the number one.

It is possible, at least in principle, for an individual to be composed of dividuals – as, for example, a piece of homogeneous and infinitely divisible matter would be composed by quantities of homogeneous and infinitely divisible matter. Dividuals, such as quantities of homogeneous and infinitely divisible matter, possess self-identity and are determinately distinct from one another and from all individuals. And yet, as we have seen, they lack unity and consequently are uncountable – not in the sense that they are uncountably *many*, like the real numbers, but rather in the sense that cardinal numbers are not assignable to them. They cannot comprise pluralities in the way that individuals do. Locke was right to say that number is a property of objects. But he was wrong to assert that 'Number applies it self to Men, Angels, Actions, Thoughts, every thing that either doth exist, or can be imagined' (II, XVI, 1). For number does not apply to dividuals and yet dividuals can at least be imagined.

5

The Absoluteness of Identity: A Defence

I shall devote this chapter to examining in some detail two important arguments presented by Geach, purporting to show that a sentence of the form '*a* is the same φ as *b*' – where '*a*' and '*b*' are non-empty particular or individual terms and 'φ' is sortal term or, in Geach's terminology, a *substantival general term* – is never analysable as '*a* is (a) φ and *b* is (a) φ and *a* is the same as (or identical with) *b*', the implication of which would seem to be that 'there is no such absolute identity as logicians have assumed'.[1] On Geach's own view, '*a* is the same as *b*' can itself only be understood as elliptical for some sentence of the form '*a* is the same φ as *b*'. Moreover, according to Geach, '*a* is the same φ as *b*' may be true while '*a* is the same χ as *b*' is false. As he says, 'On my own view of identity I could not object in principle to different [χs] being one and the same [φ]'.[2] This contention has now become known as the thesis of the *relativity of identity*.[3]

The two arguments of which I speak occur separately in successive editions – the second and third – of Geach's book *Reference and Generality*.[4]

[1] P. T. Geach, *Reference and Generality*, 3rd edn (Ithaca, NY: Cornell University Press, 1980), p. 216.
[2] Geach, *Reference and Generality*, 3rd edn, p. 181.
[3] See David Wiggins, *Sameness and Substance* (Oxford: Blackwell, 1980), p. 16, or the later incarnation of this book, *Sameness and Substance Renewed* (Cambridge: Cambridge University Press, 2001), p. 22. There is no difference of importance between the two books as far as the issues of the present chapter are concerned. However, in some places I shall refer only to the earlier book.
[4] For publication details of the third edition, see footnote 1 above. Those of the second edition are as follows: *Reference and Generality*, 2nd edn (Ithaca, NY: Cornell University Press, 1968).

The argument of the third edition is expressly intended to replace that of the second – although it would appear from Geach's remarks in the pre-face to the third edition that he has not been persuaded to regard the earlier argument as being in any way fallacious but, rather, sees it as invol-ving unnecessary complications concerning the distinction between count and mass nouns.[5]

My overall strategy will be as follows. I shall begin by presenting and discussing the argument that Geach offers in *third* edition of *Reference and Generality*, suggest a way of rebutting it, and examine how Geach might be expected to react to this sort of rebuttal. I shall then argue that if Geach *were* to take this expected line of counter-attack, then his position would lay itself open to *another* sort of objection – one which can in fact also be directed at the argument that he originally presented in the *second* edition of *Reference and Generality*.

So let us consider first of all the argument that Geach presents in the third edition of *Reference and Generality*, which I shall call – for reasons that will immediately become plain – his 'men and heralds' argument. (I shall call his other argument, of the second edition, his 'water and rivers' argument.) Geach invites us to consider the following two sentences:[6]

> (1)   Lord Newriche discussed armorial bearings with some herald yesterday and discussed armorial bearings with the same herald again today

and

> (2)   Lord Newriche discussed armorial bearings with some man yesterday and discussed armorial bearings with the same man again today.

Now, both (1) and (2) contain expressions of the form 'the same φ', where 'φ' is a sortal term, namely, 'the same *herald*' and 'the same *man*', respectively. (I am assuming here for the sake of argument that 'herald' qualifies as a genuine sortal term, although some doubt will be thrown upon this assumption later.) Geach evidently considers – and he is surely right – that if 'a is the same φ as b' were always analysable as 'a is (a) φ and b is (a) φ and a is the same as b', then (1) and (2) would have to be analysable as being equivalent to the following two sentences respectively:

---

[5]   See Geach, *Reference and Generality*, 3rd edn, p. 14.
[6]   See Geach, *Reference and Generality*, 3rd edn, pp. 174ff. I have altered Geach's numbering.

(1*)   For some x, x is a herald and Lord Newriche discussed armorial bearings with x yesterday and discussed armorial bearings with x again today

and

(2*)   For some x, x is a man and Lord Newriche discussed armorial bearings with x yesterday and discussed armorial bearings with x again today.

However, Geach argues that (1) and (2) *cannot* be analysed as being equivalent to (1*) and (2*) respectively, for the following simple reason. It is clear that

(3)   Whatever is a herald is a man

is true and is, moreover, equivalent to

(3*)   For any x, if x is a herald, then x is a man.

But (1*) and (3*) together entail (2*), whereas (1) and (3) certainly do *not* entail (2), since (2) may well be false even though (1) is true – if, for instance, there has been an overnight change of personnel in the College of Heralds. Hence, Geach concludes, it cannot be the case that (1) and (2) are equivalent to (1*) and (2*) respectively and so cannot be the case that 'a is the same herald (man) as b' is analysable as 'a is a herald (man) and b is a herald (man) and a is the same as b'. Moreover, the implication seems to be that 'a is the same φ as b' is *never* thus analysable, whatever sortal term 'φ' may be, since the man/herald example was, it appears, in no way peculiar.

When Geach concludes that (1) and (2) are not analysable as (1*) and (2*) respectively, he rests this conclusion on an extremely important assumption, which we have so far ignored. This is that the two analyses 'stand or fall together' – in other words, that (1) is analysable as (1*) *if and only if* (2) is analysable as (2*).[7] Geach mentions this in passing, but oddly enough without attempting to justify the claim. Clearly, without this assumption, the most that Geach would be entitled to infer from the fact that (1*) and (3*) entail (2*), whereas (1) and (3) do not entail (2), is that *either* (1) is not analysable as (1*) *or* (2) is not analysable as (2*). I remark on this because it seems that one very obvious line of attack on

[7]   See Geach, *Reference and Generality*, 3rd edn, p. 176.

Geach's position will be to say that, while (1) is *not* analysable as (1*), (2) certainly *is* analysable as (2*). On this view, there is a very significant difference between a sentence of the form '*a* is the same *herald* as *b*' and one of the form '*a* is the same *man* as *b*' – such that the latter *is*, whereas the former *is not*, analysable in the way Geach rejects quite generally for sentences of the form '*a* is the same φ as *b*'. Also, on this view, there is a related difference between a sentence of the form '*a* is a *herald*' and one of the form '*a* is a *man*'.

What these differences amount to, according to this anti-Geachian view, is just this. To say that *a is a herald* is not to say what *sort* or *kind* of thing *a* is, in the way that to say that *a is a man* standardly is. Rather, it is to say that *a* occupies a certain heraldic office, carrying with it certain titles and duties – and, accordingly, on this view 'herald' is not in fact a genuine sortal term. Correspondingly, to say that *a* and *b* are the *same* herald is only to say that – presumably at different times – they occupy or have occupied the same heraldic office. Hence, on this view, when it is said – as in (1) – that Lord Newriche discussed armorial bearings with *the same herald* on two successive days, it is not implied – as in (1*) – that there is any *single object of any sort* with which Lord Newriche stood in some relation on both of these days. But precisely this *is* implied, according to this view, when it is said – as in (2) – that Lord Newriche discussed armorial bearings with *the same man* on two successive days.

Observe that, on this view – which I am personally strongly inclined to endorse – it may certainly be allowed that, while 'herald' is not a genuine sortal term, only *things of a certain sort* may be heralds (that is, may occupy heraldic offices), namely, *men*. This, indeed, is what (3) may be understood as affirming. Thus, it may certainly be allowed that '*a* is a herald' *implies* '*a* is a man'. Allowing this is, in particular, quite consistent with a denial of the Geachian assumption that the two analyses 'stand or fall together'. For, while accepting the analysis of (2) as (2*), it may be urged that (1), instead of being analysed as (1*), should be analysed as, say

(1**)   For some *x*, *y*, and *z*, Lord Newriche discussed armorial bearings with *x* yesterday and with *y* today, *z* is a heraldic office, and *x* occupied *z* yesterday and *y* occupied *z* today.

So, if this view is tenable, all that Geach's argument succeeds in showing is that '*a* is the same herald as *b*' is not analysable as '*a* is a herald and *b* is a herald and *a* is the same as *b*' – which is something that upholders of the view in question would want to urge anyway. Unless Geach can prove that the two analyses really do 'stand or fall together', he has therefore done nothing whatever to give us reason to think that a sentence of the form '*a* is the same φ as *b*' is never analysable in the way he rejects.

Adherents of the view that I have just outlined may contend that such a sentence is, in fact, always thus analysable *provided that* the entailed sentence '*a* is (a) φ' is used to state what *sort* or *kind* of thing *a* is – that is, provided that '*a* is (a) φ' is what I earlier called an *instantiation sentence*.

In order to rebut objections of the foregoing type, Geach clearly has to argue that sentences of the form '*a* is a herald' and '*a* is a man' are logically isomorphous: that 'is' is not used here in two quite different senses. Now, Geach does in fact advance the view that, quite generally, a sentence of the form '*a* is (a) φ', where 'φ' is a term like 'man' or 'herald', is to be analysed as meaning '*a* is the same φ as *something*'.[8] And it may be thought that this has some bearing on the isomorphism issue. However, even someone subscribing to the anti-Geachian view that I have just outlined can in fact accept that '*a* is a herald' and '*a* is a man' are at least *logically equivalent* to '*a* is the same herald as something' and '*a* is the same man as something' respectively, without in any way compromising his contention that '*a* is a herald' and '*a* is a man' are not logically isomorphous. For he can insist that '*a* is the same herald as something' and '*a* is the same man as something' are *themselves* not logically isomorphous, on the grounds that 'same herald' and 'same man' do not function logically in the same way. In fact, of course, that '*a* is (a) φ' is *logically equivalent* to '*a* is the same φ as something' is just trivially true, in virtue of the logical truth that any φ is the same φ as *itself*.

Geach's view does, it is true, involve the more substantial claim that '*a* is a man', for instance, is a 'derelativization' of '*a* is the same man as something', in much the same way that '*a* is a mother' is derelativization of '*a* is the mother of someone'.[9] The implication of this is that sentences of the form '*a* is the same φ as something' are *logically and semantically prior* to ones of the form '*a* is (a) φ'. However, this more substantial claim relies upon the very success of Geach's argument that '*a* is the same φ as *b*' is not to be analysed as '*a* is (a) φ and *b* is (a) φ and *a* is the same as *b*', which is precisely what is now in question.

Altogether, then, nothing that Geach has to say concerning the relationship between '*a* is (a) φ' and '*a* is the same φ as something' can go any way at all towards showing, what he needs at present to show, that '*a* is a herald' and '*a* is a man' are logically isomorphous, so that we may dismiss this line of thought completely.

What needs, I think, to be made clear at this point is that Geach's commitment to the logical isomorphism of '*a* is a herald' and '*a* is a man'

---

8   See Geach, *Reference and Generality*, 3rd edn, p. 213.
9   See Geach, *Reference and Generality*, 3rd edn, p. 214.

carries with it a certain *ontological* commitment. This is that the ostensibly sortal term 'herald', no less than the sortal term 'man', really designates a *sort* or *kind* of concrete, physical object. Geach, it seems, must take the view that a heraldic name such as 'Bluemantle' – to use one of his own examples – denotes a concrete, physical object of which a series of different men may be successive 'phases'. He must suppose, moreover, that such an object may have an intermittent or interrupted existence, since there may be intervals during which no man is – that is, *is the same herald as* – Bluemantle. As Geach himself puts it, 'a herald like Bluemantle has not even spatio-temporal continuity over the years'.[10] So Geach's ontology apparently includes, in addition to men, a further sort or kind of object – *heralds*. Geach can, it seems, have no sympathy for the view that to be a herald is just to occupy some heraldic office. To speak of heraldic offices is to speak of *abstract* entities of a certain kind. What Geach is doing, in effect, is to reject talk of these in favour of talk of a hitherto unrecognized kind of *concrete* entity. Geachian heralds are *concrete*, inasmuch as their existence is spatiotemporally confined. They are, moreover, *physical*, because made of flesh and blood.

Is anything to be said in favour of Geach's unfamiliar ontology? There are, I think, serious difficulties with it, not least in connection with the notion of intermittent or interrupted existence, which it seems committed to endorsing. However, I don't want to go into such problems here, interesting though they are.[11] What I want to try to show now is that *even if we grant* Geach these ontological flights of fancy, his argument still goes no way at all towards showing that '*a* is the same φ as *b*' is never analysable as '*a* is (a) φ and *b* is (a) φ and *a* is the same as *b*'. This is because, as I shall try to explain, if we concede that '*a* is a herald' and '*a* is a man' (as the latter is standardly used) *are* logically isomorphous, then it turns out that Geach's premise

(3*)   For any *x*, if *x* is a herald, then *x* is a man

must be *false*. The consequence of this will be, of course, that the truth of (1*) is quite as consistent with the falsehood of (2*) as is the truth of (1) with the falsehood of (2), so that there will be, after all, no evidence to deny that (1) and (2) may be analysed as (1*) and (2*) respectively – accepting, still, Geach's ontological revisions.

---

[10]   See Geach, *Reference and Generality*, 3rd edn, p. 206. See also P. T. Geach, 'Existential or Particular Quantifier', in P. Weingartner and E. Morscher (eds), *Ontology and Logic* (Berlin: Duncker & Humblot, 1979), pp. 146–7.

[11]   I discuss the notion of interrupted existence in my 'On the Identity of Artifacts', *Journal of Philosophy* 80 (1983), pp. 220–32.

In order to make my reasoning plainer, it will be helpful to move at this point to a consideration of Geach's water and rivers argument in the *second* edition of *Reference and Generality*.[12] This is the argument that is replaced in the third edition by the men and heralds argument. In the water and rivers argument, Geach again presents us with two groups of three sentences, corresponding to sentences (1), (2) and (3) and (1*), (2*) and (3*) above. The sentences in question are as follows. First, the counterparts of (1), (2) and (3) respectively are:

(4)   Heraclitus bathed in some river yesterday, and bathed in the same river today,

(5)   Heraclitus bathed in some water yesterday, and bathed in the same water today

and

(6)   Whatever is a river is water.

Secondly, the counterparts of (1*), (2*) and (3*) respectively are:

(4*)   For some x, x is a river and Heraclitus bathed in x yesterday and Heraclitus bathed in x today,

(5*)   For some x, x is water and Heraclitus bathed in x yesterday and Heraclitus bathed in x today

and

(6*)   For any x, if x is a river, then x is water.

Now, once again Geach's contention is that (4*) and (6*) together entail (5*) whereas (4) and (6) do not entail (5). Similarly, his conclusion is that (4) and (5) cannot be analysed as being equivalent to (4*) and (5*) respectively, the implication being that 'a is the same river (water) as b' is not analysable as 'a is a river (water) and b is a river (water) and a is the same as b'.

The advantage of considering the water and rivers argument is that we may at least be able to agree that sentences of the forms 'a is a river' and 'a is water' *can* be interpreted in a sense in which they are logically isomorphous, whereas this was much more contentious with sentences of the forms 'a is a herald' and 'a is a man'. (As I explained earlier, in connection with the men and heralds argument, Geach's strategy – which

---

[12]   See Geach, *Reference and Generality*, 2nd edn, pp. 150–1.

is the same in both of his arguments – commits him on the logical iso-morphism issue, since opponents who dispute that the relevant pairs of sentences are logically isomorphous may object to his arguments simply by denying that the relevant pairs of analyses 'stand or fall together'.) What we may be able to agree, then, is that both '*a* is a river' and '*a* is water' can be interpreted as being, in my terminology, *instantiation sentences*, and thus as saying of a particular or individual *a* that it is a certain *sort* or *kind* of concrete, physical object. Certainly, this is a position to which I have already implicitly committed *myself*, in Chapter 3 above.

Now it is true, I concede, that others may question my assumption that '*a* is water' can be interpreted as an instantiation sentence, on a par with '*a* is a river' – simply because they do not accept, as I do, that both count *and* mass nouns qualify as sortal terms, insisting instead that they have a different logical grammar. But, on this view, '*a* is water' and '*a* is a river' *cannot* be interpreted as being logically isomorphous at all, from which it will follow that (4*) and (5*) cannot, as Geach requires, be assumed to 'stand or fall together' as analyses of (4) and (5) respectively. Someone holding such a view might accept that (4) is analysable as (4*) but not that (5) is analysable as (5*). I imagine, indeed, that it was precisely in the light of such possible objections that Geach replaced the water and rivers argument by one involving only count nouns. This, then, is a view that we are not *obliged* to take into account here, inimical as it is both to Geach's water and rivers argument *and* to an assumption that I myself am inclined to make in arguing against Geach.

Nonetheless, it is in fact possible, I believe, to modify both Geach's argu-ment and my response to it in a way which will neither do any injustice to Geach nor conflict with my own principles, but which will at the same time accommodate the sensitivities of those holding the sort of view that I have alluded to. This may be done by utilizing the fact that 'water' is used in English not *only* as a mass noun but *also* as a count noun.[13] Thus, one may quite properly speak of *a* water and of water*s*, meaning thereby a *body* or *bodies* of water. The only modification to Geach's water and rivers argument that is required in order to exploit this point of grammar is the replacement, in sentences (6), (5*), and (6*), of the predicate '— is water' by the predicate '— is a water'. I shall therefore assume, henceforth, that just such a replacement may be taken as read.

Of course, I would want to say, very much as I imagine Wiggins would, that each of the sentences '*a* is a river' and '*a* is (a) water' can *also* be used

---

[13]   *The Shorter Oxford English Dictionary* includes the following entries under 'water', both of which exemplify a count noun use: 'Water regarded as col-lected in seas, lakes, etc., or as flowing in rivers or streams' and 'A body of water on the surface of the earth'.

in distinctive *constitutive* senses: '*a* is a river' as saying that *a*, which might be a certain body of water, *constitutes* a river, and '*a* is (a) water' as saying that *a*, which might be a certain river, *is constituted by* water.[14] Geach, though, would naturally *not* want to acknowledge such a plurality of senses. Indeed, the issue between Geach (the relativist) and Wiggins (the absolutist) turns in the present case very much on the question of whether an 'is' of constitution has to be recognized – and so of course its existence at this stage cannot just be assumed. However, all that I am proposing at the moment is that the sentences '*a* is a river' and '*a* is (a) water' can at least both be interpreted as *instantiation* sentences, and in this way (but *only* in this way) be seen as being logically isomorphous, as Geach's argument requires.

But now a difficulty immediately arises for Geach. If, in (6*), '*x* is a river' and '*x* is (a) water' *are* thus interpreted as logically isomorphous, it soon becomes apparent that under such an interpretation (6*) *cannot be true*. This, at bottom, is because rivers and waters have *different criteria of identity*, and an individual of one sort or kind cannot also belong to another sort or kind with a different criterion of identity from that of the first. I shall argue this point in detail shortly, but before doing so I want to broaden the perspective of the discussion somewhat.

Let us begin, then, by asking, quite generally, when precisely it is that an individual, *x*, can simultaneously be an instance of each of two sorts or kinds, φ and χ. There must be *some* restriction here and what it is, I suggest, is this. An individual, *x*, may be an instance of each of two distinct sorts, φ and χ, only if *either* φ and χ are related as species to genus *or else* there is some further sort, ψ, instantiated by *x*, such that ψ is a sub-sort of both φ and χ.[15] Formally, we seem to have the following principle as a logical truth (I omit initial universal quantifiers and unnecessary brackets for the sake of clarity):

$$x/\varphi \ \& \ x/\chi \rightarrow \varphi = \chi \ \vee \ \varphi/\chi \ \vee \ \chi/\varphi \ \vee \ \exists\psi(x/\psi \ \& \ \psi/\varphi \ \& \ \psi/\chi)$$

For example, Fido may be an instance of both the dog kind and the mammal kind, since dogs are a species of mammal. But Fido could not be an instance of both the mammal kind and the amphibian kind, for not only are mammals and amphibians not related as species to genus, but

---

[14] See Wiggins, *Sameness and Substance*, p. 30, or *Sameness and Substance Renewed*, p. 36.

[15] Compare Wiggins, *Sameness and Substance*, pp. 201–4. Wiggins's objections to principles excluding the possibility of 'cross-classification' do not seem to touch the principle that I endorse here.

also there is not even any *sub*-species of mammal that is also a *sub*-species of amphibian, to which Fido might belong. Thus, there is not, for instance, any *hybrid* kind that is related to mammals and amphibians in the way, say, that tigons might be thought to be related to both tigers and lions.

To this it might be objected that one and the same individual, *x*, might be, say, a *caterpillar* at one time and a *butterfly* at another, even though caterpillars are not a *kind* of butterfly nor butterflies a *kind* of caterpillar, nor do they have any common sub-kind. But, then, mightn't this be precisely why *x* cannot be both a caterpillar and a butterfly *at the same time* – which, at least on one reading of it, is all that the principle implies? Read in this way, then, it seems that we don't really have a counter-example to the principle here, but if anything just further confirmation of it. However, I myself do not want to read the principle only in this temporally restricted way. For that reason, amongst others, it is important to remark that sortal terms like 'caterpillar' and 'butterfly' are in fact what Wiggins calls *phased sortals*.[16] I shall say more about phased sortals soon – and what I do say will undermine the suggestion that such sortal terms may legitimately be substituted for the sortal variables 'φ', 'χ', and 'ψ' appearing in the formal principle that I have just proposed, thus undercutting any force that the caterpillar/butterfly example might be supposed to possess.

Now, in view of the principle just stated, how could a single individual be *both* an instance of the river kind *and* an instance of the water kind? For rivers are surely not a *kind* or *species* of water – in the way, say, that heavy water is – nor water(s) of rivers. Nor does it appear that we can even say that there is some *sub*-species of river that is also a *sub*-species of water. However, I suspect that some may feel that what I say here turns on an equivocation in my use of the sortal term 'water' – in particular, an equivocation over its use as a *mass* noun and its use as a *count* noun. When I say that rivers are not a *kind* of water in the way that heavy water is, it seems clear that I must be using 'water' as a mass noun, to speak of a sort of material *stuff*. But may it not be urged that when 'water' is used as a *count* noun, it is extremely plausible to say that rivers are indeed a kind of water – other such kinds being lakes, seas, and oceans?

To this I would reply as follows. I am prepared to concede that what I said a moment ago did perhaps trade illicitly on an ambiguity. However, what I am not prepared to concede is that rivers are a kind of water *in any sense that can give comfort to Geach*. Let me explain. It seems clear that, *even used as a count noun*, 'water' has two quite distinct senses. In one of these senses, a water is something with the *same criterion of identity* as a river, but in the other sense it is not. In the first sense, a water is

---

[16] See Wiggins, *Sameness and Substance*, p. 24, or *Sameness and Substance Renewed*, p. 30.

something whose identity through time – that is, whose continuing to be the *same* water – is not impugned by the addition to it or removal from it of various quantities of water. This is the sense in which the Cumbrian lake Coniston Water is *a water*. In the second sense, this is not so. But, of course, it is the *second* sense of 'water' that must be at work in the (modified) water and rivers argument, since in the *first* sense there is no pressure at all to say that Heraclitus bathed in the same river but *not* the same water on two successive days. However, in this second sense of 'water', it is very far from platitudinous to say that a river is a kind of water – indeed, I think it is plainly *false*. And hence one may still appeal to the principle formulated earlier in order to deny that any individual could be both an instance of the river kind and an instance of the water kind (in the relevant sense of 'water kind').

I doubt, though, whether the foregoing argument would make much impression on anyone not already favourably disposed towards its conclusion. A pro-Geachian would probably be only too willing to invert it into an attempted refutation of the formal principle that I have just proposed. It would be more satisfactory, therefore, to tackle the issue head-on and try to show, quite generally, that whenever an individual, x, belongs to each of two different sorts φ and χ, these sorts cannot have *different criteria of identity*, in the way that rivers and waters – in the relevant sense of the latter – clearly do. Observe that a demonstration of this would not in itself amount to a validation of the formal principle proposed earlier, although it would at least vindicate the proposition that sorts which stand in the species–genus relationship must share the same criterion of identity. Evidently, the formal principle itself is far stronger than anything that could be established purely by considerations involving criteria of identity since – as we saw earlier – that principle imposes its restrictions even with regard to sortal terms which *do* share the same criterion of identity, such as 'mammal' and 'amphibian'.

Now, an argument of the kind we seek is not in fact particularly difficult to find. Suppose, for the purposes of a *reductio ad absurdum*, that an individual, x, *did* belong to each of two sorts, φ and χ, whose respective criteria of identity, $C(\varphi)$ and $C(\chi)$, were different. Then it seems that we could not in general rule out *a priori* the possibility that there should arise circumstances in which, according to $C(\varphi)$, say, x would *cease to exist*, whereas according to $C(\chi)$ it would *not*. That being so, anyone asserting that x instantiated both φ and χ would be laying himself open to the intolerable possibility that circumstances should arise in which he would be obliged to say that x *both did and did not* cease to exist. This presupposes, of course, that the criterion of identity for a sort φ determines the conditions under which individuals of that sort will continue or cease to exist – their *persistence* conditions – which, however, seems uncontroversial, at least in the case of contingent, concrete individuals such as those that presently concern us. I do not claim, then, that this sort of argument is directly applicable to abstract individuals like sets – although, to the extent that the argument vindicates the absolutist conception of identity in the case of concrete individuals, it renders unattractive and uneconomical any adherence to the relativist conception in the case of abstract individuals.

As far as I can see, the only way to evade the conclusion of this argument would be to relativize the very concept of *existence* itself to sortal distinctions – saying, for instance, that x might cease to exist *qua* φ but continue to exist *qua* χ. However, I need hardly say how unpalatable are the prospects of attempting to defend such a conception of existence. Indeed, it is not a conception that I can really even begin to comprehend.

Perhaps, though, it will not be immediately apparent that the prospects of relativizing existence are genuinely as repugnant as I have just suggested. After all, we are happy to talk about someone ceasing to be a *boy* but continuing to be a *human being*, or indeed of something ceasing to be a *caterpillar* but continuing to be an *insect*. But we should be careful here not to suppose that 'ceasing to be a boy' means 'ceasing to be, *qua* boy', in the sense that a relativist conception of existence would demand. For, of course, an absolutist in matters of existence and identity can quite happily handle the former sort of expression. In fact, it seems clear that a so-called phased sortal like 'boy' is really just a syntactically simple but *semantically complex* sortal term, being analysable as synonymous with some such syntactically *and* semantically complex sortal term as 'young, male human being'. As such it does not, in my view, denote a distinct *sort* or *kind* of individuals at all – a point that I shall argue for in a later chapter. Moreover, although it does have a criterion of identity associated with it, the criterion in question is just that associated with the unqualified sortal term 'human being'. For these reasons, then, it should not for a moment be imagined that examples like that of someone ceasing to be a boy but continuing to be a human being support a relativist conception of existence, according to which something can cease to exist *qua* φ but continue to exist *qua* χ, where φ and χ have different criteria of identity.

Let me now just illustrate the general argument advanced above by reference to the particular case of rivers and waters, which plainly do – at least in the relevant sense of 'water' – have different criteria of identity. Even without attempting to *state* these criteria explicitly, we can at least say that the criteria in question are such that, should *part* of a water be destroyed or removed – for example, through molecular dissociation or evaporation – then *that* water ceases to exist and what remains is a *different* water; whereas, in these same circumstances – the destruction or removal of part of the water in it – a *river* by no means ceases to exist, but merely becomes diminished in volume. This, however, means that 'Scamander', say, cannot denote an individual which is *both* a water *and* a river, since if it did we should have to say, in the circumstances just envisaged, that Scamander *both did and did not cease to exist*, which is absurd.

A philosopher of Geach's persuasion might urge at this point that it is allowable to say that Scamander *is (a) water* even though the proper name 'Scamander' has associated with it *only* the criterion of identity that is associated with the sortal term 'river' and *not* that associated with the sortal term 'water'. In other words, it may be contended that it is wrong to suppose that, where *x* is both (a) φ and (a) χ, *x* must comply with the criteria of identity of *both* these sorts or kinds.[17] *But I can agree with this.* I only maintain that where this is so and the criteria of identity in question are thus different, it follows that the two occurrences of 'is' in '*x* is (a) φ' and '*x* is (a) χ' are not univocal: they cannot *both* be the 'is' of instantiation. This is because it is abundantly clear that if '*x* is (a) φ' *is* used to say that *x* is an instance of the kind φ – that is, if the 'is' is that of instantiation – then *x* must indeed comply with the criterion of identity of φ. In short, the supporter of Geach cannot have it both ways: he cannot claim *both* that '*x* is (a) φ' and '*x* is (a) χ' may both be true, where φ and χ have different criteria of identity, *and* that the two occurrences of 'is' in these sentences are univocal. However, any lingering doubts that there may be about this I shall attempt to eliminate in the next chapter.

Now let me make fully explicit what exactly my objection to Geach's water and rivers argument is. In order for (4*) and (5*) to 'stand or fall together' as analyses of (4) and (5) respectively, it is necessary for '*x* is a river' as it appears in (4*) to be logically isomorphous with '*x* is (a) water' as it appears in (5*). And, hence, in order for (4*) and (6*) to entail (5*) it is also necessary for '*x* is a river' and '*x* is (a) water' *as they appear in (6*)* to be logically isomorphous – since otherwise the inference from (4*) and (6*) to (5*) would involve a fallacy of equivocation. But if '*x* is a river' and '*x* is (a) water' as they appear in (6*) *are* interpreted as logically isomorphous – that is, as involving in both cases an 'is' of instantiation – then, for the reason given earlier, (6*) must be regarded as *false*, contrary to what Geach requires. (6*) can be regarded as true only under an interpretation which does *not* treat both of these clauses as involving the same sense of 'is' – for example, under an interpretation which treats the 'is' in '*x* is a river' as the 'is' of instantiation but the 'is' in '*x* is (a) water' as an 'is' of *constitution*, in Wiggins's sense. However, as we have just observed, under any such interpretation the inference from (4*) and (6*) to (5*) must

---

[17]   Geach himself says something along these lines: see his *Reference and Generality*, 3rd edn, pp. 216ff.

involve a fallacy of equivocation, with 'x is (a) water' having different senses in (5*) and (6*). It is clear, then, that an argument from (4*) and (6*) to (5*) is no more available than is an argument from (4) and (6) to (5), and hence that Geach's objection to analysing (4) and (5) in terms of (4*) and (5*) respectively fails.[18]

I am now in a position to relate my criticism of the water and rivers argument to the men and heralds argument. The lesson that we may draw is that, even if we concede, for the sake of argument, that there *is* a sense of the sentence 'a is a herald' in which it is logically isomorphous with the sentence 'a is a man' – namely, a sense in which each of these sentences says of a certain individual, a, that it is something of a certain *sort* or *kind* – it is nonetheless clear that the sorts or kinds in question must have *different criteria of identity*.[19] Consequently, for the reason given earlier, when the clauses 'x is a herald' and 'x is man' in (3*) are both interpreted in *this* way, (3*) must be regarded as *false*. Even if we allow Geach his strange ontology of heraldic entities, with their intermittent or interrupted existence, it is plain that no individual instance of *this* sort or kind could *also* be an individual instance of the sort or kind *man*, any more than an individual instance of the river kind can also be an individual instance of the water kind. After all, men, unlike Geachian heralds, do *not* have an intermittent existence extending, potentially at least, over many centuries: on the contrary, they are born, live out their allotted span of some three score years and ten – without interruption – and then die. Hence, nothing can *be* both a man and a Geachian herald, in that sense of 'be' that corresponds to the 'is' of instantiation. Yet, clearly, it is precisely this sense of 'is' that has to be seen in both 'x is a man' and 'x is a herald' *as they appear in (1*) and (2*) respectively*, by anyone attempting to defend against Geach the view that (1) is equivalent to (1*) and (2) to (2*). And from this it follows, just as in the water and rivers case, that only under an interpretation which renders (3*) *false* can a fallacy of equivocation be avoided in the inference from (1*) and (3*) to (2*).

It will be recalled that the lesson that Geach himself wanted to draw was that 'a is the same φ as b' is never analysable as 'a is (a) φ and b is (a) φ and a is the same as b'. But now I don't see why we shouldn't say *precisely this* – provided, at least, that 'φ' is a genuine sortal term. We can

---

18   This diagnosis of the flaw in Geach's water and rivers argument is close to that favoured by Michael Dummett: see his *Frege: Philosophy of Language*, 2nd edn (London: Duckworth, 1981), p. 575.

19   Geach himself acknowledges as much, when he says 'There is no one criterion of identity for men and heralds': see his *Reference and Generality*, 3rd edn, p. 206.

still concede – as Wiggins would also have it – that any meaningful identity sentence of the form '*a* is the same as *b*' must in principle be expandable into the form '*a* is the same φ as *b*'.[20] But we should see this now not so much as telling us something about *identity* – for example, that there is no such thing as *the* identity relation, but only a family of sortally relativized identity relations – as telling us something about the individuation of particulars. As I have already stressed several times before in this study, particulars are only individuable *at all* as individuals *of certain sorts or kinds*, so that any comprehending use of a singular or individual term, '*a*', presupposes the existence of some sort, φ, of which *a* is an instance.[21] Hence, more specifically, given that '*a* is the same as *b*' is a meaningful identity sentence, there must at least be certain sorts, φ and χ, which *a* and *b* respectively instantiate. So the truth of '*a* is the same as *b*' will imply that there is some true sentence of the form '*a* is (a) φ and *a* is the same as *b*' and, equally, one of the form '*b* is (a) χ and *a* is the same as *b*'. But, by Leibniz's law, '*a* is (a) φ and *a* is the same as *b*' implies '*a* is (a) φ and *b* is (a) φ and *a* is the same as *b*'. And the latter is just equivalent, on the proposed analysis – rescued now from Geach's attack – to '*a* is the same φ as *b*'. (The appeal to Leibniz's law here begs no question against the relative identity theorist, since I am only trying to show that the absolutist can explain, on his own terms, why '*a* is the same as *b*' should be expandable in the way suggested – and the absolutist does, of course, accept Leibniz's law.)

So we can very readily understand why every meaningful identity sentence of the form '*a* is the same as *b*' must in principle be expandable into one of the form '*a* is the same φ as *b*', *without* taking this to imply that '*a* is the same as *b*' is somehow elliptical, or that '*a* is the same φ as *b*' is in any sense the logically prior form. We can retain the classical view that there is just *one*, univocal identity relation. And then, of course, we must also discard the thesis of the relativity of identity.

I should just mention before closing this chapter that Geach apparently has, at least by implication, *another* argument against the proposed analysis of '*a* is the same φ as *b*', in addition to the men and heralds or water and rivers argument. What Geach says in this connection is as follows. Having concluded, for the reasons that we have just been examining, that '*a* is the

[20]   See Wiggins, *Sameness and Substance*, pp. 15ff, or *Sameness and Substance Renewed*, pp. 21ff.
[21]   Such a use does not, however, require the user to have any *specific sort in mind* as being one that is instantiated by *a*, much less any specific *sortal term* by which *a* may be described: compare Wiggins, *Sameness and Substance*, p. 48. The user must, however, at least grasp any *criterion of identity* associated with '*a*', if my contentions of Chapter 3 above are correct.

same φ as b' is not analysable as 'a is (a) φ and b is (a) φ and a is the same as b', he goes on to remark:[22]

> We have already by implication rejected this analysis; for it would mean that 'the same F' always made sense, for any predicable term 'F'; and in introducing the notion of substantival general terms we explicitly denied this view, *which would make all predicable terms substantival.*

But nothing said here invalidates my earlier reasoning. To say, as I have done, that 'a is the same φ as b', where 'φ' is a *sortal* or 'substantival general' term, *does* submit to this analysis is not to imply that 'a is (an) F and b is (an) F' and 'a is the same as b', where 'F' is *any* predicable term whatever (for example, 'red thing'), can always sensibly be combined to give 'a is the same F as b'. So this additional argument of Geach's has no force and the absolute conception of identity remains unscathed.

Appendix: Some Formal Principles and Arguments

In this appendix, I shall present in a more formal way some of the theses that have been under discussion in this chapter, with a view to displaying their logical relationships as perspicuously as possible. There are, in particular, three important theses to be considered, which are as follows. First of all, there is what may be called, for obvious reasons, the *Sortal Expandability Thesis*:

$$\text{(S)} \quad a = b \leftrightarrow \exists\varphi(a =_\varphi b)$$

where 'a' and 'b' are *individual terms* (such as the proper names 'Hesperus' and 'Phosphorus'), 'φ' is a *sortal variable*, and the symbol '$=_\varphi$' is to be read as 'is the same φ as'. According to (S), then, to say that a is the *same as* (or is *identical with*) b is always to say that a is the same *something* as b – as it might be, the same *planet* or the same *man*. I take (S) to be a relatively uncontroversial thesis that can be accepted by absolutist and relativist alike (but see further my remarks at the end of this appendix).

The second important – but this time more controversial – thesis that we have to consider may be called, again for obvious reasons, the *Reducibility Thesis*:

$$\text{(R)} \quad a =_\gamma b \leftrightarrow (a/\gamma \; \& \; b/\gamma \; \& \; a = b)$$

---

[22]   Geach, *Reference and Generality*, 3rd edn, p. 176 (my emphasis added). I have used 'F' in place of Geach's 'A'.

According to (R), to say that a is the same γ as b is just to say that a is (a) γ and b is (a) γ and a is the same as b. As hitherto, I use the slash sign, '/', to express the 'is' of instantiation.

Finally, there is the *Absoluteness Thesis*:

(A) $(a =_\gamma b \ \& \ a/\delta \ \& \ b/\delta) \rightarrow a =_\delta b$

According to (A), if a is the same γ as b and a is (a) δ and b is (a) δ, then a is also the same δ as b. To deny that (A) is a logical truth is, of course, to uphold the thesis of the relativity of identity.

Concerning these three theses (S), (R), and (A), the following observations may be made. First of all, if (S) is true, then we must surely accept that (R) holds at least in the *left-to-right* direction – in other words, that the following thesis is true:

(R_1) $a =_\gamma b \rightarrow (a/\gamma \ \& \ b/\gamma \ \& \ a = b)$

For, surely, '$a =_\gamma b$' implies both 'a/γ' and 'b/γ', and it obviously also implies '$\exists\varphi(a =_\varphi b)$', which by (S) is equivalent to '$a = b$'. But it doesn't follow that (R) holds in the *right-to-left* direction, that is, that *this* is true:

(R_2) $(a/\gamma \ \& \ b/\gamma \ \& \ a = b) \rightarrow a =_\gamma b$

However, if not only (S) but also (A) is true, then clearly (R_2) must be true too. Here is the proof. Assume as hypothesis the antecedent of (R_2):

(1) $a/\gamma \ \& \ b/\gamma \ \& \ a = b$

By (S) it follows that

(2) $a/\gamma \ \& \ b/\gamma \ \& \ \exists\varphi(a =_\varphi b)$

Let $\varphi = \delta$ (say). Then we have:

(3) $a/\gamma \ \& \ b/\gamma \ \& \ a =_\delta b$

But then by (A) it follows that

(4) $a =_\gamma b$

So (1) implies (4), which is the consequent of (R_2). Hence, by conditional proof, (R_2) is true. Q.E.D. We may thus conclude that anyone accepting both (S) and (A) must also accept (R).

But what happens if one accepts both (S) and (R) – must one then also accept (A)? Clearly one must. Here is the proof. Assume as hypothesis the antecedent of (A):

(5) $a =_\gamma b$ & a/δ & b/δ

By (R) it follows that

(6) a/γ & b/γ & $a = b$ & a/δ & b/δ

from which it follows immediately that

(7) a/δ & b/δ & $a = b$

But, once more by (R), it follows from this that

(8) $a =_\delta b$

So (5) implies (8), which is the consequent of (A). Hence, by conditional proof, (A) is true. Q.E.D. (Observe, however, that this proof does not in fact appeal to (S) at all.) We see, then, that given the truth of (S), (R) is true *if and only if* (A) is true. Thus we can well understand Geach's strategy which, as we saw in the present chapter, is to argue against (A) by arguing for the falsehood of (R).

So far, I have not had any occasion to refer to *Leibniz's law* in this appendix, although that law has an obvious bearing on the debate between absolutism and relativism. Notice, then, that if Leibniz's law is accepted, then (A) follows straightforwardly from (S). Here is the proof. Assume as hypothesis the antecedent of (A):

(9) $a =_\gamma b$ & a/δ & b/δ

From this it follows immediately that

(10) $\exists\varphi(a =_\varphi b)$

and hence, by (S), that

(11) $a = b$

Now, it presumably also follows from (9) that

(12) $a =_\delta a$

But from (11) and (12), by Leibniz's law, we may infer

(13) $a =_\delta b$

So, accepting Leibniz's law, (9) implies (13), which is the consequent of (A). Hence, by conditional proof, (A) is true. Q.E.D. We see, thus, that the relativist is committed to rejecting Leibniz's law – at least in its classical, unrestricted form.

There is one further principle which is of considerable interest and importance in the present context. This is what might aptly be called the *Sortal Individuation Thesis*:

(I) $\forall x \exists \varphi (x/\varphi)$

This is the thesis that every individual instantiates some *sort* or other, or that everything is some *kind* of thing – there are no 'bare particulars'. It is worth mentioning that we can prove (S) if we assume (I), (R), and Leibniz's law. To prove that (S) holds in the left-to-right direction, assume as hypothesis the left-hand side of (S):

(14) $a = b$

Now, by (I) we know that

(15) $\exists \varphi (a/\varphi)$

Let $\varphi = \gamma$ (say). Then we have:

(16) a/γ

And from (14) and (16), by Leibniz's law, we may infer

(17) b/γ

Hence, conjoining (14), (16), and (17) we now have:

(18) $a = b \ \& \ a/\gamma \ \& \ b/\gamma$

But from (18), by (R), we may infer

(19) $a =_\gamma b$

from which we may in turn infer

(20) $\exists\varphi(a =_\varphi b)$

Thus (14) implies (20), which is the right-hand side of (S). Hence, by conditional proof, (S) holds in the left-to-right direction and the first half of our proof is complete. To prove that (S) also holds in the right-to-left direction, assume as hypothesis the right-hand side of (S):

(21) $\exists\varphi(a =_\varphi b)$

Let $\varphi = \gamma$ (say). Then we have:

(22) $a =_\gamma b$

From this, by (R), we may infer

(23) a/γ & b/γ & $a = b$

from which it immediately follows that

(24) $a = b$

Thus (21) implies (24), which is the left-hand side of (S). Hence, by conditional proof, (S) also holds in the right-to-left direction. Q.E.D.

The significance of this result is that it shows that the absolutist, who is of course already committed to both Leibniz's law and the Reducibility Thesis, (R), can establish the Sortal Expandability Thesis, (S), *merely by appeal to the Sortal Individuation Thesis*, (I). Thus, he is in a position to *explain* the truth of (S) without having to concede that its truth implies the logical or conceptual priority of sortally restricted identity relations over the non-restricted variety – in short, without having to concede that (S) must be understood as providing a *definition* of the unrestricted identity relation, '='. (This is just the point that I made more informally at the end of the present chapter.) The result is obviously quite vital, because without it someone might be able to object that (R) does not effect a genuine *reduction* or *analysis* of sortally restricted identity statements, on the grounds that the conjunct '$a = b$' on the right-hand side of (R) can itself only be understood as a shorthand way of writing '$\exists\varphi(a =_\varphi b)$', which of course employs a sortally restricted identity relation.

6

Identity and Constitution

What I hope to have made clear, in the previous chapter, is that Geach, at least, has offered no persuasive reason for thinking that the absolutist account of identity is untenable. However, it may not yet be quite so fully clear that the relativist account is not a viable alternative. It may be suspected that the two rival accounts are each internally consistent and coherent and, moreover, that they present compensating advantages and disadvantages as regards their respective ontological commitments and their respective conceptions of the logic of identity and predication. Thus, on the ontological side, it may be pointed out that the relativist can eliminate commitment to such abstract entities as heraldic offices in favour of further commitment to merely concrete ones – Geachian heralds – but only at the expense of having to countenance the notion of intermittent existence. And on the logical side it may be pointed out that the relativist economizes on the number of senses of 'is', eschewing the notion of an 'is' of *constitution* – but, again, only at the expense of having to countenance a logic of identity and predication that is considerably complicated by the absence of Leibniz's law in its classical form.

However, this irenic picture of healthy rivalry is not one that I can endorse, since I do *not* consider that the relativist conception of identity is coherent. Indeed, I believe that I have already shown, by implication, that it is not. For the relativist conception is void of interest without a commitment on its part to the *thesis of the relativity of identity* – the thesis, that is, that *a* may be the same φ as *b* and yet not the same χ. But putative examples of such relativity will, it seems clear, arise only where the sortal terms 'φ' and 'χ' are conceived as having *different criteria of identity associated with them*, as in the case of 'river' and 'water'. And we have seen that in such cases it is not in fact possible to say that either *a* or *b is*, univocally, both (a) φ and (a) χ. Nevertheless, in order to make the case against relativism still clearer, by showing that a distinctive 'is' of constitution really is unavoidable, it may be helpful at this point to examine an intriguing paradox that Geach has presented as calling for a relativist solution. Subsequently, I shall go on to say something about how I think the 'is' of constitution should be understood.

In § 110 of the third edition of *Reference and Generality*, Geach presents the following puzzle or paradox. We are to suppose that a certain cat, Tibbles, is sitting on a mat. Moreover, Tibbles is the only cat sitting on the mat. Since Tibbles is, we suppose, a perfectly normal cat, it has at least one thousand hairs. Geach continues:[1]

> Now let c be the largest continuous mass of feline tissue on the mat. Then for any of our 1,000 cat-hairs, say h_n, there is a proper part c_n of c which contains precisely all of c except the hair h_n; and every such part c_n differs in a describable way both from any other such part, say c_m, and from c as a whole. Moreover, fuzzy as the concept *cat* may be, it is clear that not only is c a cat, but also any part c_n is a cat: c_n would clearly be a cat were the hair h_n plucked out, and we cannot reasonably suppose that plucking out a hair *generates* a cat, so c_n must already have been a cat. So, contrary to our story, there was not just one cat called 'Tibbles' sitting on the mat; there were at least 1,001 sitting there!

Geach acknowledges, as one might expect, that this conclusion is absurd, but it is interesting to observe where it is that he professes to detect the fallacy, if fallacy it is. He explains:[2]

> Everything falls into place if we realize that the number of cats on the mat is the number of *different cats* on the mat; and c_{13}, c_{279} and c are not three different cats, they are one and the same cat. Though none of these 1,001 lumps of feline tissue is the same lump of feline tissue as another, each of them *is* the same cat as any other: each of them, then, is a cat, but there is only one cat on the mat, and our original story stands.

Now, I concede that this manoeuvre of Geach's saves the original story – but, as he says, there is a price to pay:[3]

> The price to pay is that we must regard '— is the same cat as . . .' as expressing only a certain equivalence relation, not an absolute identity restricted to cats.

[1]   P. T. Geach, *Reference and Generality*, 3rd edn (Ithaca, NY: Cornell University Press, 1980), p. 215.
[2]   Geach, *Reference and Generality*, 3rd edn, p. 216.
[3]   Geach, *Reference and Generality*, 3rd edn, p. 216.

Geach, of course, is happy to pay this price, since he considers that it 'must be paid anyhow, for there is no such absolute identity as logicians have assumed'.[4] And in defence of this contention he refers us to the earlier arguments in his book – arguments which we examined in the previous chapter and found to be unsatisfactory. What I want to do now, however, is to explain why I think that the truth of the original story can be saved far more plausibly without having to pay this price. At the same time, I shall try to show that Geach's resolution of the puzzle is in fact untenable.

Let me say at once what my own solution to the paradox is.[5] What I would say is that it is not merely *not* 'clear' – as Geach claims – but in fact simply *unintelligible* to suppose that the lump of feline tissue c, or any of the other lumps mentioned in the story, *is a cat* – at least in the sense in which it is correct to say that *Tibbles* 'is a cat'. *None* of the 1,001 lumps of feline tissue is a cat in this sense, so there is not even a *prima facie* case for saying that there are at least 1,001 cats sitting on the mat. The reason why I say this, of course, is that the sortal terms 'lump of feline tissue' and 'cat' have *different criteria of identity* associated with them and, as I explained in the previous chapter, I consider that no individual of a sort φ can intelligibly be said to belong also to another sort χ if φ and χ have different criteria of identity.

That these two sortal terms do indeed have different criteria of identity associated with them, and that Geach himself implicitly recognizes this fact, are things that are not difficult to show. For it is clear, on the one hand, that the criterion of identity for cats, however it might be framed in detail, is such that it implies that the removal or destruction of one of a cat's hairs is not as such sufficient for the termination of that cat's existence. It is equally clear, however, that by contrast Geach is using the expression 'lump of feline tissue' in such a way that the removal or destruction of the hair h_n *would* suffice to terminate the existence of the lump of feline tissue, c, of which the tissue in that hair formed a part. For after the removal or destruction of h_n, what would remain would be the lump of feline tissue c_n, which Geach has made clear he regards as being a *different* lump of feline tissue from c – as indeed it obviously is. So, after such removal or

[4]   Geach, *Reference and Generality*, 3rd edn, p. 216.
[5]   A modified version of the paradox, focusing on the problem of vagueness, is presented by David Lewis in his 'Many, but Almost One', in John Bacon, Keith Campbell and Lloyd Reinhardt (eds), *Ontology, Causality and Mind: Essays in Honour of D. M. Armstrong* (Cambridge: Cambridge University Press, 1993). I present my response to this version of the paradox in my 'The Problem of the Many and the Vagueness of Constitution', *Analysis* 55 (1995), pp. 179–82. That response builds on the solution that I offer here.

destruction, the lump of feline tissue c could no longer be said to exist, as there would then no longer be in existence any lump of feline tissue that could properly be said to be the *same* lump of feline tissue as c.[6] In other words, after the removal or destruction of h_n, c cannot survive as c_n, since that has been acknowledged not to be the same lump of feline tissue as c – but if c cannot survive as c_n, it equally clearly cannot survive as any of the other lumps of feline tissue still remaining after the removal or destruction of h_n.

The only way to try to evade this conclusion – that the removal or destruction of h_n would suffice to terminate c's existence – would be, once more, to attempt to relativize the very notion of *existence* itself, saying perhaps that although c might cease to exist *qua* lump of feline tissue, it could continue to exist *qua* cat: this on the grounds, presumably, that after the removal or destruction of h_n, there would still remain a cat, namely Tibbles, which was the same *cat* as c, even though there remained no lump of feline tissue which was the same *lump of feline tissue* as c. But I have already dismissed this proposal as being of doubtful coherence and, in any case, it is one that Geach himself clearly does *not* wish to endorse.[7] Of course, what I have just been saying here concerning the criteria of identity for cats and lumps of feline tissue closely parallels what I said in the previous chapter about the criteria for rivers and waters. Here, as before, I presuppose – as seems uncontroversial – that the criterion of identity for φs is a determinant of the *persistence conditions* of φs, provided at least that φs are contingent, concrete entities.

Geach, we have seen, wants to say of the lump of feline tissue c – and equally of each of the other such lumps – that it *is a cat*. Moreover, it is crucial to his position that there is no ambiguity as between saying of c that it *is a cat* and saying of Tibbles that it *is a cat*. (For Geach, the predicate '— is a cat' is an *unambiguous* 'derelativization' of the predicate '— is the same cat as something'.) Once ambiguity is conceded the game is up for the relativist, since the case for a distinction between an 'is' of identity and an 'is' of constitution can then be made out. But such ambiguity *must* be conceded, as I shall now attempt to show.

My reasoning is simple. Compare the sentences 'Tibbles is a cat' and 'c is a cat'. Let us grant that each sentence, in *some* sense, is true. It must nonetheless be the case that the senses in question are *different*. For the

---

[6]   Geach has in fact conceded in print that 'We need different criteria to decide whether Tibbles, who exists at time t, still exists at time t', and whether a lump c of feline tissue, which coincides with Tibbles at time t, still exists at time t'': see P. T. Geach, 'Reply to Lowe's Reply', *Analysis* 42 (1982), p. 32.

[7]   See again Geach, 'Reply to Lowe's Reply', for Geach's repudiation of any such proposal.

implication of saying that Tibbles *is a cat* is, clearly, that Tibbles complies with the criterion of identity associated with the sortal term 'cat' – and thus, for example, that Tibbles will not cease to exist merely upon the removal or destruction of a single hair. But, evidently, no such implication can attach to saying that *c is a cat*, in any sense in which saying this can be interpreted as being *true* – since *c will* cease to exist upon the removal or destruction of a single hair (assuming that we reject, as Geach himself does, a relativized notion of existence). So it seems that we must have here *two different senses* of '— is a cat', one of which demands that the subject of this predicate names something which complies with the criterion of identity associated with the sortal term 'cat', while the other does not. But once this is granted Geach's theory becomes untenable and we are driven, as I have said, to one like Wiggins's, which distinguishes between an 'is' of identity and an 'is' of constitution. On this view, *c is a cat* only in the sense that *c constitutes* a certain cat, namely, Tibbles.[8]

I might add that, once this is conceded, it becomes most implausible to suppose that, prior to the removal or destruction of any hairs, any of the *other* lumps of feline tissue mentioned by Geach, such as c_n, is a cat even in the sense that *c* is. For none of these other lumps does then (wholly) constitute Tibbles, although any of them might *come* to constitute Tibbles upon the removal or destruction of a single hair. Geach is right in saying, in the passage quoted earlier, that 'c_n would . . . be a cat were the hair h_n plucked out', but only in the sense that c_n would then *constitute* a cat. However, once this is understood, we can easily discern the fallacy in his going on to say 'and we cannot reasonably suppose that plucking out a hair *generates* a cat, so c_n must already have been a cat'. What plucking out a hair does is to bring it about that c_n, instead of *c*, *is a cat*, in the constitutive sense. But c_n's beginning to be a cat in this sense obviously doesn't amount to the *generation* of a cat, that is, the *coming into existence* of a cat.

Is there any way in which a defender of Geach could respond to the foregoing objection? What seems undeniable is that 'Tibbles is a cat' implies that Tibbles complies with the criterion of identity associated with the sortal term 'cat', whereas '*c* is a cat', in any sense in which it can be interpreted as true, does *not* imply that *c* complies with this criterion. Now, I have assumed that the difference between the implications of these two sentences must be attributed to an ambiguity in the predicate '— is a cat'. But could it not be attributed instead to a difference in sense between the

---

[8]   Leslie Stevenson offers a somewhat different argument for the same conclusion in his 'The Absoluteness of Identity', *Philosophical Books* 23 (1982), pp. 1–7.

two names 'Tibbles' and 'c'? After all, it may be said, any proper name, say 'N', has associated with it the criterion of identity associated with a certain sortal term (or family of such terms), the implication being that N must comply with that criterion. So it may be pointed out that 'Tibbles' and 'c' differ precisely in that the former has associated with it the criterion of identity associated with the sortal term 'cat', whereas the latter has associated with it the criterion of identity associated with the sortal term 'lump of feline tissue'. Now, may it not be argued that the reason why, for instance, 'Tibbles is a cat' implies that Tibbles is something complying with the criterion of identity associated with the sortal term 'cat' has nothing to do with the sense of the predicate '— is a cat', but everything to do with the sense of the proper name 'Tibbles' – and the same, *mutatis mutandis*, as regards 'c is a cat'? If so, it would seem to follow that '— is a cat', as it appears in these two sentences, is after all *not* ambiguous.

My answer to this line of argument is as follows. I can readily accept – as will be clear from Chapter 3 – that the proper names 'Tibbles' and 'c' have associated with them the criteria of identity associated with the sortal terms 'cat' and 'lump of feline tissue' respectively. However, I would urge that the very fact that proper names *do* have associated with them the criteria of identity associated with certain sortal terms, far from subserving the Geachian view that the predicate '— is a cat' is univocal, actually undermines that view. The point is that it is not as though most proper names wear their associated criteria of identity on their sleeves. ('Tibbles' is an atypical example in this respect, in that it is, purely by convention, rarely used as a name for *anything but* a cat.) Therefore we *need* a way of conveying to others *which particular sortal term's* criterion of identity is associated with the use of a given proper name, say 'N'. Suppose that the sortal term in question is 'cat': then what *better* way of conveying this information is there than precisely by saying 'N is a cat'? Natural language must possess a relatively simple way of conveying this important information and there is, I think, no good reason to doubt that in English it is done by a certain use of the predicate '— is a cat'. But if so, and if it is *also* claimed that a sentence like 'c is a cat' may be interpreted as true even though 'c' does *not* have associated with it the criterion of identity associated with the sortal term 'cat', but another and incompatible criterion, then it must inevitably follow that the predicate '— is a cat' is *not* being used in this latter sentence in the same way as it was in the sentence 'N is a cat'. Hence, that predicate is, contrary to the Geachian view, ambiguous. For, clearly, in the sense of the predicate '— is a cat' in which it is used to convey the information that a proper name figuring as its subject has associated with it the criterion of identity associated with the sortal term 'cat', it must be true to say that c is *not* a cat, given that 'c' does not have that criterion associated with it. And from this it follows, on pain of contradiction, that

'— is a cat' must have two different senses, in one of which it is, *ex hypo-thesi*, truly predicable of *c* but in the other of which it is not.

Of course, my own view is that the predicate '— is a cat', as it is used in a sentence like 'Tibbles is a cat', is used to say what *sort* or *kind* of thing a certain individual is – that is, that such a sentence may be classified as what I have previously called an *instantiation* sentence. But what I have been trying to do in the last few paragraphs is to argue against Geach without appealing to a semantic classification of my own, since making any such appeal in this context might very reasonably have been judged to be question-begging. This was less important in the previous chapter, where I was more concerned to defend absolutism than to attack relativism.

One aspect of Geach's theory to which I have not so far alluded, but which might be thought to be relevant to the argument that I have just been deploying, is his distinction between a name 'for' a φ and a name 'of' a φ.[9] A name is a name *for* a φ, in Geach's sense, if and only if that name has associated with it the criterion of identity associated with the sortal term 'φ'. But he takes the view that a name may still be a name *of* a φ even though it has associated with it another criterion of identity. Thus, according to Geach, 'Tibbles' is both a name *for* and a name *of* a cat. At the same time, although it is not a name *for* a lump of feline tissue, it is nonetheless a name – albeit a 'shared' one – *of* all the various lumps of feline tissue on the mat, $c_1, c_2, \ldots c_n$ and *c*. Equally, each of the names 'c_1', 'c_2', etc. is a name *for* and *of* a lump of feline tissue and, although none of them is a name *for* a cat, each of them is still a name *of* a cat – to wit, Tibbles.[10]

But when, exactly, is a name a name 'of' a φ, according to Geach? The answer, it seems, is that it is so just in case there is some φ *that it names*. Thus he says: 'A proper name is a name *of* a cat if it is not an empty name but does actually name a cat'.[11] And this is presented as definitional. The problem, however, is that I see no good reason to think that '*c*', for instance, *names* a cat all: all that it names, in my view, is a certain lump of feline tissue. Certainly, it seems clear that the suggestion that a name 'for' a φ may nonetheless be a name 'of' a χ, where φs and χs have different criteria of identity, is not one that can be motivated independently of an argument in favour of the relativist conception of identity. For the only reason that one could have to suppose that '*c*', say, is a name 'of' a cat is just that *c*, allegedly, *is the same cat as* Tibbles – which, of course, presupposes relativism.

In any case, I see nothing in this suggestion that offers a means of escape, for the relativist, from my preceding argument for the ambiguity of the

9 See Geach, *Reference and Generality*, 3rd edn, p. 70.
10 See Geach, *Reference and Generality*, 3rd edn, p. 216.
11 Geach, *Reference and Generality*, 3rd edn, p. 70.

predicate '— is a cat'. For the central claim of that argument was that there must be a distinctive sense of '— is a cat' which is tied to its use in conveying the information that a name figuring as its subject has associated with it the criterion of identity associated with the sortal term 'cat' – in other words, the information that such a name is, in Geach's terminology, a name 'for' a cat. And this can scarcely be denied. But then, *whether or not* it is supposed that '*c*' is a name 'of' a cat, given that it is *not* a name 'for' a cat it cannot be true to say that *c is a cat* in the sense just distinguished. Hence, if it *is* nonetheless true to say that *c* is a cat, it must be in some *other* sense – and we have ambiguity.

Finally, it is questionable whether Geach's doctrine concerning names is ultimately even intelligible or, at least, to any degree credible as a serious semantic proposal. For consider some condition that is true of Tibbles the cat, but *not* true of *c* the lump of feline tissue – such as that it will not cease to exist if just a single hair is removed or destroyed. The problem now is that if, as Geach holds, '*c*' is a name 'of' Tibbles – that '*c*' *names* Tibbles – then it is hard to see why the manifestly *false* sentence '*c* will not cease to exist if just a single hair is removed or destroyed' should not also be *true*, since its subject allegedly names something (to wit, *Tibbles*) of which its predicate is undoubtedly true. Perhaps in an artificial or suitably regimented language this difficulty could be overcome by exploiting certain technical devices, but it seems clear enough that *natural* languages like English simply do not work in the way that Geach's doctrine demands.[12] Altogether, then, it appears that this doctrine concerning names is one that a relativist should regard as being an embarrassment rather than a strength, to be avoided if at all possible. Geach himself, however, appears to think that relativism is committed to it – and if he is right, then this is yet another nail in the coffin of relativism.

Having argued that the distinction between the 'is' of identity and the 'is' of constitution is semantically well motivated, I shall now go on to say something positive about the latter kind of 'is', but also to comment on a rival absolutist theory which appears to offer a way of diminishing the importance of any such 'is'. I shall approach the matter by returning to Heraclitus's famous problem. Heraclitus, of course, is commonly supposed to have held that one cannot step into the same river twice.[13] This is no

---

[12]   Geach himself seems to recognize this sort of difficulty, though rather makes light of it: see *Reference and Generality*, 3rd edn, p. 218.

[13]   Plato at *Cratylus* 402 attributes this opinion to Heraclitus: see G. S. Kirk and J. E. Raven, *The Presocratic Philosophers* (Cambridge: Cambridge University Press, 1957), p. 197, and their ensuing discussion, pp. 197–9. See also Jonathan Barnes, *The Presocratic Philosophers*, 2nd edn (London: Routledge and Kegan Paul, 1982), pp. 65ff.

place for me to enter into questions of Presocratic exegesis, which I am not in any case equipped to answer. However, the relevant Heraclitean text, whatever we are to make of it, is as follows:[14]

> Upon those that step into the same rivers different and different waters flow . . . It scatters and . . . gathers . . . it comes together and flows away . . . approaches and departs.

Now Geach, as we have seen, implicitly charges the absolutist with being committed to the paradoxical view that I have just described as being commonly attributed to Heraclitus: that one cannot step into (or indeed 'bathe in') the same river twice – unless, indeed, in doing so one were to step into in the same *water* twice, which, given the mutable nature of rivers, one is unlikely to do. I have defended the absolutist against this charge, arguing with Wiggins that the right response to make to Heraclitus's alleged claim is simply to refuse to *identify* a river with the water which, at any given time, may properly be said to *constitute* it. As Wiggins himself puts it:[15]

> Rivers are indeed water but this means that water goes to make them up. 'Same water' is not therefore a covering concept for an identity statement identifying a river with something.

What he means by this last assertion is just that, where the individual terms '*a*' and '*b*' refer to *rivers* – and hence, as I should say, have the criterion of identity associated with the sortal term 'river' incorporated into their sense – the identity statement '*a* is the same as *b*' cannot be expanded as '*a* is the same *water* as *b*', in the way that it undoubtedly *can* be expanded as '*a* is the same *river* as *b*'. With '*a*' and '*b*' thus understood, the sentence '*a* is the same water as *b*' could indeed conceivably be regarded as *true* – but only if interpreted as affirming that the same water *constitutes* both *a* and *b*, not literally as an *identity* statement concerning *a* and *b*.

My only dissatisfaction with Wiggins's treatment of these matters lies not in his views about them, with which I almost entirely agree, but only in certain aspects of his defence of those views, which seems to me to fall short of a completely adequate response to the relativist opposition. In my opinion, Wiggins's defence places rather too much reliance on appeals to Leibniz's law in its classical form, which the relativist may fairly object to as question-begging. He is furthermore hampered, I consider, by his

---

[14] See Kirk and Raven, *The Presocratic Philosophers*, p. 196.

[15] David Wiggins, *Sameness and Substance* (Oxford: Blackwell, 1980), p. 35, repeated in his *Sameness and Substance Renewed* (Cambridge: Cambridge University Press, 2001), p. 43.

failure to recognize a distinctive 'is' of *instantiation*. However, it will become clear later in this book that, on issues other than that of the correctness of absolutism, I am often by no means in agreement with Wiggins and consider, in particular, that as an absolutist he takes a mistaken line on the question of personal identity.[16]

I spoke a moment ago of a *rival* absolutist theory which makes no significant appeal to an 'is' of constitution. The theory in question is Quine's. Quine is an absolutist who equally believes that he can avoid the paradoxical 'Heraclitean' position that one cannot bathe in the same river twice. What he says, more precisely, is this:[17]

> The truth is that you *can* bathe in the same *river* twice, but not in the same river stage . . . A river is a process through time, and the river stages are its momentary parts.

He goes on to explain:[18]

> Let me speak of any multiplicity of water molecules as a *water*. Now a river stage is at the same time a water stage, but two stages of the same river are not in general stages of the same water. River stages are water stages, but rivers are not waters. You may bathe in the same river twice without bathing in the same water twice, and you may, in these days of fast transportation, bathe in the same water twice while bathing in two different rivers.

From what Quine says, it does not appear that he need positively *reject* the notion of an 'is' of constitution, but it seems clear that it cannot play any very fundamental theoretical role for him in the resolution of problems like that of Heraclitus. It is open to Quine, perhaps, simply to *define* 'Water x constitutes river y at time t' as meaning something like 'There is some water stage z of x such that z is a river stage of y at time t' – although, very arguably, this will not quite do as it stands, because it fails to imply

---

[16]   My disagreements with Wiggins in the latter regard survive the very considerable changes that he makes to his account of personal identity in *Sameness and Substance Renewed*, whose chapter on the subject entirely supersedes that of *Sameness and Substance*. I discuss *Sameness and Substance Renewed* in my review of it, *Mind* 112 (2003), pp. 816–20, and in my 'Is Conceptualist Realism a Stable Position?', *Philosophy and Phenomenological Research* 71 (2006), pp. 456–61.

[17]   See W. V. Quine, 'Identity, Ostension and Hypostasis', in his *From a Logical Point of View*, 2nd edn (Cambridge, MA: Harvard University Press, 1961), p. 65.

[18]   Quine, 'Identity, Ostension and Hypostasis', pp. 65–6.

that the constitution relation is an *asymmetrical* one, as it surely is. However, when Quine blithely asserts that 'A river is a process through time, and . . . river stages are its momentary parts', I am immediately impelled to ask: but just what *are* these 'river stages' of which he so readily speaks? *Rivers* are a species of thing with which we are all quite familiar, but hardly so *river stages*. Why, indeed, should Quine feel any need to resort to the extravagance of introducing such peculiar entities in response to Heraclitus's problem?

The only reason that I can suggest is this. Quine must assume that if I bathe in a certain river *and* at the same time in a certain 'water', then – since these individuals are, *pace* Geach, *different* things – there must be some *one* thing that I bathe in at that time, by virtue of bathing in which I may be said to bathe in both the river and the water, *because this one thing is a 'common part' of both the river and the water*. An obvious analogy, I suppose, is provided by the fact that I can simultaneously stand in both of two different shadows, because they *overlap* and consequently have a common spatial part – although Quinean thing-stages are, of course, meant to be *temporal* parts of things. Only this assumption seems to explain why Quine introduces 'river stages' and 'water stages' – namely, so that he can go on to *identify* entities of these sorts, despite the fact that we cannot, as he rightly insists, identify rivers and waters themselves. As he himself puts it, 'River stages are water stages, but rivers are not waters': and the 'are' here is plainly the 'are' of *identity*.

But why should we accept the assumption? I can see no reason to, because we can reach Quine's common-sense conclusion – 'You may bathe in the same river twice without bathing in the same water twice, and . . . in the same water twice while bathing in two different rivers' – without countenancing any sorts of entities other than ordinary rivers and waters. The fact in virtue of which I may be said to bathe simultaneously in a certain river *and* in a certain water, despite their distinctness, need not be that these two individuals have some 'common part' in which I bathe, but quite simply that *they exist simultaneously in the same place*, at the time and place at which I bathe.[19] And it is, moreover, precisely because they are *non-identical* that these two individuals, nonetheless, need not *always* coincide spatially, thus securing for us our common-sense answer to Heraclitus's

[19]   Of course, there have been plenty of philosophers who have tried to cast doubt on the idea that two different material objects can exist in the same place at the same time, even if they are objects of different kinds, but I find none of their arguments at all persuasive: see further my 'Coinciding Objects: In Defence of the "Standard Account"', *Analysis* 55 (1995), pp. 171–8, and my 'Substantial Change and Spatiotemporal Coincidence', *Ratio* 16 (2003), pp. 140–60.

problem. But since these are facts that Quine himself is committed to acknowledging, it seems that he really gains nothing by additionally postulating
the existence of 'river stages' and 'water stages'. Certainly, no reason has
been given – and I don't see how one could – for supposing that two distinct individual things can exist in the same place at the same time *only* if
they share a common 'temporal part'.

Here, however, it may be protested on Quine's behalf that by introducing
reference to river stages and water stages he effects a considerable economy,
by doing away with any reliance upon an undefined 'is' of constitution.
That might be a fair objection against anyone who, in rejecting the Quinean
doctrine of temporal parts, took the 'is' of constitution to be logically primitive. But that is not my own position. We saw, indeed, that for Quine,
defining an 'is' of constitution may be a relatively easy matter, given his
acceptance of river stages and water stages – provided, at least, that the
asymmetry of this 'is' can be duly acknowledged. But while anyone who,
like myself, looks askance at the doctrine of temporal parts will not – for
that very reason – find a definition along those lines at all illuminating,
it does not follow that such a philosopher should reject altogether the prospect
of achieving a reductive analysis of constitution statements. Indeed, one
element required in such an analysis has already become apparent, at
least in the case of concrete, physical entities: simultaneous existence
in the same place. If x is to be constituted by y at a certain time – say, a
river by a water – then at that time the spatial locations of x and y must
exactly coincide.

Of course, there must be *more* to constitution than mere simultaneous
co-location, not least because constitution is an asymmetrical relation:
if x is constituted by y, then y is *not* constituted by x – whereas spatiotemporal
coincidence is symmetrical. Another plausibly essential feature of constitution that has emerged from previous discussion is this: if x is to be
constituted by y, then it seems that x and y must have different and indeed
incompatible criteria of identity, as do rivers and waters. But this still
does not explain the asymmetry of constitution. Exactly how to fill out the
logically necessary conditions suggested so far into a plausible logically
necessary *and sufficient* condition for x to be constituted by y is, I acknowledge, not a perfectly straightforward task. But I see no reason to suppose
that the task cannot be accomplished without recourse to the doctrine of
temporal parts.

One proposal that I have explored elsewhere is the following, although
it is restricted to cases in which x and y are composite objects possessing
various lesser component parts, such as the *molecules* that make up both
rivers and waters. (It may be, of course, that *simple* – that is, non-
composite – objects *cannot* stand in the constitution relation, in which case

this proposal is not really a restricted one after all.) The proposal is that
x constitutes y at time t just in case x and y coincide spatially at t and
every component part of x at t is also a component part of y at t, but not
every component part of y at t is also a component part of x at t.[20] Thus,
for example, when a certain water, a, constitutes a certain river, b, all of
the molecules that compose a at that time are also component parts of
b at that time: but the river, b, also appears to have certain parts that
cannot intelligibly be regarded as being *parts* of the water, a, such as its
river-mouth. The river-mouth is, no doubt, *constituted* by part of the water,
a, at the time in question, but doesn't itself seem to *be* a part of that water.
It is not my intention to extend my defence of this proposal here, although
I certainly think that it has considerable merits. But, in any case, we do
not need to wait until we have a water-tight analysis of the constitution
relation before we can reasonably appeal to a distinctive 'is' of constitution for semantic and metaphysical purposes. For those purposes, we may
legitimately rest our case on intuitively compelling illustrative examples,
such as that of a river and its constituent water, or that of a bronze statue
and its constituent bronze.

We are, then, under no pressure to follow Quine's lead in attempting to
change the ontological category of things like rivers and waters from that
of *continuants* to that of *processes*.[21] Continuants, on my understanding of
the term, may have spatial but not temporal parts – but need not even
have the former, as in the putative case of non-extended Cartesian egos,
whose existence is at least conceptually possible.[22] Processes, by contrast,
seemingly must have temporal parts, but not necessarily spatial parts, even
if they occur in an extended region of space. (It is not obvious, for example,
that a particular performance of a play must have spatial parts, just
because it takes place on a *stage* that is spatially extended.) Quine's proposed ontological revision, so casually advanced by him, is in fact one of

---

[20] See my *A Survey of Metaphysics* (Oxford: Oxford University Press, 2002),
pp. 73–4, and also my 'Identity, Composition, and the Simplicity of the Self',
in Kevin Corcoran (ed.), *Soul, Body, and Survival: Essays on the Metaphysics
of Human Persons* (Ithaca, NY: Cornell University Press, 2001). For other
proposals, see, for example, F. C. Doepke, 'Spatially Coinciding Objects', *Ratio*
24 (1982), pp. 45–60, and Peter Simons, *Parts: A Study in Ontology* (Oxford:
Clarendon Press, 1987), pp. 237ff.
[21] The term 'continuant' we owe to W. E. Johnson, who contrasted it with the
term 'occurrent': see his *Logic, Part I* (Cambridge: Cambridge University
Press, 1921), p. 199.
[22] In fact, I myself consider that persons are *extended* simples: see again my 'Identity,
Composition, and the Simplicity of the Self'.

enormous magnitude and even of doubtful intelligibility. Certainly, then, it is not one that should be contemplated as long as the prevailing common-sense ontological scheme can be defended as viable, as I believe it can.

My own view about the doctrine of temporal parts is that it is questionable whether clear and determinate sense can be made of the notion that something like a river has such parts – and that such attempts as philosophers have made to give sense to this notion are implicitly parasitic upon a prior understanding of the category of continuants.[23] For example, it seems that many of these philosophers trade upon an implicit conflation between continuants and *their life-histories*. Of course, the *life-history* of a tree, say, has its early, middle, and late stages: but the *tree* itself doesn't have such stages. Nor am I able to make much sense of the idea of an 'object-at-a-time' – something such as *Napoleon-in-July-1798* – as a supposed way of thinking of a temporal part or 'time-slice' of an object such as a man or a tree. For objects like men and trees don't have temporal *locations* – that is, *dates* – at all, in the way that events do. Events in the life of a man – such as his birth – certainly have dates, but no 'part' of a man has a date, any more than the man himself does. Of course, a man's *existence* will extend over some definite period of time and so its beginning and end will be datable: but a man is no more to be identified with his own *existence* than he is with his own life. Moreover, even if some sort of sense *could* be conferred upon the notion of a 'man-at-a-time', it seems clear that our understanding of it would still be parasitic upon our prior understanding of what a *man* is, since it explicitly draws upon the latter notion. However, I shall say no more here in opposition to the doctrine of temporal parts, since I have already done so elsewhere at considerable length.[24]

Altogether, then, it seems to me that the cost at which the Quinean theory eliminates any special appeal to an 'is' of constitution is much too high. For if the elimination is not to be merely cosmetic rather than real, an enormous task of ontological revision needs to be accomplished. That task may be made to appear deceptively easy by resorting to such subterfuges as the notion of an 'object-at-a-time', when what is really required is an entirely new way of thinking about spatiotemporal reality which does not illicitly rely upon our existing, common-sense conceptual scheme, in which the category of continuants has a central place. As for that scheme

[23]   I sympathize, then, with D. H. Mellor's forthright rejection of this notion: see his *Real Time* (Cambridge: Cambridge University Press, 1981), pp. 126ff., or his *Real Time II* (London: Routledge, 1998), pp. 85ff.

[24]   See, especially, my *The Possibility of Metaphysics: Substance, Identity, and Time* (Oxford: Clarendon Press, 1998), pp. 98–105, 114–18 and 127–35.

itself – in the words of the well-known saying – 'If it ain't broke, don't fix it'. My firm conviction is that, indeed, it ain't broke.

I shall say more about the *parts* of continuants in the next chapter: but only about their *spatial* or *component* parts – which, in my view, is the only type of parts that they may have. These parts are *themselves* always continuants and at most only *spatially* smaller than the wholes whose parts they are.

7

Parts and Wholes

It is often said that certain 'wholes' are 'greater than the sum of their parts'. Since it is not entirely clear what 'greater than' is supposed to mean in this context, I would prefer simply to say that some wholes are *distinct from* the sum of their parts – or, more accurately, distinct from *any* sum of their *proper* parts, since we may need to allow that there is more than one way of individuating a thing's 'parts' and hence, perhaps, no such thing as *the* sum of its parts. But this is not true, it seems, of *all* wholes. By a 'whole', I should explain, I just mean a thing which *has* proper parts, or is 'composite', and I shall restrict my attention almost entirely to *concrete* wholes. (Henceforth, I shall drop the qualification 'proper' to avoid prolixity and so should be understood to be using the term 'part' in a sense in which it is *not* the case that any thing is, trivially, a part of itself.) I shall begin by defending the claims that I have just made. Later, I shall go on to examine their implications for the views of certain other philosophers, in particular those who adhere to a relativist conception of identity.

Consider again our old friend, Tibbles the cat. Tibbles is a composite thing: he certainly has parts. Tibbles's tail – call it 'Tail' – is a part of Tibbles.[1] But is there an object which is, so to speak, Tibbles *minus* Tail? I rather think there is and that this object is also a part of Tibbles, albeit a very

---

[1] Some philosophers, notably Peter van Inwagen, would deny this: see his 'The Doctrine of Arbitrary Undetached Parts', *Pacific Philosophical Quarterly* 62 (1981), pp. 123–37, and his *Material Beings* (Ithaca, NY: Cornell University Press, 1990). However, this is certainly a counter-intuitive opinion, which I think we should eschew if the common-sense view of the matter can be defended, as I believe it can.

large part. Let us, following Noonan, call this part 'Tib'.[2] (Many, I concede, will find the suggestion that there *is* such an object as Tib highly dubious – and to *some* extent I sympathize, as I shall explain in due course.) Now, granted all this, it seems that we may affirm the following identity, appropriately understood:

(1)   Tib = (Tibbles – Tail)

But the use of the minus sign here, even if it is legitimate, is a distinctly peculiar one, because it apparently doesn't conform to anything like the laws of arithmetic. For it seems that we cannot derive from (1) anything like

(2)   Tibbles = (Tib + Tail)

The problem is not that '(Tib + Tail)' does not denote an object – I think it *does*: it denotes the 'sum' of two parts of Tibbles, the object that is Tib *plus* Tail. The problem, rather, is that this object is *distinct from Tibbles*.

Of course, one could simply *stipulate* that the plus sign in (2) has whatever sense is required to make (2) just an alternative way of writing (1). But then my point would be that this sense would have to differ from any sense that we could intuitively attach to it in talking about a 'sum' of an object's parts – and hence, once more, that the intuitive notions of 'subtraction' and 'addition' at work in the present context are not very closely related to the arithmetical notions going by the same names. (It may legitimately be inquired here what bearing these remarks have on the logistical system known as 'mereology' and, indeed, I shall address this question later in the chapter.)

That (Tib + Tail) is distinct from Tibbles may be shown in the following familiar way. If Tail were to be annihilated – but no other part of Tibbles not included in Tail – then Tibbles would continue to exist, but (Tib + Tail) would cease to be. A sum of certain parts ceases to be when one of those parts ceases to be.[3] Suppose this is denied: suppose it is claimed

---

[2]   See Harold W. Noonan, *Objects and Identity* (The Hague: Martinus Nijhoff, 1980), p. 22.

[3]   Peter van Inwagen, in his 'Can Mereological Sums Change Their Parts?', *Journal of Philosophy* 103 (2006), pp. 614–30, while acknowledging that '[m]any philosophers think not' (p. 614), maintains that mereological sums *can* change their parts. He also cites what I say in *Kinds of Being*, Chapter 6, as possibly exemplifying the position that he rejects – only *possibly* because he takes me to deny that mereological sums *have* parts, at least in the 'ordinary' sense of 'part' in which things like cats have them. However, despite what I may have

that even if Tail were annihilated, (Tib + Tail) would continue to exist. This seems to lead to absurdity. For, surely, if Tail were annihilated, *Tib* at least would, *ceteris paribus*, continue to exist – and Tib is distinct from (Tib + Tail). But if *both* Tib *and* (Tib + Tail) were to continue to exist after the annihilation of Tail, what would then distinguish Tib from (Tib + Tail)? Perhaps it could be answered: *their different past histories* – for instance, things that happened to Tail would be included in the past history of (Tib + Tail), but not in that of Tib. But this seems to put the cart before the horse, for the question at issue is precisely whether (Tib + Tail) would *have* a past history subsequent to the time of Tail's annihilation. I think it is clear that it would not, for it would no longer exist.

The next question is this: is Tib *a cat*? Indeed, is (Tib + Tail) *a cat*? If the answer is 'yes' in either case, then we are, of course, in trouble. For we are obliged to deny both

(3)   Tibbles = Tib

and

(2)   Tibbles = (Tib + Tail)

so that, it seems, we must have, in the same place at the same time, *two* or even *three* different cats. One putative remedy, as we saw in the preceding chapter, is to reject the notion of absolute identity and say that Tibbles, Tib and (Tib + Tail) are all the same *cat*, but that Tibbles and Tib are different *lumps of feline tissue*, while Tibbles and (Tib + Tail) are different relative to some other appropriate sortal classification of them. But I hope I have already shown that this remedy is a desperate one indeed.

Why, however, should we be at all *tempted* to suppose that either Tib or (Tib + Tail) is a cat? (By 'is a cat' I mean, of course, exactly what I mean in saying that *Tibbles* 'is a cat': that is, I am using the 'is' of *instantiation*.) Well, consider Tib. There are readily conceivable circumstances in which Tib would continue to exist if Tail were annihilated, as would Tibbles.

said in *Kinds of Being*, I don't now deny this, nor do I now think that the word 'part' is ambiguous in this respect. What I *do* think is that mereological sums and things like cats have different *principles of composition*, just as they have different *criteria of identity*, and that the principle of composition for mereological sums is simply that some things, the *x*s, have a mereological sum, *y*, just so long as the *x*s (all of them) *exist*. Hence, I maintain, if one or more of the *x*s ceases to exist, so does *y*. Things like cats have a much more complicated and interesting principle of composition.

But, it may be urged, Tib and Tibbles would then be spatially indistinguishable (despite differing in their past histories): and hence, since Tibbles would still be a cat, so too would Tib then be a cat.[4] And if Tib would be a cat after the annihilation of Tail, then why not also before that?

But this argument is unsatisfactory. The mere spatial indistinguishability – that is, exact spatial coincidence – of two objects at a given time is by no means sufficient to show that they fall under the same sortal concepts at that time, much less at other times. This is a lesson that we should by now have learned from the discussions of previous chapters. Nor should we be unsettled by the fact that, according to the view I am defending, we may not be able to tell simply *by looking* that Tibbles is a cat but Tib is not. For sortal concepts like that of a *cat* are just not in this sense purely observational.[5]

But what then *is* Tib, subsequent to the annihilation of Tail, given that Tib is not then – much less previously – a *cat*? My answer is that Tib remains what it was before, namely, a *part* of the cat Tibbles – albeit a part which now *wholly composes* Tibbles ('wholly composes' Tibbles in the sense that Tibbles now has no other part that is not materially included in Tib).[6] It should not really surprise us that an object can come to be wholly composed by a part of it which at one time only partially composed it, as the following somewhat macabre example should help to make clear. It is at least conceivable that Tibbles should meet with a dreadful accident, in which his body and legs are run over and have to be amputated from his head, which – through the miracles of modern science – can be kept alive on a life-support machine. In these circumstances, I suggest, Tibbles will have *survived* the accident, albeit terribly maimed, having lost everything except his head. Call this 'Head'. Are we then to say that

(4)   Tibbles = Head

is true in these circumstances? Surely not. A *cat* cannot be identical with a *cat's head*, even though it may *have* no more than a head. A cat's head

---

4   Compare Noonan, *Objects and Identity*, p. 22.

5   See further my 'Substantial Change and Spatiotemporal Coincidence', *Ratio* 16 (2003), 140–60.

6   This answer requires me to deny what is known, by mereologists, as the *weak supplementation principle*, according to which, if an object has a proper part, then it also has *another* proper part which is not a proper part of that first part. For some discussion, see my 'Identity, Composition, and the Simplicity of the Self', in Kevin Corcoran (ed.), *Soul, Body, and Survival: Essays on the Metaphysics* of *Human Persons* (Ithaca, NY: Cornell University Press, 2001) – although in that paper I am more sympathetic to the principle than I am here.

cannot be a *cat*, but at most only a *part* of a cat, even though it may be the *largest* remaining part in certain extreme circumstances. In like manner, then, if it is conceded that Tib is indeed a genuine object and a cat-part prior to the annihilation of Tail – a proposition that I shall examine more closely later on – it should also be conceded that Tib *remains* only a cat-part after the annihilation of Tail and is not a *cat* either before or after that.

Tibbles, as I hope we have now been persuaded, is the sort of 'whole' that is distinct from any sum of its parts. But not *all* wholes are like this. (Tib + Tail) is not, since it obviously *is*, by definition, the sum of its parts – relative, at least, to that way of individuating its parts which identifies these as Tib and Tail. One might suppose that objects such as *heaps* and *lumps* – call them *aggregates* – can be likened to (Tib + Tail). Thus, it might seem that a heap of sand is – that is, is *identical with* – the sum of its individual grains and that a lump of butter is identical with any sum of particular butter portions into which that lump may be divided without remainder. But to this it may be objected that a heap of sand ceases to exist if all of its grains are *scattered* – or, indeed, even if only *one* grain is removed, where-upon we have a *different* heap – whereas the *sum* of the grains continues to exist provided that each grain does. I think that this objection is a sound one and consequently that what we should say is that an aggregate, although it is *constituted* by a sum of its suitably individuated parts, is not *identical* with any such sum, because a further constraint on its persistence conditions is imposed by the requirement that these parts should *adhere to* one another, so as to compose a *connected* – and thus not a *scattered* – whole.

Let us say, then, that a *collective* is a composite object which is identical with a certain sum of its parts, individuated in a certain way, whereas an *aggregate* is constituted by a collective whose appropriately individuated parts are united by adhesion. (Of course, it is not necessary for every such part to adhere *directly* to every other, so long as any two which do *not* adhere directly to one another belong to a single chain of parts adjacent members of which *do*. Just what counts as 'adhesion' need not trouble us for present purposes: it may amount to little more than *contact* in the case of a heap of sand, or to something much more robust in the case of something like a lump of stone.) A *collective*, I should point out, is not as I understand it the same as a *set*. For collectives are *concrete* objects whereas *sets* are abstract. A familiar everyday example of a collective would be a *herd of sheep*. And the key distinction between collectives and aggregates resides in the fact that the former are, whereas the latter are not, *scatterable*, in the sense that they can survive the separation of their appropriately individuated parts. I should point out, if it isn't already sufficiently obvious, that the qualification 'appropriately individuated' is very important here, for reasons that I shall discuss further shortly.

Now, in contrast with both collectives and aggregates, we have objects like Tibbles the cat, which we may call, for want of a better word, *integrates* – although, in fact, my notion of an 'integrate' is quite close to the traditional one of an *individual substance*. Integrates, as I understand this term, are composite objects which are *not* identical with any sum of their parts, nor with any aggregate constituted by any sum of their parts. Thus, one mark of an integrate is that it may survive the destruction or removal of at least some of its parts and their replacement by new ones, however these parts may be individuated – although, obviously, some parts of an integrate may play such a vital role in its make-up that their removal or replacement is effectively precluded. Of course, it may not always be possible to remove a part of an integrate 'all in one go': sometimes, this may need to be done gradually, by successively removing and replacing *parts* of that part. Notice, too, that some integrates may in fact be *scatterable*, unlike aggregates: those that are *artefacts*, such as clocks and ships, surely often are, for it seems clear that they may be taken to pieces and put together again without their ceasing to exist during the time in which their parts are separated.[7] By contrast, the mark of a collective is that it cannot survive the destruction of *any* of the parts with whose sum it is identical, while the mark of an aggregate is that it cannot even survive the *separation* – much less the destruction – of any of the parts whose sum constitutes it. And corresponding to these different persistence conditions for integrates, collectives, and aggregates, there are of course different *criteria of identity* for objects in these different categories – although even within each category there may be further differences between the criteria of identity of different kinds of objects since, for example, not all integrates share the same criterion.

It is important to observe that even a collective or an aggregate *may* survive the destruction or removal of one of its parts, *provided that* this part is not one of those whose sum is identical with the collective or which constitutes the aggregate. For instance, a heap of sand, which is constituted by the sum of a number of different grains of sand, clearly contains as a 'part' an *electron* in an atom of silicon in one of those grains: but the removal or destruction of that electron is surely consistent with the survival of the heap, given at least that it is consistent with the survival of the grain, as it certainly seems to be. Here I should acknowledge that, as this remark already demonstrates, I am not using the term 'sum' in exactly the same way that many other philosophers currently understand the term

---

[7] See my 'On the Identity of Artifacts', *Journal of Philosophy* 80 (1983), pp. 220–32.

'mereological sum'. For, according to their usage, any two sums of parts into which the same object can be completely 'decomposed' are in fact *identical*, so that we may always refer uniquely to *the* sum of an object's parts. Thus, these philosophers would say that the sum of all the *grains of sand* in a heap is identical with the sum of all the *subatomic particles* in the heap. But this way of individuating sums seems much too crude to me. When we sum certain objects – such as a number of different grains of sand, or a number of different sheep in a field – then I don't think that we should regard this operation as necessarily having the same outcome as that of summing, say, all the *subatomic particles* in those grains or those sheep. As I see it, the sum, *y*, of some objects, the *x*s, has *only the x*s as its *summands*, not just *any* plurality of objects into which the *x*s may be exhaustively partitioned. Thus, in my usage, an electron in a grain of sand is, like the grain itself, a *part* of the sum of grains which constitutes a certain heap of sand: but only *the grain* is one of the *summands* of that sum.

Another thing that I should acknowledge here is that there may well be *another* sense of 'heap' in which heaps belong to the category of integrates: a sense in which it is legitimate to speak of one and the same heap *growing* or *diminishing* by the addition or removal of grains of sand. We do not really have to *choose* between saying that heaps are aggregates and saying that they are integrates: rather, we can say that 'heap' in one sense denotes a kind of aggregate and in another sense denotes a kind of integrate. A *single* heap in the *integrate* sense which undergoes growth or shrinkage is successively constituted by a series of *different* heaps in the *aggregate* sense, these latter heaps being of different sizes.

I turn now to the implications of these conclusions for the views of certain other philosophers. I have already indicated what it is that I regard as the main issue at present: the debate between 'absolute' and 'relative' identity theorists. A number of arguments for the relativist position can be scotched by appeal to the distinctions that I have drawn. Consider, for instance, Zemach's argument to the surprising conclusion that 'the overwhelming majority of the objects actually referred to [by us], objects such as Jimmy Carter, this shirt, the man on my right, etc., are *not* ontologically complete'.[8] By an object's being 'not ontologically complete' he means that it is *not* the case that 'with respect to every property *F*, either it has it, or it does not have it'. The following passage will give us the flavour of his position:[9]

[8] Eddy M. Zemach, 'Schematic Objects and Relative Identity', *Noûs* 16 (1982), pp. 295–305, at p. 295.

[9] Zemach, 'Schematic Objects and Relative Identity', p. 297.

Does the referent of 'this table' include, e.g., the nail and thumb tack which were driven into it? Does it, or does it not, include the paper pasted on it? Yet surely table A, which includes nail, thumb tack and paper, is a very different object (it has a different weight, history, mass, etc.) from table B which does not include them as parts.

For Zemach, then, there are at least two – and in fact many more than two – distinct 'ontologically complete' objects in the region occupied by this table, all of which are *tables*, but all of which may be counted as the *same* table. (This is how his argument leads to a version of the relative identity theory.) 'This table', however, denotes an 'ontologically incomplete' or 'schematic' object, of which it may not be true to say, for instance, either that it weighs more than fifty pounds or that it does not weigh more than fifty pounds.

Here again I think we see confusion concerning the relations between parts and wholes. Let us suppose, for the sake of argument, that the nail, thumb tack, and paper are indeed parts of a certain 'complete' object, which we shall continue to call 'table A', on the understanding that this object really is a *table*. (I shall, however, query this assumption in a moment.) Now, tables are *integrates*, in my terminology: they are not identical with any sum of their parts and they may lose or gain at least some parts without ceasing to be. So, in particular, table A may presumably lose the nail, thumb tack, and paper that – we have assumed – are parts of it and continue to exist without them. We may also agree that there is an object which is table A *minus* the nail, thumb tack, and paper – an object that Zemach calls 'table B'. But is table B really a *table*? I think not, *given that table A is*. B is just a very large part of table A – and a part of a table, no matter how large a part, is not a table. (I exclude here as irrelevant the special case of tables made by *joining together* two or more smaller tables.) We should not be misled by the fact that if the nail, thumb tack, and paper are removed, table A will become spatially indistinguishable from the object that Zemach has called 'table B', any more than we should be misled by the comparable circumstance in the case of Tibbles and Tib.

In fact, however, I think that we were mistaken to allow that the nail, thumb tack, and paper could really be *parts* of a *table*, in the way that one of its legs, or the knob on one of its drawers, certainly is. There may indeed be an object which is the sum of a table, a nail, a thumb tack and a piece of paper: but such an object is *not* a table, because it is not even an integrate. Such an object ceases to be if, say, the thumb tack is destroyed: but no *table* can cease to exist for so trivial a reason. Equally, an *aggregate* constituted by the sum of these items does not qualify as a table.

I conclude that there can be no such two objects as Zemach calls 'table A' and 'table B', *both* of which are tables. Either table A is a table, in which case 'table B' is just a large table-part; or else, as seems much more plausible, table B is a table and 'table A' is just an *aggregate* which is constituted by the sum of table B, the nail, the thumb tack and the paper – and such an aggregate, I repeat, cannot be a table. And so it will be with regard to any other 'complete' objects that Zemach cares to identify in this case (table C, table D, and so on): only *one* of the objects can be a *table*, whereas others will either be *parts* of that table or else *aggregates* of such table-parts or of such table-parts and other objects that are not table-parts. For instance, if table B is indeed a table, then the object that is table B *minus* the bottom half-inch of one of its legs will be a table-part, albeit a large one. It may perhaps be the case that it is to some degree arbitrary precisely how we individuate the table – and consequently that there is 'no fact of the matter' as to whether, say, there is a table in the room weighing more than fifty pounds. All I am claiming is that *not more than one* object in the location can simultaneously qualify as a table: tables can't 'overlap'.[10] And therefore we don't need to resort to the relative identity theory in order to justify the common-sense conviction that there is only *one table* in the room. We don't have to say that several different objects, all of them tables, may be one and the same table, because we don't have to concede that any more than one of these objects *is* a table.[11]

It should now be explained why I have made no use in this chapter of the so-called *calculus of individuals*, or *mereology*, in one or other of its versions: for this, after all, is usually regarded as providing the classic treatment of the part–whole relation.[12] The simple reason is that this calculus is plainly quite inadequate for my purposes. For instance, according to the calculus, an individual, x, is a sum of the individuals y and z if and only if y is a part of x and z is a part of x and every part of x has a part in common with either y or z. But on this definition it would appear that Tibbles *is* a sum of Tib and Tail: for Tib is a part of Tibbles and Tail is a part of Tibbles and every part of Tibbles has a part in common with either Tib

---

[10] Compare my 'The Problem of the Many and the Vagueness of Constitution', *Analysis* 55 (1995), pp. 179–82.

[11] David Wiggins has said some things with which the view developed here is broadly in sympathy: see his 'Mereological Essentialism: Asymmetrical Essential Dependence and the Nature of Continuants', in Ernest Sosa (ed.), *Essays on the Philosophy of Roderick M. Chisholm* (Amsterdam: Rodopi, 1979).

[12] See, for example, H. S. Leonard and Nelson Goodman, 'The Calculus of Individuals and its Uses', *Journal of Symbolic Logic* 5 (1940), pp. 45–55, Nelson Goodman, *The Structure of Appearance*, 3rd edn (Dordrecht: D. Reidel, 1977), pp. 33ff., and Alfred Tarski, *Logic, Semantics and Metamathematics*, 2nd edn (Indianapolis, IN: Hackett Publishing Company, 1983), pp. 24–9.

or Tail. (This is true even if, as the calculus demands, we regard Tibbles himself as a 'part' of Tibbles.) However, precisely what I *deny* is that Tibbles is a sum of Tib and Tail.

My conclusion must therefore be that *either* the 'is a part of' relation utilized by the calculus under its intended interpretation does not correspond to the ordinary sense of this expression as it is used to say, for example, that Tail *is a part of* Tibbles, *or* the notion of 'sum' defined in the calculus does not correspond to the notion that I have invoked in characterizing collectives as being 'sums' of certain of their parts. This disjunction is not exclusive, but in point of fact I have already acknowledged that my understanding of the term 'sum' differs importantly from that of standard mereology. Certainly, I cannot accept that the calculus provides an adequate framework for discussion of the issues raised in this chapter. For it fails to provide the resources with which to articulate the very distinctions that I have been trying to draw between what I call *integrates*, on the one hand, and *collectives* and *aggregates* on the other. Furthermore, it takes no proper account of the fact, emphasized throughout this chapter, that there may be many more ways than one of individuating a thing's 'parts'. (In fact, to speak of *the* parts of a thing is not even to speak fully determinately, because the general term 'thing which is a part of *a*', where *a* is some individual, is only what is known as a *dummy* sortal: it conveys no criterion of identity and hence, although grammatically a count noun, it carries with it no principle for counting the items to which it applies.)

I do not pretend to have rendered perfectly transparent, in this chapter, all of the subtle distinctions that can be drawn concerning our ways of talking about 'parts' and 'wholes', much less to have *defined* the expression 'is a part of'. But I hope at least that I have made it clear that the concepts involved are considerably more complex and sophisticated than any that can be handled purely in terms of the calculus of individuals, or mereology, at least in its classical, extensional form.[13]

Finally, I turn to an interesting question which I have so far set on one side. Is there *really* an 'object' which is the cat Tibbles 'minus' Tail? Many, as I acknowledged earlier, will view the suggestion with suspicion: and their suspicion is, I think, partly well founded, although not completely so. I think that Tib – that is, (Tibbles – Tail) – *is* a genuine object, but nonetheless one which is, from a logical point of view, rather peculiar. It is significant that both Tibbles and Tail are relatively uncontentious objects

---

[13]   Compare Peter Simons, *Parts: A Study in Ontology* (Oxford: Clarendon Press, 1987). I find myself in substantial agreement with Simons's critique there of standard extensional mereological theory.

of quite familiar sorts: a *cat* and a *cat's tail*, respectively. But what sort of thing is Tib? I suggest that what is logically peculiar about Tib is that, to the extent that we can individuate this object *at all*, we can only do so precisely as the 'difference' between two *bona fide* objects, Tibbles and Tail. Tib is not *independently* individuable as a *bona fide* object of any sort. And this, fundamentally, is why, even after the annihilation of Tail, Tib cannot be *identified* with Tibbles. For even then Tib is still only individuable in a way which presupposes the independent individuability of Tibbles the cat. Tib is still only a *logically dependent* object, as we might call it, in stark contrast with Tibbles, even though they now coincide spatially. An object which is introduced to us as a logically dependent one cannot subsequently become a logically *independent* one: an object cannot change its logical status. I believe that the puzzles posed by Noonan, Zemach, and others at least partly trade upon a blurring or ignoring of this distinction.

Perhaps a geometrical example will help to clarify the distinction that I have just drawn. Suppose that AB is the straight-line interval between points A and B which includes A and B as its end-points. And suppose that X is a point somewhere in AB between A and B:

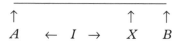

Then XB, like AB, is a straight-line interval with two end-points, X and B. But if we consider the straight-line interval, call it I, which is obtained by *subtracting XB* from AB – that is, the interval consisting of all the points that are in AB but not in XB – then it is obvious that this interval does *not* have two end-points. I is a 'half-open' interval, closed at only one end, by point A. Hence, I is not to be identified with the closed interval AX, even though I and AX have exactly the same length. Now, I itself is, in our sense, a *logically dependent* object, inasmuch as it can only be individuated as the 'difference' between two closed intervals or, alternatively, as the 'difference' between a closed interval and a point – that is, as what 'remains' when either the closed interval XB is 'subtracted' from the closed interval AB or the point X is 'subtracted' from the closed interval AX. And, although the closed interval AX can in turn be individuated as the result of 'adding' the point X to I, it can nonetheless *also* be individuated independently of I and without appeal to any operation of 'addition' or 'subtraction', namely, as the closed straight-line interval whose end-points are A and X. Hence, AX, unlike I, is *not* a logically dependent object in our sense.

The analogy with the case of Tibbles and Tib should be obvious: Tib is to Tibbles rather as I is to AB. And the fact that Tib and Tibbles *exactly coincide* after the annihilation of Tail no more makes them *identical* at that time than the fact that I and AX have *exactly the same length* makes *them* identical. Of course, the parallel is not perfect, but it was not intended to be. Tib and Tibbles, after all, are concrete rather than geometrical objects. However, with regard to the key distinction that I was seeking to illustrate, the two cases are the same: I and Tib are examples of *logically dependent* objects in our sense, in contrast with AB and Tibbles.

8

Persons and Their Bodies

What is the relationship between a living organism and the collection of material particles composing it at any given time? What is the relationship between a person and his or her body? Is either of these relations simply that of *identity*? If not, are we at any rate faced with the *same* relation in each case? Questions like these are amongst the most difficult and interesting that can arise in metaphysics and I hope to cast some light on them in the course of this chapter, making full use of the semantic, logical and ontological findings of the preceding chapters.

Matter and Organisms

I have, of course, already implicitly answered our first question, 'What is the relationship between a living organism and the collection of material particles composing it at any given time?': this relationship is one of *constitution* rather than *identity*. It cannot be one of identity simply because living organisms and collections of material particles have different *criteria of identity* and so cannot be identified, for reasons that I have tried to make clear in previous chapters. That the relevant criteria are different is something that Locke must be credited with having understood particularly clearly – although where he would have elected to stand in the modern debate between absolute and relative identity theorists is a moot point, since he does not explicitly raise the issue and says things in different places which could be interpreted as favouring each of these positions. Certainly, however, we can still look with much profit at what Locke says in the opening sections of Chapter XXVII, 'Of Identity and Diversity', of Book II of the *Essay Concerning Human Understanding*.

In § 3, Locke offers us what is effectively a criterion of identity for what he calls a 'body', 'mass', or 'parcel of matter' – such a lump of gold – as follows:[1]

> [W]hilst a [number of atoms] exist united together, the Mass, consisting of the same Atoms, must be the same Mass, let the parts be never so differently jumbled: But if one of these Atoms be taken away, or one new one added, it is no longer the same Mass or the same Body.

Locke, then, understands a 'mass' or 'parcel of matter' to be, in my terminology, an *aggregate of atoms*. And the criterion of identity that he gives us here for such objects may simply be stated as follows:

> If x and y are *parcels of matter*, then x is identical with y if and only if x and *y consist of the same atoms united together.*

Now, we may reasonably query Locke's assumption that the criterion of identity for parcels of matter implies that matter is *atomic* rather than, say, infinitely divisible. For that it is atomic is surely not inherent in the very *concept* of matter, nor is this apparently a semantic implication of the term 'matter' as it is ordinarily used by English speakers, whether in Locke's day or ours. Rather, what we have here is just a thesis advanced by a particular *scientific theory* concerning the *nature* of matter – although, to be quite fair to Locke, we should not necessarily assume that he himself was in any way concerned to express a *semantic* principle in articulating the criterion as he did. We may, nonetheless, agree with Locke that parcels of matter, according to *any* satisfactory conception of what they are, have the ontological status of *aggregates* and as such are constituted by 'sums' of certain of their *parts*, while also recognizing the need to examine further precisely *which* of the constituents of a parcel of matter – say, of a lump of gold – are to *count* as its 'parts' for the purpose of framing an adequate criterion of identity for such an object. Does an *electron*, for instance, qualify? Very plausibly, it does *not*.

What I myself am inclined to say is that the relevant parts of a lump of gold in this context are just the various smaller *bits of gold* into which it may be divided – and *not*, thus, the atoms or smaller sub-atomic particles composing it. (There are, of course, very many – perhaps indefinitely many and maybe even infinitely many – ways of carrying out such a division: a fact which may or may not pose a difficulty for the current proposal.) For,

---

[1]   John Locke, *An Essay Concerning Human Understanding*, ed. P. H. Nidditch (Oxford: Clarendon Press, 1975), II, XXVII, 3.

very plausibly, it *is* a semantic fact, grounded in the sense of the term 'lump of gold', that if any *part* of the gold in a lump of gold is removed or replaced, what remains is a *different* lump, on the understanding that 'part of the gold' here means something that is itself *golden*, that is, *consists of gold*. But, on this understanding, it would seem that an *atom* of gold does *not* qualify as 'part of the gold' in the relevant sense: for – at least according to modern physics – gold atoms do not *consist of gold*, but rather of protons, neutrons and electrons.

What I am suggesting, then, is that we ordinarily conceive of a lump of gold as being an aggregate of smaller lumps, or 'bits', of gold: a conception which we no doubt acquire from our experience of being able to join and divide such lumps to make larger or smaller ones – if not in the case of gold itself, then at least in the case of lumps of commoner and cheaper sorts of stuff, such as clay. However, this already seems to create a problem when we try to frame a *criterion of identity* for lumps of gold in terms of this conception. It would scarcely do, for instance, to say:

> If x and y are *lumps of gold*, then x is identical with y if and only if x and y *are divisible into the same smaller lumps of gold.*

For this is blatantly circular. And there are, besides, other difficult questions concerning lumps of matter or stuff as we ordinarily seem to conceive of them. For instance, if two separate lumps of gold, x and y, are conjoined and their united matter is thoroughly mixed – say, by melting and stirring – are we to say that x and y themselves *continue to exist*? Indeed, more generally, to what extent do we want to say that all of the various lumps of gold into which a given lump is potentially divisible *actually* exist prior to any actual division – or can we intelligibly speak of their merely 'potential' existence?[2] Again, what do we or should we say about mixtures of *different* sorts of stuff, homogeneous or otherwise, such as gold and silver or flesh and bone?[3]

Perhaps, in the light of these difficulties, Locke's corpuscularian presuppositions saved him a good deal of trouble and at least freed him to discern the crucial fact that parcels of matter, whatever their precise criterion of identity should be deemed to be, certainly do *not* share the same criterion as living organisms. This, too, is the only fact that I would

---

[2]   Some of these questions are interestingly addressed by Eli Hirsch in his *The Concept of Identity* (Oxford: Oxford University Press, 1982), pp. 113ff.

[3]   For an illuminating discussion of some of the issues arising here, see Richard Sharvy, 'Aristotle on Mixtures', *Journal of Philosophy* 80 (1983), pp. 439–57, and also Kit Fine, 'Mixing Matters', in David S. Oderberg (ed.), *Form and Matter: Themes in Contemporary Metaphysics* (Oxford: Blackwell, 1999).

wish to emphasize at this point, for the purpose of pursuing the questions raised at the outset of this chapter. So I shall attempt no further resolution at present of the problem of framing an adequate criterion of identity for 'parcels of matter'. Indeed, I deliberately formulated those initial questions in terms of *collections of material particles* rather than 'parcels of matter', in part simply to deflect the problem that I have just identified. Locke himself might have been advised to do likewise, since the criterion of identity that he gives for parcels of matter is, of course, much more acceptable if it is taken instead as a criterion of identity for collections of material particles – or, more precisely, for aggregates of atoms.

Having offered us a criterion of identity for parcels of matter, Locke goes on to make the following observation:[4]

> In the state of living Creatures, their Identity depends not on a Mass of the same Particles; but on something else. For in them the variation of great parcels of Matter alters not the Identity.

The point that he is making, of course, is quite simply that living organisms, such as an oak tree, can lose or gain material particles – for instance, through metabolic processes – while retaining their identity, that is, without thereby ceasing to exist: and that therefore living organisms must have a *different* criterion of identity from the one that he has just assigned to 'parcels of matter'. He even goes so far as to suggest what this criterion might be, in § 4, where he writes:

> We must therefore consider wherein an Oak differs from a Mass of Matter, and that seems to me to be in this; that the one is only the Cohesion of Particles of Matter any how united, the other such a disposition of them as constitutes the parts of an Oak; and such an organization of those parts, as is fit to receive, and distribute nourishment, so as to continue, and frame the Wood, Bark, and Leaves, *etc.* of an Oak, in which consists the vegetable Life.

This is slightly obscure and perhaps even has a misleading air of circularity, in view of the way in which the sortal term 'oak' is itself used – 'so as to continue, and frame the Wood, Bark, and Leaves, *etc.* of an Oak' – in Locke's attempt to explain the criterion of identity associated with that sortal term. Nonetheless, two obviously important features of the continuing identity through time of a living organism do emerge from Locke's remarks: the maintenance of a certain *form* or *organization of parts* and the maintenance, by means of that organization, of certain *biological functions*

---

[4]   Locke, *An Essay Concerning Human Understanding*, II, XXVII, 3.

and processes which serve to preserve that organization or form. Of course, we must be prepared to be quite flexible in talking about the preservation of 'form' here, given the sorts of alteration that normally occur as a sapling grows into a mature tree. What is more fundamental than mere continuity of form is the maintenance of a system of biological functions, such as respiration and photosynthesis, which contribute to their own preservation: a system of functions which renders the organism relatively autonomous, despite the constant interchange of matter between it and its environment, by conferring upon it a considerable degree of *control* over that process of interchange. In short, a living organism is a *homeostatic* mechanism.

Locke succeeds in conveying that this is the crucial point, when he goes on to advance the following criterion of identity for *man*, conceived purely as a species of animal, that is, as a kind of living organism:[5]

> [T]he Identity of the same *Man* consists . . . in nothing but a participation of the same continued Life, by constantly fleeting Particles of Matter, in succession vitally united to the same organized Body.

Spelling this out more in line with my own style and terminology, we might say that Locke is here endorsing a criterion of identity for living organisms – and so, more specifically, for 'men' or human beings – which could be stated thus:

> If x and y are living organisms, then x is identical with y if and only if x and y are constituted by collections of material particles participating of the same continued life.

where the notion of 'participation of the same continued life' is to be explained in terms of the engagement of material particles in the metabolic and other vital processes that together constitute the workings of the sort of self-sustaining or homeostatic system of biological functions mentioned earlier.

It is perhaps worth remarking, incidentally, that although the last quoted passage from Locke may not make this quite clear, other passages indeed indicate that for Locke it is not so much *organisms* as the *material particles* constituting them that may said to 'participate of the same life' – not that I think that a great deal turns on this terminological point, since it would be easy enough to define organisms as sharing 'the same life' just in case their constituent particles do. The only awkward feature of Locke's proposal, as he himself states it – apart from its undoubted vagueness – lies in his use of the phrase 'the same organized Body': for this can only be

---

[5]   Locke, *An Essay Concerning Human Understanding*, II, XXVII, 6.

understood to mean something like 'the same *living organism*'. Plainly, it cannot be taken just to mean 'the same *body*', in the sense of 'the same *mass*, or *parcel of matter*'. But then circularity again threatens, since 'man' is here being understood precisely to denote a species of *living organism* and hence something with precisely the latter's criterion of identity. However, I consider Locke's use of the offending phrase to be superfluous for his purposes, as will be apparent from my suggested paraphrase of his proposed criterion.

An objection which might be raised against the foregoing proposal is that it would not permit us to rule out *a priori* one and the same living organism changing from being an organism of one animal kind or species, say a *dog*, to being one of another, say a *cat* – or even, more radically, from being an *animal* to being a *plant*, unless perhaps 'life' can be understood in different senses as applied to animals and plants respectively. However, in my view, it would indeed be wrong to see such changes as being *conceptually* or even *metaphysically* impossible, as opposed to being, perhaps, *physically* or *naturally* impossible. For who, after all, would have thought, prior to experience, that caterpillars might turn into butterflies? If a dog's turning into a cat could be excluded *a priori*, then surely a change as radical as that of a caterpillar into a butterfly would be too – and yet we know that it is not. The sort of change that clearly *is* conceptually and indeed metaphysically impossible is – to use an example of Wiggins's – one in which a human being turns into a pillar of salt, as is said to have happened to Lot's wife: and then only if we understand 'turns into' as implying 'continues to exist as'. But this, of course, is just because living organisms and parcels of matter (such as pillars of salt) have different and incompatible criteria of identity.

Incidentally, these considerations again serve to show that it would be mistaken to place too much emphasis on the preservation of *form* as far as the identity of living organisms is concerned – although, no doubt, *sudden and extreme* changes of form are inimical to the homeostatic mechanisms that are essential to life. Of course, I do not mean to deny that an organism's form is relevant to the question of what *species* or *kind* of organism it instantiates: something with four legs and a tail could hardly qualify as an *oak tree*! The question is only whether such specific facts about such an individual's form bear upon its *criterion of identity* and consequently upon its *persistence conditions* – and it is my view that they do not.

My own opinion, I should say, is that the criterion of identity for living organisms that I have ascribed to Locke is one that is broadly along the right lines, although it suffers from a certain amount of vagueness over what constitutes 'the same life' and consequently may leave the answers to some important identity questions underdetermined. For example, do conjoined twins share 'the same life' and so constitute a single living organism?

Do a pregnant woman and her unborn child? To answer that 'inseparable' conjoined twins do, or that a woman and her 'non-viable' foetus do, is merely to invite further difficult questions. However, I shall not attempt to render the notion of sameness of life and therewith the Lockean criterion any more precise here, since my main concern once more is merely to emphasize the *difference* that must be acknowledged to obtain between any adequate criterion of identity for living organisms and any adequate criterion of identity for either parcels of matter or collections of material particles – the consequence of this difference being, of course, the *non-identity* of individuals belonging to sorts or kinds governed by these different criteria.

A further implication of this difference, as we have seen, is that we must allow that two or more different individual things not only may, but very often do, exist in the same place at the same time: the 'parcel of matter' occupying the region of space in which a certain oak tree is situated at a given time, and that oak tree itself, are two such individual things. To this a relative identity theorist might object that it makes no determinate sense to speak of 'two different things' existing in the same place at the same time, unless we can specify what *sort* or *kind* of thing it is of which they are, supposedly, *two*. And this, of course, we can't do with the present example. Such a theorist may claim that it makes sense to talk of two different *oak trees*, or of two different *parcels of matter*, but not of two different 'things', one of them an oak tree and the other a parcel of matter.

However, this objection rests on a confusion. Certainly, counting makes sense only when we have countable sorts of thing: we cannot simply count 'things', but only things of this or that countable sort. But it doesn't follow that we can count only relative to a *single* sortal distinction.[6] 'How many things?' is an indeterminate question, unlike 'How many φs?', where 'φ' is a sortal term. But it doesn't follow that 'How many φs *and* χs?' is indeterminate, even when there is no sort ψ of which both φs and χs are subspecies – that is, even when the answer 'There are n φs and χs' cannot be recast in the form 'There are n ψs', in the way, for example, that 'There are ten boys and girls' can be recast as 'There are ten children'. The *most* that is required for the question 'How many φs and χs?' to make determinate sense is that nothing should qualify *both* as a φ *and* as a χ, that is, that φ and χ should be *disjoint* sorts or kinds – which is why, for example, the question 'How many dogs and animals?' seems ill-formed. And this condition *is* satisfied, of course, in the case of the sorts *oak tree* and *parcel of matter*. It is not necessary for there to be some *higher* sort or kind of which both φ and χ are sub-kinds.

6 Compare Jonathan Bennett and William Alston, 'Identity and Cardinality: Geach and Frege', *Philosophical Review* 93 (1984), pp. 553–67.

Another objection that might be raised is that Locke himself seems to rule out simultaneous existence in the same place, in §§ 1–2 of Chapter XXVII of Book II of the *Essay*. In fact, however, he is careful to say there only that it is impossible that 'two things *of the same kind* should exist in the same place at the same time',[7] and indeed specifically allows that different sorts of substances 'do not exclude one another out of the same place'.[8] Nonetheless, it may be conceded that, in making this latter remark, the 'sorts of substances' that he has in mind are God, 'finite intelligences', and bodies – and he insists indeed that different *bodies* cannot exist in the same place at the same time. However, by 'body' here he just means, of course, 'parcel of matter', and he has not yet extended his discussion to a consideration of 'organized bodies', that is, living organisms or 'living creatures'. So nothing that Locke says in §§ 1–2 about simultaneous existence in the same place implies that he would have been obliged to *deny* that an oak tree and a parcel of matter existing in the same place at the same time could be distinct objects, even though the question of their identity or distinctness does not seem to have occurred to him.

Moreover, it may in any case be pointed out that it is at least debatable whether the existence in the same place at the same time even of two different *parcels of matter* can be ruled our *a priori*, as Locke seems to think when he asserts that 'could two Bodies be in the same place at the same time; then those two parcels of Matter must be one and the same'.[9] Certainly, if parcels of matter are conceived to be *aggregates of atoms*, as Locke himself would have it, then it is not at all obvious why it should be impossible for one such aggregate to pass intact through another, provided at least that there are big enough interstices between the atoms in each aggregate. We allow, after all, that water may seep through an earthenware pot without loss of identity. (It is true that this observation does not apply to the *atoms* themselves, but even in their case it might be deemed *conceivable* for them to merge temporarily whilst preserving their separate identities, with putative empirical evidence for the occurrence of this phenomenon being provided by a temporary doubling of material density in the region of space concerned – though I mention this only in a speculative vein, since there are obvious questions to be raised about *how* the identities of atoms could be preserved across such events.)

A living organism, then, such as an oak tree, and the parcel of matter or collection of material particles existing in the same place at a given time,

---

[7]   Locke, *An Essay Concerning Human Understanding*, II, XXVII, 1 (my emphasis added).

[8]   Locke, *An Essay Concerning Human Understanding*, II, XXVII, 2.

[9]   Locke, *An Essay Concerning Human Understanding*, II, XXVII, 2.

are *distinct* individuals, the latter of which *constitutes* the former at that time, but may not do so at another time in the course of the organism's life. And here it may be observed that when an individual, x, of one sort, φ, is constituted at a certain time by another individual, y, it is not in general a purely contingent matter what *sort* of thing y itself is, even though it is contingent that it is y, rather than some other individual, z, of the same sort as y, that constitutes x at that time. There will in general be, then, some non-contingent and quite possibly even *a priori* principle to the effect that φs are constituted by χs. For instance, it is not contingent that rivers are constituted by water, nor that human organisms are constituted by flesh and bone, nor that trees are constituted by wood.

Perhaps not all such necessities can be regarded as being purely *a priori* in character, because we may well need to accord an epistemic role to empirical scientific investigation in such matters. Nonetheless, it *is*, I suggest, an *a priori* truth that, for example, *living organisms are constituted by matter* – the reason being that this is implied by the very *criterion of identity* for living organisms. This is why, although we can *perhaps* conceive of discovering that oak trees are not in fact constituted by wood but instead by some kind of synthetic material imported from Mars – provided, of course, that this is consistent with our still regarding them as being *alive* – the notion of an *immaterial* oak tree is just incoherent and absurd. If departed oak trees have ghosts, their ghosts certainly aren't *trees*! Living organisms are *essentially* material beings. For if a living organism were to lose *all* of its matter without replacement, the very criterion of identity for living organisms implies that it would thereby cease to exist. (I should perhaps remark that, by an 'essential' property of an individual, in the present context, I just mean a property which that individual *cannot lose without thereby ceasing to be*. There is another notion of 'essence' according to which an essential property of an individual is one which that individual *could not have lacked*, or which it possesses 'in every possible world in which it exists'. Important and interesting though this distinction is, however, it does not presently concern me.[10])

Notice, however, that while I leave it open that certain *a posteriori* necessary truths of constitution may also obtain – truths that are not derivable purely from criteria of identity, such as that human organisms are constituted by flesh and bone – these necessities attach only to the *sorts* or *kinds* in question, not directly to the *individuals* instantiating them. For, while it may necessary that φs are constituted by χs, it may not be

---

[10]   I discuss the history of the distinction in my chapter 'Substance', in G. H. R. Parkinson (ed.), *An Encyclopaedia of Philosophy* (London: Routledge, 1988). See also my *A Survey of Metaphysics* (Oxford: Oxford University Press, 2002), pp. 79–80 and 96–7.

necessary that a given individual, which is now a φ, should *always* be constituted by a χ, provided that the necessity is not one that arises from that individual's very criterion of identity – although, of course, should that individual cease to be constituted by a χ, it will necessarily no longer qualify as a φ. Thus, despite the fact that human organisms are necessarily constituted by flesh and blood, it is not perhaps *inconceivable* that an individual which is *now* a human organism should come in time to be constituted by synthetic materials, with the consequence that that individual would thereby cease to be a human organism. What *is*, however, inconceivable is that such an individual should cease altogether to be *made of matter*, or cease to be *alive*, and yet continue to exist: for this would be contrary to its very criterion of identity.

Organisms and Persons

We are now in a position to start looking at the second question raised at the outset of this chapter: what is the relationship between a person and his or her body? By a 'body', here, I mean what Locke would call an 'organized body' and thus – at least in the case of *human* persons – what I have hitherto called a 'living organism'. I am concerned, then, as Locke himself is, with the relationship between *person* and *man*, the latter being understood as a species of animal and so of living organism.[11] There are two issues to be dealt with: (1) can an individual man or human living organism be *identified* with an individual person, and (2) if not, may we at least say that an individual man or human living organism can *constitute* an individual person, or even that the collection of material particles or parcel of matter constituting an individual man at any given time may also constitute an individual person at that time? I shall argue that both answers should be negative. The relation between a person and his or her 'organized body' – and likewise the relation between a person and any parcel of matter constituting such a body – is *neither* that of identity *nor* that of constitution.

If previous arguments of mine are correct, the most direct way to establish that an individual person is identifiable neither with his or her 'organized body', nor with the parcel of matter constituting that body at

---

[11]   Since Locke, as was customary in his day, regularly uses the word 'man' where we would now prefer to use the gender-neutral term 'human', and I want to relate my own discussion closely to his text, I shall have to adopt his usage more frequently than I would otherwise choose to. Note, moreover, that 'human being' is not unambiguously a modern-day equivalent of Locke's 'man', since it may also be taken to mean 'human *person*', as opposed to 'human *animal*' or 'human *living organism*'.

any given time, is simply to show that *persons do not have the same criterion of identity as either living organisms or parcels of matter.* Of course, determining precisely what criterion of identity persons *do* have – if indeed they have one, which cannot just be assumed without argument – is no easy business. But, fortunately, it may not be necessary to do this in order to show that they do *not* have either of the other criteria of identity now under consideration. Let us begin more optimistically, however, by inquiring how we should approach the problem of trying to find a criterion of identity for persons, if one exists.

Here Locke is again surely right in saying that we should start from a consideration of the meaning of the sortal term 'person'. As he puts it:[12]

> This being premised to find wherein personal Identity consists, we must consider what Person stands for; which, I think, is a thinking intelligent Being, that has reason and reflection, and can consider it self as it self, the same thinking thing in different times and places; which it does only by that consciousness, which is inseparable from thinking, and as it seems to me essential to it: It being impossible for any one to perceive, without perceiving, that he does perceive.

And I largely agree with Locke's characterization of the concept of a *person* here. A person is, essentially, something that acts and perceives and knows that it does so: it is a *perceiving, self-conscious agent*, or, equivalently, an *active, self-conscious percipient.* By 'acting', here, I mean, of course, performing *intentional* actions. I should also stress that I demand of persons only the *capacities* for action, perception, and self-reflection, not the continual *exercise* of those capacities.

However – turning aside for the moment from the quest for a criterion of personal identity – I think we can already say that if the foregoing characterization of persons is even approximately correct, then it does *not* follow from the very concept of a person that a person must be something embodied or material. And, indeed, there is *not* apparently any absurdity in speaking of an immaterial person, in the way that there is in speaking of an immaterial oak tree or an immaterial river. At least, if there *is* any incoherence here, then it must be buried very deep – which would be enough in itself to set 'person' widely apart from biological sortals such as 'oak tree'. I say this in view of the long history, in human thought, of the notion of personal survival after bodily death and of the supposed existence of immaterial but personal spirits, demons and gods: all of which testifies to the fact that our concept of a person is not one which *obviously* excludes,

---

[12]   Locke, *An Essay Concerning Human Understanding*, II, XXVII, 9.

a priori, the possibility of an individual person existing without a body.[13] (This observation, I should stress, is made entirely without prejudice regarding the question of whether such disembodied personal existence is an empirical *scientific* or *natural* possibility.)

Let me expand a little on this important point. When we consider what kinds of evidence we look for if we want to detect the presence of a *person* in some situation, we see that we do *not* in fact necessarily look for bodily characteristics of any kind: we look, rather, for *intelligent activity* – and where we find it, we attribute its source to a *person*. Thus, if we hear a message tapped out on a wall, we assume the presence of a person responsible for it. We may well, of course, *also* assume the presence of an 'organized body' associated with that person and through which that person may be supposed to act: but this is *not*, I would urge, a *conceptual* requirement without which we cannot make even sense of the notion of a person's presence and agency. Persons are not, I repeat, essentially material in the way that oak trees and rivers plainly are.[14] But then, for this very reason, persons cannot be regarded as a *species of living organism*, since living organisms *are* essentially material.[15]

Another reason for denying that persons are a species of living organism would be, of course, that we can plausibly envisage certain *non-living* mechanisms – 'robots' – embodying persons: I won't say *being* persons, for reasons that will immediately become plain. That we really can envisage this is sometimes denied. Thus, Wiggins writes of 'our . . . conviction that

[13]   One quite well-known attempt to demonstrate the incoherence of the notion of disembodied personal existence is by Terence Penelhum, in his *Survival and Disembodied Existence* (London: Routledge and Kegan Paul, 1970). However, I think that his arguments are vitiated, not least, by an assumption that 'person' must have a criterion of identity and that, in the absence of a 'bodily' criterion, a 'memory' criterion would have to suffice – which he argues, it could not. If, as I suspect, 'person' denotes what I called in Chapter 2 a *basic* sort, such arguments are beside the point.

[14]   I cannot, then, agree with David Wiggins's claim that 'A person is material in the sense of being essentially constituted by matter': see his *Sameness and Substance* (Oxford: Blackwell, 1980), p. 164.

[15]   Thus, I cannot accept Wiggins's assertion that 'by *person* we mean *a certain sort of animal*': see again his *Sameness and Substance*, p. 187. However, it should be borne in mind here that the chapter on personal identity that appears in *Sameness and Substance* is replaced by an entirely new one in Wiggins's recent reworking of that earlier book, *Sameness and Substance Renewed* (Cambridge: Cambridge University Press, 2001). So passages cited from the earlier book should not be assumed to be indicative of Wiggins's current view concerning the matters in hand. I cite them, nonetheless, as exemplifying a view that has been seriously held by at least one important philosopher.

. . . such artifacts as robots and automata have no title to any kind of civil right', of 'the depth and passion of most people's resistance to the idea that automata can approximate to life or sentience' and of our belief that 'to have genuine feeling or purposes or concerns, a thing must *at least* be an animal of some sort'.[16] But, to the limited extent that we *do* have any such convictions, I suggest that they can be explained by a proper reluctance to allow that one might *identify* a person with a robot. The evidence of people's reactions to science-fiction stories and films is, *pace* Wiggins, that we find it *only too easy* to suppose that robots or automata might nonetheless *embody* persons – that is, that persons could have robotic 'organized bodies', entirely composed of non-biological and, in that sense, non-living material. There is, in my view, no *deeper* mystery in understanding how *electronic* mechanisms, say, could be involved in sentience than there is in understanding how *biological* mechanisms could be.

I should emphasize that, in saying that persons are not essentially material, I do not want to deny that they can be bodily beings *at all*: that is to say, I do not want to deny that they can genuinely have various bodily or physical characteristics. I certainly do not want to draw the conclusion – to do which would plainly be fallacious – that persons are essentially *non*-material or *im*material and hence have an ontological status akin to that of 'Cartesian egos' or souls. From 'φs are *not* essentially *F*' we cannot legitimately infer 'φs are essentially *non-F*'. I do not even want to accuse Descartes himself of committing this fallacy: for although he clearly regarded the *mind* as being essentially non-extended, it is at least questionable to represent him as regarding the terms 'mind' and 'person' as being synonymous, or as identifying *himself* with his mind. On the other hand, while the inference that I have just mentioned would indeed be fallacious, that in itself does not, of course, exclude the possibility that its conclusion *might* nonetheless be true. However, my own view is that it is in fact *false* and that persons can indeed *have bodily characteristics*, in a strict and literal sense.[17]

Now, if what I have just been saying about the concept of a person is correct, then even without endeavouring to formulate a precise criterion

---

[16] Wiggins, *Sameness and Substance*, pp. 174–5.

[17] To a considerable extent, then, although not entirely, I can agree with P. F. Strawson's characterization of persons in his *Individuals: An Essay in Descriptive Metaphysics* (London: Methuen, 1959), Chapter 3. Here it is worth recalling that Strawson does allow for the conceptual possibility of disembodied personal survival: see pp. 115–16. For a fuller account of why and how I think that persons can have at least *some* 'bodily characteristics' without *being* bodies, see my *Subjects of Experience* (Cambridge: Cambridge University Press, 1996), Chapter 2.

of identity for persons, we can at once see that any such criterion would at least have to *differ* from the criteria for either living organisms or parcels of matter. This is because the latter criteria imply that anything answering to them is *essentially* material, so that if persons are *not* essentially material, they must answer to a *different* criterion, if indeed they answer to any criterion at all. But from this, of course, we can immediately conclude, for now familiar reasons, that no person can be *identified* with any living organism, nor with any parcel of matter.[18] And, indeed, this is a conclusion to which we are plausibly driven quite independently of my contention that the ontological status of persons is one of beings that are *not essentially material*. For if the Lockean account of the concept of a person advanced earlier is even remotely correct, it is clear that this concept so *differs* both from the concept of a living organism and from the concept of a parcel of matter that, in view of the intimate semantic and metaphysical linkage between sortal concepts and their associated criteria of identity, there is really no good reason to suppose that the criterion of personal identity – if indeed there is one – *should be* the same as either of the other criteria of identity at issue. Certainly, the burden of proof must lie entirely with those who think otherwise. But then, once more, a difference between two criteria of identity is sufficient to warrant the denial that we can intelligibly *identify* individuals answering to one of those criteria with individuals answering to the other.

Here it may perhaps be objected that it is just *absurd* to deny that a particular man or human living organism may be a person: for cannot a living organism *act* and *perceive* and engage in *self-reflection* – in which case, how can it fail to have all that is required to make it a person, according to the Lockean conception?[19] In my view, several quite compelling responses to this objection may be offered. First of all, we may ask, *is* it in fact especially obvious that a *living organism* – as opposed, as I would say, to the *person* that it embodies – may act and perceive and possess self-consciousness?

---

[18]   In point of fact, we can reach this conclusion even without appealing to the principle that nothing can answer to two different criteria of identity: for if anything answering either to the criterion of identity for living organisms or to that for parcels of matter is *essentially material*, and persons are *not* essentially material, then Leibniz's law on its own licenses the conclusion that persons *do not* answer to either of those criteria and hence are neither living organisms nor parcels of matter. However, I forgo appeal to this more direct inference for reasons that are about to be made clear in the main text.

[19]   It is a thought along such lines that seems, in large measure, to motivate the position now commonly known as 'animalism', for a clear exposition and defence of which see Eric T. Olson, *The Human Animal: Personal Identity without Psychology* (New York: Oxford University Press, 1997).

Not, I suggest, unless we confuse these properties with certain properties which living organisms obviously *do* have – that is, with certain of their physiological features. After all, intentional action and perception, very arguably, are not just *the same* as bodily movement and sensory stimulation, nor is self-consciousness plausibly just *the same* as any kind of neurological activity in the brain. Again, it is surely the *person* who thinks, feels, desires and so on, not his or her *body*, nor any part of it such as his or her *brain*.

It is currently fashionable, I know, to distinguish in this context between 'type–type' and 'token–token' identity theories – the suggestion often being made that while there may be no kind or *type* of neurological activity that is identifiable with a given *type* of mental activity, such as self-reflection or perceptual experience, particular instances or *tokens* of the former might nonetheless be identifiable with *tokens* of the latter.[20] My response to this suggestion, however, is that I do not, of course, concede that questions concerning the identity or diversity of *particulars* can be so divorced in this way from questions concerning what *kinds* of particulars they are. Mental and physical *events* and *processes* – no less than those particulars that belong to the category of *continuants*, such as persons and their bodies – can be individuated and identified only as particulars *of some kind*: and their criteria of identity will be determined by what kinds of particular they are.

It is true that Davidson – perhaps the most famous proponent of a 'token–token' identity theory, in the shape of his doctrine of 'anomalous monism' – once proposed a quite general criterion of identity for events, according to which particular events are identical if and only if they have the same causes and effects.[21] However, while not explicitly circular, this criterion is unsatisfactory, because questions of event identity arise in determining the identities of causes and effects.[22] Indeed, I find very plausible Tiles's suggestion that 'there is no single criterion of identity for everything that may be called "an event" '.[23] Thus, there seems to me no more sense in the idea that one might set about counting the *events* that occurred in a certain room over the course of an hour than there is in the idea that one might set about counting the *things* that are now in it. What one *may*

---

[20] See, for example, Colin McGinn, 'Anomalous Monism and Kripke's Cartesian Intuitions', *Analysis* 37 (1977), pp. 78–80, and his *The Character of Mind* (Oxford: Oxford University Press, 1982), p. 27.

[21] See Donald Davidson, 'The Individuation of Events', in his *Essays on Actions and Events* (Oxford: Clarendon Press, 1980), p. 179.

[22] See further my 'Impredicative Identity Criteria and Davidson's Criterion of Event Identity', *Analysis* 49 (1989), pp. 178–81, and the discussion of such circularity issues in Chapter 2 above.

[23] J. E. Tiles, 'Davidson's Criterion of Event Identity', *Analysis* 36 (1976), pp. 185–7: see p. 185.

intelligibly count are the events *of this or that sort* – such as the door-closings or glass-breakings – that occurred in the room during that period, not the events *tout court*. And the search for a general criterion of identity for *intentional actions* seems to me to be similarly misconceived.

Unless, therefore, it can be convincingly argued that mental typology and physiological typology are capable of being appropriately *matched*, the proposal that one might – 'barely', as it were – *identify* token events of various mental types with those of various physiological types is devoid of determinate sense. Consequently, in the absence of the required arguments, such a 'token–token' psychophysical identity theory amounts to nothing more than an empty gesture, which may give emotional satisfaction to the committed physicalist, but has no intellectual substance to it.

Against me, at this point, it may be urged that such a token–token identity theory can in fact be supported on empirical grounds, given in addition some allegedly plausible assumptions concerning causal relations between mental and physical events.[24] Very roughly, the sort of argument that I speak of goes like this. *First*, we must accept, on pain of having to endorse a most implausible kind of epiphenomenalism, that mental events sometimes cause physical events, such as bodily movements. *Second*, it is plausible to suppose that empirical scientific investigations will eventually show such physical events to be fully accountable for by wholly physical causes, such as neural events in the brain. *Therefore*, on pain of having to allow a most implausible kind of systematic causal overdetermination of the physical effects in question, we must accept that their mental causes just *are* – that is, are *identical* with – certain of their physical causes. The weak link in this argument, however, is the bland assumption that empirical investigation *can* show what it is alleged to be capable of showing, prior to a resolution of the very identity question at issue. For, while it is still an open question whether the accepted mental causes of a given physical effect are distinct from any physical events, empirical investigation obviously cannot establish that a *wholly physical* causal account of that effect exists, since any complete causal account of the effect must acknowledge the causal contribution which, *ex hypothesi*, the mental events in question make.[25]

---

[24]   The sort of argument that I have in mind here may be found, for example, in Christopher Peacocke, *Holistic Explanation* (Oxford: Clarendon Press, 1979), pp. 134ff., and in Robert Kirk, 'From Physical Explicability to Full-Blooded Materialism', *Philosophical Quarterly* 29 (1979), pp. 229–37. Many other variants of the argument have appeared since these relatively early versions.

[25]   See further my 'Against an Argument for Token Identity', *Mind* 90 (1981), pp. 120–1, and, for a more general elaboration of the difficulties attending such arguments for physicalism, Part I of my *Personal Agency: The Metaphysics of Mind and Action* (Oxford: Oxford University Press, 2008).

The more general objection that I have been addressing, it will be recalled, was that a living organism might qualify as a person simply in virtue of possessing the requisite 'Lockean' properties – the capacities to act, perceive and engage in self-reflection. However, quite apart from my responses of the preceding paragraphs, I would point out that – according to my own precepts, as set out in Chapter 3 – if *persons* qualify as a genuine *kind* of individuals at all, then the general term 'person' is to be construed as a *semantically simply sortal term*, and as such not reducible by analysis or definition to some complex general term incorporating a conjunction of 'defining characteristics'. That is to say, when I announced earlier my sympathy with the Lockean conception of a person, I was not proposing to endorse – even if Locke himself was – any suggestion to the effect that the sentence '*a* is a person' might be *analysed as meaning* either '*a* is a thing which acts and perceives and is self-conscious' or even '*a* is a φ which acts and perceives and is self-conscious', where 'φ' is some specific sortal term. On the first of these analyses, of course, 'person' is not a genuine sortal term at all, since 'thing' is not. On the second, it is a semantically *complex* sortal term, as such terms were characterized in Chapter 3. Now, to adopt the first proposal would be very radical indeed, since it flies in the face of our apparent readiness and ability to *individuate*, *distinguish* and *count* persons.[26] To this it might be replied, I suppose, that some of the bizarre clinical evidence arising from pathological cases of 'multiple personality syndrome', such as the famous case of 'Miss Beauchamp', supports this radical view.[27] And a similar appeal might be made to some

[26] One philosopher who has shown a willingness to deny that 'person' is a genuine sortal term is Bernard Williams, in his *Ethics and the Limits of Philosophy* (London: Fontana, 1985), his grounds being that 'The category of person, though . . . it looks like a sortal or classificatory notion . . . in fact . . . signals characteristics that almost all come in degrees – responsibility, self-consciousness, capacity for reflection, and so on' (p. 114). But although these characteristics 'come in degrees', that is no reason to suppose that *being a person* is a matter of degree, unless one supposes – as I do not – that being a person is *definable* in terms of possessing these characteristics. And, in any case, the existence of *borderline cases* of things satisfying a general term is not generally thought to be incompatible with that term's qualifying as a sortal – the term 'heap' providing a paradigm illustration of this point. Indeed, forbidding borderline cases would probably leave us with very few 'genuine' sortal terms in everyday language. I remark on this not in an attempt to dismiss the proposal as absurd, but only to emphasize its radical nature.

[27] For discussion, see Kathleen V. Wilkes, 'Multiple Personality and Personal Identity', *British Journal for the Philosophy of Science* 32 (1981), pp. 331–48.

of the evidence arising from cases of so-called 'split-brain' patients.[28] But on the whole I am most reluctant to let our responses to pathological cases dictate to us concerning the meaning or use of well-entrenched concepts, like that of a person.

The second proposal, however, is also seriously flawed. And here the difficulty lies in deciding, in a principled way, precisely *which* sortal term 'φ' should figure in the analysis. 'Living organism' will *not* do, for reasons which we have already discussed: persons are arguably not essentially material and, less contentiously, are at any rate not essentially *alive*, in the literal, biological sense.[29] To suggest that any of a range of unrelated sortal terms may do service for 'φ', or to hold that '*a* is a person' means 'For *some* φ, *a* is a φ which acts and perceives and is self-conscious', is again to give up a well-entrenched idea – namely, that persons, even if they may divide into different 'species', do not form a heterogeneous class of entities governed by a variety of different criteria of identity and hence by various different principles for *counting* them.

My own view, then, is that – pending satisfactory arguments to the contrary – 'person' should be accepted at its face-value as being a semantically simple sortal term and hence as being *unanalysable*.[30] When I announced, earlier, my sympathy for the view that persons are *essentially* percipient, self-reflective agents, I was not, then, advancing the case for any particular *semantic analysis* of the term 'person' – and so, to the extent that the general objection that I have been considering presupposes the contrary, it is misconceived. And here I would add that, in my opinion, any attempt to confer upon something the status of *person* by trying to ascertain *first* whether it can act, perceive, and engage in self-reflection is, in any case, going to be implicitly question-begging. This is because positive

[28]   See, for instance, Thomas Nagel, 'Brain Bisection and the Unity of Consciousness', in his *Mortal Questions* (Cambridge: Cambridge University Press, 1979). I shall review the evidence later, however, and argue that it at most creates problems for individuating *minds* rather than *persons*. See also my 'Can the Self Disintegrate? Personal Identity, Psychopathology, and Disunities of Consciousness', in J. Hughes, S. Louw, and S. Sabat (eds), *Dementia: Mind, Meaning, and the Person* (Oxford: Oxford University Press, 2006).

[29]   I reject, then, what Wiggins calls the 'animal attribute view' of persons, according to which '*person* is a non-biological qualification of *animal*': see his *Sameness and Substance*, p. 171. But my reason for rejecting it is diametrically opposed to his. He does so on the grounds that the concept of a person is a wholly biological one – that 'by *person* we mean *a certain sort of animal*' (p. 187) – whereas I do so because I think that it is a wholly *non*-biological one.

[30]   Wiggins also seems to endorse this view in his *Sameness and Substance*, pp. 171ff. Where I differ from the view that he takes there is in refusing to accept, as he does, that 'persons are a class of organisms' (p. 187).

answers to such questions very arguably already *presuppose* personhood. For instance, in deciding whether we can interpret our words *literally* or only *metaphorically*, when we speak of a robotic device as 'seeing' intelligently with its electronic 'eye' or as 'acting' intentionally with its mechanical 'arm', we very arguably have to come to a prior decision precisely as to whether the object of our descriptions has the status of a *person* or *subject* – although if we decide that it *does*, then, of course, I would want to urge that it is not after all *the robotic device* as such that perceives and acts, but rather *the person that it embodies*. The reason for this is that ascriptions of agency, perception and self-consciousness to a subject cannot be made *independently* either of each other or of ascriptions to it of indefinitely many other appropriately interrelated psychological states of suitable kinds, such as beliefs, desires and intentions – states which together go to make up the complex network of phenomena necessary to constitute the mental life of a single *person*. Thus, for example, a subject cannot genuinely be said to *perceive* unless it can also be said to *believe, intend, imagine*, and so forth. In short, what we have to contend with here is nothing less than the so-called *holism of the mental*.[31]

How we *are* to come, in a principled way, to a decision that something is or embodies a person is, I confess, no easy question to answer – although in practice, of course, we make many such decisions quite spontaneously every day, whenever indeed we encounter a new human face or hear a new human voice. But one lesson that we can draw from these practical encounters is that our decision to confer the status of *person* upon something is *not*, apparently, one that we arrive at by observing the satisfaction of any determinate list of necessary and sufficient conditions: and to this extent, my suggestion that the concept of a person is unanalysable gains some empirical support. Of course, we *do* decide on the basis of *observational evidence* – evidence precisely of agency, perception, and self-consciousness, I should say – but my point is that such evidence is apparently quite *non-uniform* from case to case and is, moreover, always *defeasible*. The basis for such decisions cannot be captured, it thus seems, by any sort of algorithm or rote procedure. And indeed, our ability to make them is just one more sign of our own personhood: *persons recognize other persons*.

I have been arguing that a human person can never be *identified* with the living organism that is his or her 'organized body', much less with the parcel of matter or collection of material particles which constitutes that organism at any given time. But this, of course, raises the following question: what then *is* the relationship between a person, on the one hand, and his

---

[31]　I borrow the phrase, of course, from Donald Davidson: see his 'Mental Events', in his *Essays on Actions and Events*, p. 217.

or her 'organized body' and its material constituents on the other? Before addressing that question, however, I need to clear up a minor point. My contention, in Lockean terms, is that a *person* is never identifiable with a *man*. Put this way, it does indeed seem rather paradoxical, since we often use 'man' and 'person' pretty well interchangeably.[32] And we have no hesitation in saying, for instance, that if 'John Smith', say, is the name of a *man*, then it is *ipso facto* the name of a *person*. But I take such facts to show only that 'man', in ordinary usage, is *not* employed simply to denote a certain species of animal and so of living organism: on the contrary, it means something like 'adult, male, human person' – in other words, or so I would urge, 'person who has an adult, male, human body'. Used in this sense, then, 'man' is a semantically complex sortal term which is governed by no other criterion of identity than that – if there is one – which is associated with the simple sortal term 'person'.

Here it may be asked why, this being so, we do not have names *both* for human persons *and* for the human organisms which I refuse to identify with them. The answer is that, being persons ourselves, our primary interest lies with the assignment of *personal* names, but that we have at the same time a simple and satisfactory method of referring uniquely to human organisms which dispenses with the need for a distinctive set of names for them. We simply speak of '*N*'s body', where '*N*' is a personal name, relying on the empirical fact that, at least in the common experience of the vast majority of us, there is a one-to-one relation between persons and human organisms. The very existence and ubiquity of this form of expression, '*N*'s body', testifies indeed to our common-sense refusal to identify a person and his or her 'organized body': a refusal which we have now seen, I think, to be wholly justified.

Returning, however, to the question raised a moment ago, can we perhaps say that the relationship between a person and a certain living organism – that person's 'organized body' – is, like the relationship between this organism and the parcel of matter that is spatiotemporally coincident with it, one of *constitution* rather than identity? Is a person plausibly constituted by his or her body, in anything like the way in which a river is constituted by water? Plainly *not*, if my earlier remarks about constitution and the concept of a person were correct.[33] For I pointed out earlier that it is not in general a purely *contingent* affair that things of one sort, φ, are constituted

---

[32] Locke addresses this objection in much the way that I am about to, when discussing his imaginary example of the prince and the cobbler: see Locke, *An Essay Concerning Human Understanding*, II, XXVII, 15.

[33] I disagree fundamentally, then, with Lynne Rudder Baker's position, as developed in her *Persons and Bodies: A Constitution View* (Cambridge: Cambridge University Press, 2000).

by things of another sort, χ. It is not contingent, thus, that *rivers* are constituted by *water*, nor that *oak trees* are constituted by *wood*. I concede that, in the case of *artefacts*, such as tables, it is contingent whether they are constituted by, say, *wood* or *plastic* or *metal*: but even here it is not contingent that they are constituted by *matter* of some sort.[34] And in the case of *natural* kinds, as we have just observed, there is not even this degree of flexibility regarding constitution. So if persons were *constituted* by living organisms, it surely ought to make as manifestly little sense to speak of *disembodied* persons, or even of *non-living* persons, as it does to speak of an immaterial oak tree or river. But, on the contrary, it *does* seem to make sense to speak of such persons, whether or not we believe that any *exist*, purely as a matter of fact. Furthermore, the relation of constitution would appear to be *transitive*: if x is constituted by y and y by z, then x is constituted by y. So if persons were constituted by living organisms, then they would equally be constituted by the *matter* constituting those organisms and hence be *essentially* material, which I have already argued they are *not*.

Nor can we plausibly suppose that there might be various different *kinds* of *differently* constituted persons – for example, *human* persons that are constituted by living organisms, *artefactual* persons that are constituted by robotic devices and, perhaps, *disembodied* persons that have no material constitution at all. For these three 'kinds' of person would surely all have to have *different criteria of identity*, in view of the intimate relationship between such criteria and the necessities of constitution attaching to kinds: and hence it would be improper, after all, to speak of them all as being species of a single genus, *person*. (It would be rather like saying that real living oak trees and plastic replica oak trees are species of a single genus.) The supposition that one and the same person might survive bodily death as a disembodied person would also have to be manifestly absurd, as would the supposition that a person with a living human body might, through successive artificial replacements of body-parts, eventually come to have a wholly artefactual non-living body. Yet, surely, neither of these suppositions *is* manifestly absurd.

Altogether, then, I can see no prospect at all for successfully modelling the relationship between persons and living organisms on that between living organisms and parcels of matter or collections of material particles. Persons stand to their 'organized bodies' and to the matter constituting

---

[34]   It has, of course, famously been argued by Kripke that, in the case of a *particular* table, it is not even contingent that it is – or, at least, *was originally* – constituted by wood, if that is *in fact* what it was originally constituted by: see Saul A. Kripke, *Naming and Necessity* (Oxford: Blackwell, 1980), pp. 113–14. However, for reasons which need not be gone into here, I am not ultimately convinced by his arguments.

those bodies *neither* in the relation of identity *nor* in that of constitution. Indeed, I don't believe that persons are *constituted* by anything at all. I can see little alternative, in fact, to recognizing a *sui generis* relationship of *personal embodiment*, because I cannot see that the relation between a person and his or her body – whether the latter be human, animal but non-human, or indeed altogether non-biological – is remotely like that between objects of any other two kinds. This should not, however, be seen as a concession to obscurantism, nor even to Cartesian dualism, since I am by no means denying that facts about a person's body – whether they be biological facts or facts pertaining to some other branch of physical science, such as electronics – can cast light on and help to explain psychological facts concerning that person. At the same time, I am committed, of course, to repudiating the possibility of any 'reduction' of psychology to any of the physical sciences – biology, chemistry, electronics, and so forth – either separately or in conjunction. It may even be that in the light of such psychophysical explanations we could some day come to establish that the existence of disembodied – or even non-living – persons, although a conceptual and even a metaphysical possibility, is not an empirical scientific possibility. But I would add that such a day is, in my view, still a very long way off.

Is There a Criterion of Personal Identity?

It will be noticed that these conclusions, while turning on considerations concerning criteria of identity, have been arrived at without any attempt so far to formulate a criterion of personal identity. Indeed, the quest for such a criterion was deferred quite early on in the present discussion. My reason for proceeding in this indirect fashion is that, as I have indicated previously, I am rather doubtful whether this quest can succeed. I suspect that persons do not in fact *have* an informative criterion of identity: in other words, that *person* may be a 'basic' sort, in the terminology of Chapter 2 above.

To see why this might be so, we need to return to Locke. Before we do so, however, it should just be observed that the non-existence of a criterion of personal identity would not vitiate those arguments of the preceding part of this chapter which turned on the non-identity of individuals belonging to sorts differing with respect to their criteria of identity. For two sorts can differ in this respect not only through *each* of them having a *different* criterion, but also through *one* of them having such a criterion while the other does *not*. Wherever I spoke earlier of two sorts *differing* in their criteria of identity, I should be understood to have included this possible source of their difference.

Now, I agreed earlier with Locke that, in order to discover a criterion of personal identity – or, as he puts it, to 'find wherein *personal Identity* consists' – we need to examine the concept of a person, or 'what *Person* stands for'. And I substantially agreed with him also as to what persons essentially *are*: they are thinking, self-conscious beings with a capacity for perception and action. Locke himself, it is true, is not perfectly explicit about the need for perception and agency, although I think that he is implicitly committed to regarding them as essential characteristics of persons – and, certainly, I myself believe that they are.[35] Let us look, then, at the criterion of personal identity that Locke himself proposes, since if any proposal can be satisfactory it must, I think, be one that is formulated along broadly Lockean lines. (We have already seen, of course, that no 'bodily' criterion of personal identity can hope to succeed.)

The criterion that Locke proposes is stated in his own words as follows:[36]

[S]ince consciousness always accompanies thinking, and 'tis that, that makes every one to be, what he calls *self*; and thereby distinguishes himself from all other thinking things, in this alone consists *personal Identity*, *i.e.* the sameness of a rational Being: And as far as this consciousness can be extended backwards to any past Action or Thought, so far reaches the Identity of that *Person*; it is the same *self* now as it was then; and 'tis by the same *self* with this present one that now reflects on it, that that Action was done.

And a little later he puts it thus:[37]

[*P*]*ersonal Identity* consists . . . in the Identity of *consciousness* . . . If . . . *Socrates* waking and sleeping do not partake of the same *consciousness*, *Socrates* waking and sleeping is not the same Person.

It is clear, as this last passage itself suggests, that Locke was to some extent modelling his criterion of personal identity on his earlier criterion of identity for living organisms, with the notion of 'participation of the same consciousness' playing a role analogous to that of the notion of

---

[35]   In the very section of the *Essay* (II, XXVII, 9) in which Locke characterizes a person as 'a thinking intelligent Being, that has reason and reflection, and can consider it self as it self, the same thinking thing in different times and places', he goes on to speak of both perceptions and actions as properties of persons, quite as a matter of course. And although Locke used 'perception' in a broad sense to include thinking, it is clear that in this section he also means it to include *sense*-perception. Thus, having commented that it is 'impossible for any one to perceive, without perceiving, that he does perceive', he immediately adds, obviously as a gloss on this, 'When we see, hear, smell, taste, feel, meditate, or will anything, we know that we do so'.

[36]   Locke, *An Essay Concerning Human Understanding*, II, XXVII, 9.

[37]   Locke, *An Essay Concerning Human Understanding*, II, XXVII, 19.

'participation of the same life'. At one point he even draws a direct parallel, in these words:[38]

> Different Substances, by the same consciousness (where they do partake in) [are] united into one Person; as well as different Bodies, by the same Life are united into one Animal, whose *Identity* is preserved, in that change of Substances, by the unity of one continued Life.

It would appear that the 'different substances' referred to by Locke at the beginning of this passage are understood by him to be different *immaterial* or *spiritual* substances, or 'souls'. For it seems to be entities of *this* kind that, here at least, he takes to 'participate of the same consciousness', by analogy with the way in which different *material* substances – bodies, or particles of matter – are taken by him to 'participate of the same life'. I do not know, however, to what extent Locke intended this analogy to be taken seriously, since he frequently openly admits our almost total ignorance concerning spiritual substances, remarking that we are 'in the dark concerning these Matters'.[39] Certainly, elsewhere he speaks as though it is *persons*, rather than souls or immaterial substances, that may be said to 'participate of the same consciousness' and thereby be the *same* person: see, in particular, his earlier-quoted remark concerning Socrates waking and sleeping. And, indeed, it is in these terms that I propose to interpret Locke's suggested criterion of personal identity – in common, I think, with most other commentators. For if the analogy just mentioned is taken too seriously, Locke cannot easily be represented as making a contribution of much value to our modern understanding of personal identity.

Accordingly, I shall take it that the criterion that Locke wishes to endorse may be stated in my own style, of Chapter 2 above, as follows:

> If *x* and *y* are *persons*, then *x* is identical with *y* if and only if *x* and *y* *participate of the same consciousness* at all times at which they are conscious.

(As we shall shortly see, I shall, purely for the sake of brevity, soon replace Locke's somewhat cumbersome talk of *x* and *y* 'participating of the same consciousness' by talk of *x* and *y* being 'co-conscious'.)

Of course, interpreting what this criterion actually *amounts to* is a considerable problem in itself. But this much, at least, is surely clear enough: 'participation of the same consciousness' cannot simply be supposed to mean *possession of the same conscious states*, not least because the *same* person

---

[38]   Locke, *An Essay Concerning Human Understanding*, II, XXVII, 10.
[39]   Locke, *An Essay Concerning Human Understanding*, II, XXVII, 27.

possesses *different* conscious states at different times – such states being transient, whereas persons persist.

It is worth remarking here that Locke's famous critic Bishop Butler is, I think, grossly uncharitable to Locke in suggesting, at one point, this unsatisfactory interpretation.[40] Obviously, I am not denying that if x and y *are* the same person, then any conscious state possessed by x must also be possessed by y: Leibniz's law already demands as much. And it is equally true that possession of the same conscious states by both x and y is logically sufficient for the identity of x and y, in virtue of the logically *non-shareable* character of individual conscious states. However, as will become clear in due course, no *adequate*, because *non-circular*, criterion of personal identity can be grounded on these truths, since the conscious states of persons *depend for their identity* on the persons whose conscious states they are – which is precisely *why* such states are logically non-shareable. My criticism of Butler as being 'uncharitable' turns on a quite different matter, namely, his unwarranted suggestion that on Locke's criterion a person existing now could, strictly speaking, only be said to have persisted for as long as his present state of consciousness – in other words, that a Lockean person couldn't survive a *change* of consciousness.[41]

Instead, then, I interpret 'participation of the same consciousness' to mean what I propose to call *co-consciousness*: a notion which, as I understand it, demands that if persons x and y are conscious at times t_1 and t_2 respectively (where $t_1 \leq t_1$), then x and y are *co*-conscious at those times only if, for any item, z, such that x is conscious of z at t_1, y is (at least *potentially*) conscious of z at t_2. So, for example, suppose we let t_1 = noon on 1 January 1805 and t_2 = now. Then if Napoleon Bonaparte and I were to be co-conscious at those times, I would now be conscious of (or, at least, be *capable of calling to consciousness*) everything of which Napoleon was then conscious. This, then, is a condition which may evidently be satisfied in respect of any such item, z, by the occurrence at *different* times of two distinct acts of consciousness: for example, by a conscious *perception* of z at one time and by an 'experiential memory' of z at a later time.[42] So, clearly, what is at issue here is not so much the identity of *conscious states* as the identity of *objects* of consciousness – although it is natural to presume that conscious states may *themselves* be such objects and, indeed, that they *must*

---

40   See Joseph Butler, 'Of Personal Identity', in John Perry (ed.), *Personal Identity* (Berkeley, CA: University of California Press, 1975), pp. 102–3.

41   A similar criticism may be levelled at Thomas Reid's 'Of Mr. Locke's Account of Our Personal Identity': see Perry (ed.), *Personal Identity*, pp. 116–17.

42   For more on the notion of 'experiential' (or 'personal', or 'autobiographical') memory in play here, see my *An Introduction to the Philosophy of Mind* (Cambridge: Cambridge University Press, 2000), pp. 277–82.

be in the case of self-reflecting beings, such as Locke takes persons by definition to be. For recall, here, Locke's assertion, quoted earlier, that it is 'impossible for any one to perceive, without perceiving, that he does perceive', which seemingly commits *him*, at least, to such higher orders of consciousness, apparently indeed *ad infinitum*.[43]

However, I take it that co-consciousness also demands the satisfaction of *another* condition, which is harder to state clearly, but which might be expressed loosely in the following way. Suppose that persons x and y are co-conscious at a certain time (so that this is the 'synchronic' case, in which $t_1 = t_2$): then, if w and z are any two items of which x and y respectively are conscious at that time, x must be conscious of w and z 'together', as the combined object of a single act of consciousness, as must y. This might be called the 'unity of consciousness' condition. No doubt much more could be said about the notion of co-consciousness that Locke seems implicitly to be operating with, but I have said enough for my present purposes – and I should, in any case, make it plain that I have no stake in claiming that the notion is ultimately either a very useful one or even a wholly coherent one.[44]

Now, many commentators dwell on the *diachronic* implications of Locke's proposed criterion of personal identity – that is, its implications for the identity of persons *through* or *across* time – and various apparent problems arising from these implications. But, naturally enough, the criterion also has *synchronic* implications, concerning the identity of persons *at one and the same time*. Indeed, any remotely plausible criterion of identity for any sort of *continuant* may be expected to have synchronic as well as diachronic implications, since such entities exist both *at* times and *through* time. However, even in the case of synchronic identity questions, Locke's proposal meets with difficulties.

It is true that the so-called 'unity of consciousness' has seemed to many philosophers to play an important role in our understanding of what makes one person distinct from another at a given time. One may be strongly tempted to say that one is, necessarily, *jointly* conscious of each of *one's*

[43] The spectre of an infinite regress here is obviously a potential embarrassment for Locke's account and maybe the lesson is that we shouldn't, after all, conceive of 'self-reflection' in terms of higher-order consciousness or *perhaps* even regard our own conscious states as being possible *objects* of consciousness at all – although this latter suggestion seems excessively radical and indeed highly implausible. For discussion of some of these issues, see my *An Introduction to the Philosophy of Mind*, pp. 288–95.
[44] I say a good deal more about these matters in my 'Can the Self Disintegrate? Personal Identity, Psychopathology, and Disunities of Consciousness'.

own present conscious states but not at all conscious – or, at least, not 'directly' conscious, or conscious 'from the inside' – of any of *another person's* present conscious states. But then we have to contend with the evidence arising from studies by Sperry and others of so-called 'split-brain' patients, who *seem* to be subject to a bifurcation of consciousness.[45] Interpreting this evidence is, certainly, a contentious matter – some experimenters holding that consciousness in fact resides only in the dominant left hemisphere of the brain, others that even prior to commissurotomy there are two distinct centres of consciousness, and yet others that a genuine bifurcation of consciousness is brought about by the operation, with one mind 'splitting' into two.[46] But, whatever we should ultimately say about the possibility of a 'split mind' or a 'bifurcation of consciousness', what we surely *cannot* say, with any degree of plausibility, is that either biologically normal human organisms, or even those with 'split brains', embody two distinct *persons*. My reasons are as follows.

In the first place, we shouldn't rashly suppose that the terms 'mind' and 'person' are simply *co-designative*, although this is indeed often tacitly assumed in philosophical discussions of split-brain phenomena. Secondly, to suppose that all biologically normal human organisms embody two distinct persons simply runs completely counter to common sense and our well-entrenched use of the term 'person'. Moreover, genuinely distinct persons could not, I suggest, tolerate the degree of mutual dependence that co-embodiment of the kind now being envisaged would impose upon them – a degree of dependence inestimably higher than any imposed on inseparable conjoined twins, even in the most extreme examples of that condition. And this latter consideration also counts against the proposal that commissurotomy *divides one person into two*. In consequence, it appears, only the hypothesis that consciousness is restricted to the dominant left hemisphere permits the evidence to be interpreted in a manner compatible with Locke's co-consciousness criterion of personal identity. But this hypothesis is certainly not a very plausible one, in the light of some of the patently intelligent actions that seem on occasion to be performed, in 'split-brain' cases, solely through the medium of the right hemisphere.

Thus, the Lockean co-consciousness criterion of personal identity appears to fail even before we consider its application to diachronic identity questions concerning persons. In the latter context, of course, Locke is usually

---

[45]   For a description and discussion of Roger Sperry's results, see Karl R. Popper and John C. Eccles, *The Self and Its Brain* (London: Springer Verlag, 1977), pp. 313ff.

[46]   Eccles suggests the first possibility and reports that Sperry favours the second: see Popper and Eccles, *The Self and Its Brain*, pp. 325ff.

interpreted as advancing a so-called 'memory' criterion of personal identity and, certainly, much of what he says supports that interpretation. I do not, however, propose to traverse once more this well-trodden area of debate, making reference to all the standard objections raised by Locke's critics from Butler and Reid onwards. I think that it has been sufficiently well established, by modern authors such as Wiggins and Parfit, that many of these objections either fail or else can easily be circumvented by modifications true to spirit of Locke's approach.[47] For instance, one can replace the requirement for identical persons to be co-conscious at *all* times at which they are conscious – and hence for a person to remember his very earliest experiences throughout his life – with the weaker and much more plausible requirement that such memory need only extend across times within overlapping intervals of some minimum duration. Again, one can relax the very strong requirement – if indeed Locke himself ever really meant to endorse it – that a person's memory should embrace *all* of the items of which that same person was conscious at a given earlier time, as opposed to just *some* of them.

However, rather than discuss such points of detail, I shall instead try to explain why I do not think that anything remotely along the lines of Locke's criterion of personal identity can have any hope of success. We have seen, indeed, that Locke's own co-consciousness criterion appears to fail on empirical grounds even in the synchronic case. But in what follows I shall not be concerned with merely *empirical* reasons for dissatisfaction with a criterion formulated along Lockean lines. What I want to contend, rather, is that there is a *defect of principle* in 'Lockean' accounts of personal identity, which cannot be overcome by any amount of tinkering with the details. And here I may remark that, for my purposes, I can lump together 'Humean' accounts with 'Lockean' ones, since both approaches attempt to provide an account of personal identity purely in terms of *psychological states and their interrelationships*.[48]

---

[47] See Wiggins, *Sameness and Sustance*, Chapter 6 and Derek Parfit, *Reasons and Persons* (Oxford: Clarendon Press, 1984), chs 10 and 11. See also the useful anthology, Perry (ed.), *Personal Identity*.

[48] Hume, of course, differs from Locke in thinking that personal identity is, strictly speaking, 'fictitious', and perhaps even more importantly in emphasizing the role of *causal* relationships between psychological states of the 'same' person, in contrast with Locke's emphasis on *cognitive* relationships and especially those involving *memory*. See David Hume, *A Treatise of Human Nature*, ed. L. A. Selby-Bigge and P. H. Nidditch (Oxford: Clarendon Press, 1978), Book I, Part IV, Section VI.

It will be recalled from our general discussion of criteria of identity in Chapter 2 that an adequate criterion of identity for things of a given sort φ must specify the truth-conditions of identity statements concerning φs *in an informative way* – and, more particularly, that a putative criterion cannot in general be deemed to inform us 'wherein identity consists' for φs if it makes appeal, however tacit, to φ-*identity* in its expression of the relevant criterial condition, C_φ. It may also be recalled that I allowed that this requirement might be circumvented in certain exceptional cases, such as that of sets in 'pure' set theory. However, there is no reason to suppose that this sort of consideration has a bearing on our present concerns, so I shall ignore it in what follows.

Now, I furthermore suggested that – such exceptional cases aside – a criterion of identity for φs can be informatively supplied only in terms which presuppose the identity of things of one or more *other* sorts. This is certainly true of the criterion of identity for (impure) *sets*, which presupposes determinable identity-conditions for their (non-set) members, but it is equally true of the Lockean criteria of identity for *parcels of matter* and *living organisms*, to both of which I have lent my qualified endorsement earlier in this chapter. Thus, the criterion of identity for parcels of matter presupposes an account of the identity of *atoms*, while the criterion of identity for living organisms presupposes an account of the identity of *collections of material particles*. We saw, indeed, that a defect in the former is its very presumption of atomism, although we also saw that it is no easy task to formulate an informative, non-circular criterion of identity for parcels of matter which does *not* presuppose atomism. And I suspect that similar difficulties would arise for atomism itself, if its advocates were pressed to provide an informative, non-circular criterion of identity for *atoms*. I speak here, of course, of seventeenth-century atomism of the sort that Locke and Boyle favoured, not the modern theory in which 'atom' is a complete misnomer. Today the difficulties in question arise instead with regard to the latest candidates for the status of 'fundamental particle' – formerly including protons and neutrons, but now quarks and electrons.

Observe here that it would be naïve indeed to suppose that mere considerations of 'spatiotemporal continuity' might resolve such difficulties. For, first of all, this would be to ignore the thorny issue of whether *interrupted existence* is possible. But, more fundamentally still, there is the problem that we must always be in a position to answer, in a non-question-begging way, the query 'spatiotemporal continuity *of what?*'. Thus if, in the atomic case, say, we simply appeal to spatiotemporal continuity of *the presence of an atom*, then we just seem to be begging the question at issue by *presupposing* certain determinable identity-conditions for atoms. On the other hand, if we appeal instead to spatiotemporal continuity of putative 'atom-stages', then we are committed to the extravagant and contentious doctrine of temporal parts.[49] The underlying lesson, I suggest, is that any system of ontology must take *some* sorts or kinds to be 'basic': these are the sorts or kinds for which informative identity criteria simply *cannot be given*, because there are no *other* sorts or kinds of things available in the system whose identity can be presupposed in specifying the truth-conditions of identity statements concerning things of these sorts.[50]

Now, why might it be thought that *person* is a basic sort? First of all, it should be observed that, very plausibly, persons are not *constituted* by anything.[51] I have argued already that they have no *material* constituents. Locke, it is true, seems to have flirted with the idea that persons have *immaterial* or *spiritual* constituents, in his attempt to draw an analogy between the notions of 'participation of the same consciousness' and 'participation of the same life'. But we saw that this analogy could not easily be taken seriously, not least because we have no knowledge of the existence of 'spiritual' substances of any sort. Now, *if* persons had constituents, *person* could not reasonably be expected to be a basic sort, since we would then expect to be able to formulate a criterion of identity for persons in terms presupposing the identity of these constituents, whatever they might be. But, to repeat, it doesn't seem that they do. And this, I think, is why we find it so difficult to comprehend how a *person* could literally divide or split, since only things possessing parts seem capable of division. (Here, indeed, we may discern an element of truth in the Cartesian doctrine of the indivisibility of the 'soul', once it is shorn of its immaterialist assumptions.)

However, even if persons do not have constituents, they do have *states*, seemingly both mental and physical – although the latter only if they are embodied. So why may we not hope to supply an informative criterion of personal identity framed in terms of such states? The states in question would, apparently, at least have to *include* mental ones, since a criterion

---

[49]   For fuller discussion, see my *The Possibility of Metaphysics: Substance, Identity, and Time* (Oxford: Clarendon Press, 1998), Chapter 5. Note, incidentally, a certain irony in the very notion of an 'atom-stage', given that atoms, as their very name implies, are classically supposed *not* to be composed of parts of any kind. However, it is equally incongruous to suppose that quarks, say, if indeed they are *fundamental* particles, are composed of 'quark-stages'. If there really were such entities as 'quark-stages', then *these* rather than quarks would qualify as 'fundamental particles'. But modern particle physicists recognize the existence of no such entities and are unlikely to be impressed by philosophical arguments for positing them.

[50]   The point that I am making is quite closely related to Strawson's claim that there must be a class of 'basic particulars', as he calls them. See Strawson, *Individuals*, pp. 38ff.

[51]   Here again I distance myself from Lynne Rudder Baker's view, as expressed in her *Persons and Bodies*.

framed in wholly physical terms has already been ruled out, to all intents and purposes. And, indeed, it is just such a criterion – one framed in terms of *mental* and, more specifically, of *conscious* states – that Locke proposes, on the interpretation of his position that I have defended.

But – and here is the key difficulty – the co-consciousness criterion that I have attributed to Locke is clearly one that *presupposes the identity of conscious states*. I am not forgetting here my earlier denial that 'participation of the same consciousness' just *means* 'possession of the same conscious states'. I am only pointing out that questions concerning the identity of conscious states do require to be settled in determining whether persons are co-conscious in the Lockean sense. For answers to questions concerning the co-consciousness of persons turn on answers to questions concerning the identity of *objects* of consciousness – and, according to Locke, at least some of these objects must themselves be *conscious states*.[52] Thus, for example, according to a Lockean account, answers to diachronic identity questions concerning persons will sometimes turn on such matters as whether a person *a* consciously remembers at a time t_1 some conscious state – such as a particular *sensation of pain* – experienced by a person *b* at an earlier time t_2. And this presupposes that we have to hand some account of the *identity-conditions* of such items as particular sensations of pain. It is evidently not enough, on a Lockean account, that *a* should consciously remember a sensation of pain *qualitatively indistinguishable* from the one experienced earlier by *b*: *a* must consciously remember *that very sensation of pain*, if *a* is to be identified with *b* according to Locke's criterion.

This is precisely why, quite apart from the question of its empirical plausibility, the Lockean criterion – and, more generally, any criterion of personal identity formulated along broadly Lockean lines – cannot be deemed *informative* in the sense in which any adequate criterion of identity is required to be so. For conscious states – and, indeed, mental or psychological states quite generally – cannot themselves be individuated or identified save in terms which presuppose the identity of the persons (or conscious subjects) whose states they are.[53] Thus there is, for instance, no generally applicable

---

[52] I have not forgotten here my earlier querying of Locke's apparent presumption that *self-reflection* involves higher-order consciousness of lower-order conscious states. However, one can reject this conception of self-reflection without having to deny that one's own conscious states *can* sometimes be objects of one's consciousness: that, for instance, one can consciously *remember* a past conscious experience that one once had. In fact, denying that one can do this would be a very radical proposal indeed and is not a line of thought that I am inclined to take at all seriously here.

[53] Compare Strawson, *Individuals*, pp. 41ff. It is particularly unfortunate that Parfit, while acknowledging the existence of Strawson's arguments to this effect,

way of identifying a particular *sensation of pain* save as the pain-sensation of such-and-such a character experienced on a certain occasion *by a given person* – for example, the toothache that I experienced at noon yesterday. Character and occasion alone may clearly be insufficient to identify a pain-sensation uniquely, as an easily imagined example involving conjoined twins will testify: if both feel pain in some shared part of their bodies, each nonetheless experiences a numerically distinct sensation of pain. Nor will reference to a pain-sensation's *causes and effects* do more, at best, than to shift the question of identification on to other items in the same category as the pain-sensation itself, that is, on to *other mental or psychological states*: for in view, once more, of the *holism of the mental*, no psychological state can be said to have purely *non*-psychological causes and effects. And in the case of 'non-locatable' conscious states, such as thoughts and desires, the dependence of their identity upon the persons (or conscious subjects) whose states they are is still more evident.[54]

Those modern philosophers who have felt sympathy for a mentalistic criterion of personal identity formulated along broadly Lockean lines have, I suspect, been guilty of implicitly hypostatizing mental states and treating them effectively as constituting some, or even all, of the *constituents* of persons. Hume, of course, did this quite explicitly, regarding a person as being 'nothing but a bundle or collection of different perceptions'.[55] But, clearly, the *constituents* of objects precisely *do* need to be conceived of as entities that can be individuated and identified independently of the objects whose constituents they are supposed to be – a possibility that we have just seen to be ruled out in the case of mental states and their conscious subjects, *persons* included. This tacit hypostatization of mental states has conferred upon them, I suggest, a superficial *appearance* of ontological independence which has served to disguise, from friend and foe alike, this fatal flaw in the Lockean approach to personal identity.

Perhaps it will be suspected, however, that my argument of the preceding few paragraphs proceeded rather too quickly. In particular, some may want to urge that a *physicalist* in matters of the mental could overcome the difficulty that I have been dwelling on by contending that each psychological state

---

elects to defer discussion of them in his *magnum opus, Reasons and Persons*: see p. 225. For unless Parfit can counter these arguments, his entire approach to personal identity in that book is vitiated. The same criticism may be levelled against John Perry: see his 'Personal Identity, Memory, and the Problem of Circularity', in Perry (ed.), *Personal Identity*, pp. 136–7.

54   For a more detailed argument in defence of this dependence thesis, see my *Subjects of Experience*, pp. 22–32.

55   Hume, *A Treatise of Human Nature*, p. 252.

is identifiable, *at least in principle*, with some physiological state – even if only on a 'token–token' basis – and that the physiological state in question will itself be capable of being individuated by reference to its causes and effects as described in certain purely physical terms.

However, quite apart from the fact that this proposal threatens to reduce what was intended to be a psychological account of personal identity to a physiological one, the qualification 'at least in principle' should certainly not be allowed to pass unchallenged. All that its employment here really signifies is a pious hope that what I say cannot be done *might* somehow be achieved by a neurophysiologist in the future. But, as I tried to make clear earlier in this chapter, it would be utterly facile to suppose that such an achievement could issue purely from empirical inquiry, no matter how detailed or intensive. Before one can even begin to consider what kinds of empirical evidence there might be in support of the thesis that each or any psychological state is identifiable with some physiological state, one must not only have some grasp of the identity-conditions of *physiological states* – whether stated in terms of their causes and effects, or in some other terms – one must also have some *independent* grasp of the identity-conditions of *psychological* states.

So we can see already that the physicalist proposal now under consideration presents no *solution* to the current difficulty – that of finding some way to circumvent reference to the *person who possesses* a particular psychological state in order to identify the latter – since no reason has been offered to doubt that such reference will still be needed in order to specify *which* psychological state is supposedly identifiable with any given physiological state. But, furthermore, this very fact seems to vitiate altogether the sort of psychophysical identity thesis now under consideration. For, as I have stressed so often before, individual entities, whether they be objects or states, are *not even in principle* identifiable if they belong to sorts possessing *different criteria of identity*: and yet this now appears to be precisely how matters stand with regard to *psychological* states and *physiological* states, since the former but not the latter possess a criterion of identity involving reference to *persons or subjects whose states they are*.

There is another reason, however, why it may be felt that my condemnation of mentalistic criteria of personal identity formulated along broadly Lockean lines was too swift. It may be thought that the kind of objection that I raise fails to undermine the capacity of such a criterion to determine answers to *diachronic* identity questions concerning persons, even if it shows that answers to *synchronic* identity questions concerning persons must be presupposed for the purpose of individuating and identifying mental states. But to adopt such a defence is effectively to regard persons as four-dimensional 'spacetime worms'. According to this approach, what we should do when trying to frame a criterion of identity for persons is to look for some relationship between *person-stages* – 'time-slices' of persons – which is logically necessary and sufficient for their being *stages of the same person*.[56] I am, however, completely opposed to this sort of approach to the diachronic identity of continuants quite generally, for reasons set out in Chapter 6 above. I wholly repudiate the 'four-dimensional view' which it embodies, since I find the very notion that things such as tables, trees, and indeed persons *have* 'stages' or 'time-slices' at best ontologically extravagant and at worst doubtfully comprehensible.[57]

More crucially – since not all other philosophers share my distaste for four-dimensionalism – I can see no prospect of our being able to introduce the notion of a 'person-stage' in a way which would make the individuation and identification of person-stages possible without reference to the *persons* whose stages they would supposedly be. In consequence, I see can no prospect of our being able to formulate an *informative*, because *non-circular*, criterion of personal identity framed in terms of person-stages.[58] If my scepticism on this point is warranted, then it provides an answer to the objection raised at the beginning of the preceding paragraph: for the implication would be that, contrary to the supposition of that objection, *synchronic* identity questions concerning persons – which, on the four-dimensional view, are tantamount to identity questions concerning person-stages – are not answerable independently of *diachronic* identity questions concerning persons and that, indeed, any acceptable criterion of identity for persons should be capable of delivering answers to *both* diachronic *and* synchronic identity questions concerning persons, in terms of a *unitary* criterial condition embracing both kinds of case. Locke's co-consciousness criterion of personal identity, it should be remarked, does at least have the merit of attempting to meet this requirement.

In connection with the crucial point at issue, then, I suggest that any attempt to formulate identity-conditions for person-stages will be compelled to presuppose answers to diachronic identity questions concerning *persons*

---

[56] See, for example, David Lewis, 'Survival and Identity', in his *Philosophical Papers, Volume I* (Oxford: Oxford University Press, 1983).

[57] See further my *The Possibility of Metaphysics*, chs 4 and 5.

[58] One leading advocate of the four-dimensional approach, Sydney Shoemaker, has conceded that, on this approach, the diachronic identity-conditions of continuants quite generally cannot be non-circularly specified: see 'Identity, Properties, and Causality', in his *Identity, Cause, and Mind* (Cambridge: Cambridge University Press, 1984). But I cannot agree that a circular specification, even if *non-trivial*, may legitimately be regarded as an account of what identity through time *consists in* – a verdict that is shared by Colin McGinn in his review of Shoemaker's book, *Journal of Philosophy* 84 (1987), pp. 227–32.

– in other words, that person-stages will at best prove to be identifiable and distinguishable only by reference to different periods in the *careers or histories* of the persons to which they supposedly belong. This, at root, is because I consider that persons are *essentially* things with a past and at least a potential future. The essential historicity of persons promises to defeat, thus, any attempt to see their careers as merely being constructed compositionally from short-lived or momentary elements and consequently prevents us from seeing 'person-stages' as being anything else than, at best, mere abstractions from the histories of persons. One way of making the point would be to deny that any genuine sense could be made of the notion that a *person*, or indeed anything even temporarily *simulating* a person, could exist for only the span of a few moments or minutes. The generation of a person is, I suggest, something that *necessarily* takes time, because it involves processes of education, socialization, and the accretion of experience whose end-products *could not even in principle* be reproduced in any 'instantaneous' fashion – the fanciful imaginings of some science-fiction writers and philosophers notwithstanding. This is, admittedly, a large claim, which I cannot undertake to defend in depth just here. At the same time, the burden of argument in this matter surely lies squarely with my opponents, since it is they who seek to invoke entities of a hitherto uncountenanced kind – 'person-stages'.

My overall conclusion is that 'person' *does* in all probability denote what I call a basic sort, for which no adequate, because non-circular, criterion of identity can be supplied. It is true that I have arrived at this conclusion by the elimination of alternative possibilities rather than by the perhaps more secure method of deduction from first principles – although what could such 'first principles' *be*, in the present case? Moreover, it may be worried that I have not surveyed all of the possible alternatives. But here again it falls to my opponents to propose such alternatives if they can and to argue for their merits.

Meanwhile, it is incumbent upon me to say something about how it is, in the supposed absence of any informative criterion of personal identity, that we nonetheless seem able to identify and distinguish persons as relatively easily as we apparently do. The sort of response that is available to me here should be clear, however, once we recall the distinction made in Chapter 2 between identity criteria proper, which are *semantic-cum-metaphysical* principles, and the merely *heuristic* or *evidential* rules that often guide us in making judgements of identity.

There are many principles of the latter sort that we can call upon where judgements concerning personal identity are concerned. For instance, since – to the best of our knowledge – we actually have dealings only with *human* persons and confidently believe that a one-to-one relationship almost

PERSONS AND THEIR BODIES   139

universally obtains between human persons and human organisms, we generally regard the identity of human organisms as providing a reliable, albeit not infallible, guide to personal identity. Thus, because apparently unique physical characteristics such as fingerprints are a reliable guide to the identity of human organisms, they are derivatively also taken by us to be a reliable guide to personal identity. Hence, in an *evidential* sense of 'criterion', we can indeed legitimately speak of 'bodily criteria' of personal identity. And in the same evidential sense we may equally legitimately speak, say, of a 'memory criterion' of personal identity. The various 'puzzle cases' and thought-experiments indulged in by writers on the topic of personal identity, beginning with Locke himself, only serve to show – what philosophical analysis more directly serves to show – that neither 'bodily' nor 'memory' criteria of personal identity can have the status of semantic-cum-metaphysical principles, but at most only that of defeasible rules of evidence. In other words, these 'criteria' do not tell us, in Locke's phrase, 'wherein personal identity consists', but only help us to decide what judgements of personal identity we are best advised to make in the light of such empirical evidence as may be available to us.

Here, however, the following sort of objection may perhaps be raised. While it is true that most of us may *confidently believe* that, as I put it, a one-to-one relationship almost universally obtains between human persons and human organisms, how can we possibly *justify* this belief, in the absence of a proper – and properly justified – criterion of personal identity? More generally, how, in the absence of this, can we be entitled to regard any of the evidential 'criteria' of personal identity that we use as being at all *reliable*, even if only defeasibly so? However, it is not in fact so difficult to argue that we have good reason to believe in this almost universal one-to-one relationship, without presupposing that we must have at least implicit recourse to some well-founded criterion of personal identity.

One fairly compelling piece of evidence is simply this. Each human person who has mastered a natural language has mastered the proper use of the first-person pronoun – 'I', in English – to refer exclusively to *himself*. And we generally find that when sentences containing this pronoun issue from the mouths of human organisms, the sentences thus uttered are very rarely suggestive of the possibility that 'I', in the mouth of a single human organism, has more than one referent. Cases that *are* suggestive of this possibility – for instance, extreme cases of so-called multiple-personality syndrome – are very striking indeed and quite out of the ordinary. In these cases, 'I'-sentences issuing from the mouth of a single human organism express assertions which would be straightforwardly and blatantly *contradictory*, if 'I' in these cases always had the same referent. Of course, it might still be speculated that every normal human organism also houses one or more wholly inarticulate and almost entirely submissive 'persons', all dominated by the one who refers to himself as 'I'. This possibility cannot be conclusively ruled out by the empirical evidence available to us. Even so, the speculation is an utterly fanciful and empirically unsupported one and so not a consideration that should be allowed undermine our confidence in using the identity of human organisms as an everyday guide to the identity of human persons.

Wherein *does* personal identity consist, then? The only tenable answer that I can see at present is that *it can consist in nothing but itself* – that personal identity is, as we might put it, *primitive and ungrounded.*[59] If this really turns out to be so, the further implications for metaphysics and psychology will be very far-reaching indeed. Here, however, I must leave this topic for the purposes of the present book. In the remaining chapters, I shall turn to more general questions concerning the logic and ontology of sortal terms and concepts, focusing especially on their connection with dispositions and natural laws.

[59]   In recent times, much the same conclusion has been arrived at by, amongst others, Geoffrey Madell: see his *The Identity of the Self* (Edinburgh: Edinburgh University Press, 1981). For more on the notion of primitive identity and an argument that at least some identities must be ungrounded, see my *The Possibility of Metaphysics*, Chapter 7.

9

Sortal Terms and Natural Laws

That there is a distinction of some importance to be drawn between 'law-like' and 'accidental' generalizations has long been recognized by philo-sophers of science.[1] There is disagreement, however, as to whether the source of the distinction lies in some subjective diversity of our attitudes towards statements bearing a single underlying form or, instead, in some objective difference between the truth-conditions of two types of statement.[2] An import-ant ontological question that arises for the second of these views is this: does the assertion of lawlike or 'nomic' generalizations invoke the existence of entities that are not invoked by the assertion of accidental generaliza-tions? In particular, does it presuppose a universe of discourse embracing more entities than just the *actually existent individuals* countenanced by the classical nominalist – and, if so, what is the nature of these supplement-ary entities? Will it do, for instance, merely to expand the nominalist's ontology by the addition of *possible* individuals, or must entities of a quite different order be acknowledged?

In this chapter, I shall argue in favour of the objectivist thesis that law-like statements have distinctive truth-conditions and that a satisfactory answer to the ontological question will require us to invoke, as additional entities, not possible individuals but *actual sorts or kinds*, as items distinct from the individuals that may be said to instantiate them. My approach will take as its starting point a consideration of the grammatical form of lawlike sentences in natural language – a point of departure which I justify on the grounds that natural language is the primary vehicle of human thought, at

---

[1] See, for example, William Kneale, *Probability and Induction* (Oxford: Clarendon Press, 1949), pp. 70ff.

[2] For the former view, see, for example, A. J. Ayer, *Probability and Evidence* (London: Macmillan, 1972), pp. 129ff.

least in the case of thought of the level of sophistication with which we are presently concerned. And, even if natural language is not an infallible guide to ontology, there is no reason to suppose that it is a wholly unreliable one.

In a natural language, natural laws are most naturally expressed – or so I wish to claim – as *dispositional predications with sortal terms in subject position*. Concerning sortal terms, enough has already been said by way of introduction in previous chapters, but some brief reminders may be of service here. Sortal terms may be either *simple* or *complex* – although we may set aside, for the time being, my earlier distinction between *syntactical* and *semantic* simplicity or complexity, relying on the presumption that, for the most part, syntax may be expected to reflect semantics in this regard. In English, the chief varieties of *simple* sortal terms are *mass nouns*, such as 'wood' and 'water', and *common* or *count nouns*, such as 'tree' and 'horse'. *Complex* sortal terms are then formed from simple ones by the adjunction of adjectives or adjectival phrases, as in 'rusty iron', 'wild horse', 'wood which has been soaked in water' and 'tree which sheds its leaves in winter'.

As I explained in Chapter 2, the *indefinite article* or a *plural suffix* is often appropriately regarded as being a logically redundant part of a sortal term containing a count noun, so that I shall commonly describe noun-phrases of the form '*a* φ' or 'φ*s*' simply as being sortal terms in their own right – for example, '*a* tree' or 'wild horse*s*'. One widely applicable test for such redundancy, which I shall often exploit in what follows, is that it should be a matter of merely stylistic difference whether the singular or plural form is used – as, for instance, in the case of the logically equivalent sentences 'A horse is a mammal' and 'Horses are mammals'.

Finally, we may compare and contrast sortal terms with *individual terms*, which in a natural language like English may also be either simple or complex. The simple ones are chiefly exemplified by *proper names*, such as 'Dobbin' and 'Scott', while the complex ones are exemplified by definite descriptions, such as 'the horse in Farmer Brown's stable' and 'the author of *Waverley*', and also by demonstrative noun-phrases, such as 'that horse' and 'this piece of salt'.

Dispositional – as opposed to *occurrent* – predication is indicated, in English at least, either by certain conventions of tense and aspect or by certain conventions of adjective-formation. Thus, compare the two sentences 'Dobbin *eats* grass' and 'Dobbin *is eating* grass', the first of which is dispositional in force and the second occurrent. Or, again, compare the two sentences 'This piece of salt *dissolves* in water' and 'This piece of salt *is dissolving* in water'. In present-tense predications, as these examples show, English generally uses the continuous present to indicate occurrent predication and the simple or absolute present to indicate dispositional predication. In past-tense predications, the corresponding distinction is between the continuous or imperfect past, as in 'was eating' or 'was dissolving', and the habitual past, as in 'used to eat' or 'used to dissolve'.

Alternatively, English often uses the adjectival suffix '–able' and variants of this to express dispositional predication, as in 'This piece of salt is water-soluble', which is clearly equivalent to 'This piece of salt dissolves in water'. But some adjectives appear to be ambiguous with respect to the dispositional/occurrent distinction, such as the English colour-adjectives. Thus, when asked to describe the colour exhibited by a ripe tomato, when it is illuminated by light at the blue end of the visible spectrum, many speakers will readily describe it as being *black*. But they will generally recognize that there is also a sense in which the tomato's colour hasn't changed from its normal hue and so is still *red* – and, indeed, that it is red in this sense even when it is placed in a darkened room. This suggests that 'red' and 'black' have both dispositional and occurrent senses. Some philosophers may protest that the tomato illuminated by blue light only *looks* black. Of course, it *does* look black, but to insist that there is no sense in which it *is* black is, I think, just a philosophical prejudice.

How the dispositional/occurrent distinction is ultimately to be explicated is a difficult issue, which I cannot yet go into in any detail. So far, I have characterized the distinction for English in purely syntactical terms, but that there is an important underlying semantic distinction cannot be in doubt. Of course, one theory that was once very popular, but is now less so, is that disposition statements may be analysed in terms of *conditional* statements involving only occurrent predication. Thus, it might be suggested that 'This piece of salt is water-soluble' can be analysed, at least to a first approximation, as meaning something like 'If this piece of salt were currently immersed in water, then it would be dissolving'. Although I cannot go into my reasons at the moment, my own view is that *any* such attempt to eliminate dispositional predication in favour of the occurrent variety is doomed to failure. And thus it seems to me that Aristotle, if I interpret him rightly, was correct in viewing the distinction between the 'actual' and the 'potential' as being ultimate and irreducible.[3]

Unfortunately, this means that I cannot yet profess to explain, in any non-circular fashion, precisely in what the distinction consists. For the time being, then, I shall simply have to appeal to linguistic intuition to support any claim of mine that a certain predicate has dispositional or occurrent force. Nonetheless, in due course I shall be in a better position to offer

---

[3]   See Aristotle, *Metaphysics*, Book θ, in W. D. Ross (ed.), *The Works of Aristotle Translated into English, Volume VIII: Metaphysica*, 2nd edn (Oxford: Clarendon Press, 1928).

some theoretical insight into the nature of the distinction, when I shall suggest that the irreducibility of the dispositional/occurrent distinction is ultimately grounded in the irreducibility of the distinction between *individuals* and *sorts*. However, for my immediate purposes what is important is that there *is* a distinction between dispositional and occurrent predication, whatever its underlying explanation might be.

In ordinary English, both individual and sortal terms may figure as the grammatical subjects of sentences, whether involving dispositional or occurrent predication. We have already seen how the individual terms 'Dobbin' and 'this piece of salt' may serve as the subjects of the dispositional predicates '— eats grass' and '— dissolves in water' respectively, but equally as the respective subjects of the corresponding occurrent predicates '— is eating grass' and '— is dissolving in water'. But sortal terms, such as '(a) horse' and 'salt', may also serve as the subjects of these predicates, as in the dispositional sentences 'A horse eats grass' and 'Salt dissolves in water' on the one hand and the occurrent sentences 'A horse is eating grass' and 'Salt is dissolving in water' on the other. All of these sentences are grammatically well-formed in English and fluent English speakers will be well aware of circumstances in which their utterance would be appropriate.

We are now better placed to evaluate my claim that, in a natural language, natural laws are most naturally expressed by dispositional predications with sortal terms in subject position. This claim may be corroborated by the following simple and commonplace examples of lawlike English sentences: 'Fire burns', 'Bread nourishes', 'Arsenic is poisonous', 'Ravens are black', 'Lightning precedes thunder', 'Horses eat grass', and 'Water dissolves salt' or, equivalently, 'Salt is water-soluble'. At a further remove from everyday concerns and more clearly within the realms of natural science, we have: 'Sulphuric acid reacts with copper to form copper sulphate', 'Protons carry unit positive electrical charge', 'A planet moves in an ellipse with the sun at one focus' (Kepler's First Law of Planetary Motion), 'A gas at constant temperature varies in volume in inverse proportion to the pressure exerted upon it' (Boyle's Law), 'A body upon which no external force is impressed continues in its state of rest or uniform motion in a straight line' (Newton's First Law of Motion), 'An electrical charge attracts or repels another with a force directly proportional to their product and inversely proportional to the square of the distance between them' (Coulomb's Laws).

Inspection will show that all of these sentences contain sortal terms – sometimes complex and sometimes, where the predicate is relational rather than monadic, more than one – in subject position and verbs or adjectives having dispositional rather than occurrent force. (More complex scientific laws usually need to be expressed with the aid of mathematical symbols for the sake of clarity, but even these can in principle be formulated in the foregoing fashion, as indeed the example of Coulomb's Laws shows.) Take, for instance, the sentence just cited as expressing Kepler's First Law: 'A planet moves in an ellipse with the sun at one focus'. The grammatical subject here, 'a planet', is clearly a simple sortal term, consisting of a common or count noun preceded by the logically redundant indefinite article. (The redundancy of the article is shown by the equivalence of this sentence, understood as expressing a law, with the sentence 'Planets move in ellipses with the sun at one focus', in which the plural form of the noun is used.) And the predicate is clearly dispositional in force, as may perhaps be seen most clearly by substituting the individual term 'Mars' for 'a planet' and comparing the resulting sentence, 'Mars *moves* in an ellipse with the sun at one focus', with the corresponding occurrent sentence, 'Mars *is moving* in an ellipse with the sun at one focus'. (Here, as I explained above, I appeal to linguistic intuition to confirm my judgement that these two sentences do indeed have dispositional and occurrent force respectively, the former describing Mars's *tendency* to move in a certain fashion and the second its *actual* motion.)

Even so, the claim that I have just made concerning the natural expression of natural laws is insufficiently general inasmuch as it only accommodates lawlike sentences in which only sortal *terms* occur, neglecting those in which sortal *variables* appear – or, more precisely, the sortal *quantifier phrases and pronouns* which, in a natural language, do duty for the corresponding quantifiers and variables in a formal logical language. For example, we have already noticed the equivalence between 'Water dissolves salt' and 'Salt is water-soluble': but this should draw our attention to the corresponding equivalence between the simpler nomic generalization 'Salt *is soluble*' and '*Something* dissolves salt'. In the latter sentence, 'something' is evidently a *sortal existential quantifier expression*, because 'Something dissolves salt' is clearly entailed by any sentence differing from it only in that 'something' is replaced by a *sortal term*, such as 'water', or 'alcohol', or 'oil'. (I describe it as an *existential* quantifier expression because the sentence in question would standardly be semi-formalized as '$\exists\varphi(\varphi$ dissolves salt)' and it is customary to call '$\exists$' the 'existential' quantifier – although, for reasons mentioned in the Introduction, I no longer favour this nomenclature myself.) The use of sortal variables, or their natural language counterparts, is a natural and inevitable extension of the use of sortal terms, just as the use of individual variables is a natural and inevitable extension of the use of proper names and other individual terms.

I am now in a position to present a straightforward – albeit still contentious – answer to the question of the ontological implications of laws of nature. If Quine's criterion of ontological commitment is accepted, according to which 'to *be* is to be the value of a variable',[4] and if statements of natural law inevitably involve the use of sortal variables (or their natural-language counterparts), then such statements apparently carry a commitment to the existence of *sorts* or *kinds*, as the potential *values* of such variables – a commitment, moreover, to sorts or kinds conceived as entities quite distinct from those that are the potential values of *individual* variables, with the latter being regarded as particular *instances* of such sorts or kinds. In short, they apparently carry a commitment to the existence of *universals* of a certain type, however much Quine himself might have regarded this consequence with repugnance.

This still leaves open, of course, whether this is a commitment to 'Platonic' (or 'transcendent') universals or only to 'Aristotelian' (or 'immanent') universals – and much else besides.[5] But it is clearly a major ontological commitment, nonetheless. Thus, even the humble law 'Horses eat grass', to the extent that it is equivalent to the semi-formalized statement '$\exists\varphi\exists\chi(\varphi$ eats χ & $\varphi = $ (a) horse & $\chi = $ grass)', will apparently commit anyone asserting it to the existence of the species *horse* and the stuff *grass*, as items existing over and above any *individual* horse or blade of grass. Nor is the appeal to a semi-formalized equivalent here really necessary, since even in ordinary English the inferences from 'Horses eat grass' to 'Horses eat *something*', and '*Something* eats grass', in which the quantifier expressions are clearly not *individual* in character, are readily accepted as valid. This conclusion will, as I say, be repugnant to those with Quinean or, more generally, nominalist sympathies. It remains to be seen, however, whether there is any way in which it can plausibly be avoided.

---

[4] See, for example, W. V. Quine, 'A Logistical Approach to the Ontological Problem', in his *The Ways of Paradox and Other Essays* (Cambridge, MA: Harvard University Press, 1976).

[5] It may be urged, perhaps, that *immanent* realism is not in fact open to us here, as the following example – for which I am indebted to John Heil, who attributes it to C. B. Martin – seems to show. Suppose that research is being conducted to create a solvent for a certain kind of mineral, M, but that, just as success is near, funding is cut off and the project is never completed. Is it not still true to say that M is soluble in the never-to-be-manufactured solvent? My answer is that it is just not clear to me that it *is* true to say this, or whether it is only true to say that M *would have been soluble* if the project had been completed. In any case, however – to anticipate points that will be made later in this chapter – I myself am not ultimately committed to the falsehood of claims of the form 'S dissolves M', where 'S' names a *non-existent* kind of substance, nor need I deny that in these circumstances 'S dissolves M' entails '$\exists\varphi(\varphi$ dissolves $M)$', since I don't regard the quantifier '$\exists$' as expressing *existence*.

There are, I think, three possible strategies whereby one might hope to evade the foregoing conclusion. One is to question whether the usual modes of expressing natural laws in ordinary language adequately display their true logical form. Another is to query Quine's criterion of ontological commitment. And the third is to argue that sortal quantification does not necessarily extend the *domain* of the variables of quantification beyond that needed for individual quantifiers, on the grounds that sortal variables take as their values not sorts or kinds conceived as *non*-individuals, but instead only *pluralities* of individuals. On this view, although sortal terms *refer*, they do not refer *singularly* to universals of a certain type, but rather *plurally* to individuals – to the very same individuals, indeed, that would ordinarily be described as being the particular 'instances' of the referents of sortal terms. Hence, according to this strategy, the distinction between the semantic roles of sortal and individual terms lies not in an *ontological* distinction between their referents, but merely in a *linguistic* distinction between their modes of reference to the *same* entities, all of them individuals. Of these three strategies, I shall pay most attention to the last, because it seems to me the most interesting and also the most promising, even though I shall firmly reject it myself. But first I need to examine the other two strategies.

The first strategy would be adopted by those who, following Popper, consider that natural laws are most perspicuously formulated as 'all-statements',[6] translatable into the language of modern predicate logic as universally quantified conditionals all of whose variables of quantification are *individual* variables, ranging over some suitable and potentially infinite domain of individuals – thereby apparently excluding any role for *sortal* variables in the expression of natural laws. For instance, the putative law-statement 'Ravens are black' should, according to this approach, first be reformulated as an *all*-statement, 'All ravens are black', and then be translated canonically as '$\forall x$(if x is a raven, then x is black)', in which 'x' is an individual variable and, presumably, the colour-adjective is dispositional in force. (Insisting on a dispositional interpretation of 'black' seems unavoidable here, because no one would suppose the putative law to be falsified by, say, the discovery of a raven whose feathers had been dyed green or bleached white.)

And, indeed, at first blush such a translation may not seem unreasonable. For one thing, it looks as though it is interestingly paralleled by an analogous and very plausible translation of *occurrent* sentences with sortal terms in subject position, such as 'A horse is eating grass' and 'Salt is dissolving in water'. For these seemingly go over into *existentially quantified*

---

[6]   See K. R. Popper, *The Logic of Scientific Discovery* (London: Hutchinson, 1968), where he defines this expression thus: '[A]n *all-statement* . . . [is] a universal assertion about an unlimited number of individuals' (p. 63).

conjunctions, namely, '∃x(x is a horse and x is eating grass)' and '∃x(x is salt and x is dissolving in water)', in which the variables are once again *individual* variables. Why not, then, correspondingly translate lawlike sentences – that is, *dispositional* sentences with sortal terms in subject position – as *universally quantified conditionals*, with 'A horse eats grass' going over into '∀x(if x is a horse, then x eats grass)' and 'Salt dissolves in water' going over into '∀x(if x is salt, then x dissolves in water)'?

Unfortunately, this attractively simple proposal runs into a host of difficulties, some of which are well known, others less so. One of the lesser known difficulties is this. Take a lawlike sentence containing more than one sortal term, such as 'Water dissolves salt'. According to the Popperian approach, this may be translated as '∀x(if x is water, then x dissolves salt)', although it could equally well be translated as '∀x(if x is salt, then water dissolves x)' – so that the fullest translation would be '∀x∀y(if x is water and y is salt, then x dissolves y)', where the last predication is still dispositional in force, meaning 'x is disposed to dissolve y'. Now, clearly, one cannot claim to have captured the logical form of lawlike sentences unless one can show how, in virtue of that form, one lawlike sentence entails another. But the Popperian cannot explain, consistently with his own constraints on the logical form of a law, why the lawlike sentence 'Water dissolves salt' should entail the lawlike sentence '*Something* dissolves salt'.

This is because it is hard to see how any remotely adequate translation of the lawlike sentence 'Something dissolves salt' can be found which *both* conforms to the Popperian requirements – that is, which contains only *individual* variables and is bound by an initial universal quantifier – *and* is entailed by the Popperian translation of 'Water dissolves salt'. (Of course, if Popper's constraints are lifted and *sortal* quantification is admitted, then the entailment may simply be taken at its face value as a case of existential generalization.) Clearly, '∃x∀y(if y is salt, then x dissolves y)' will not do for the Popperian, because it is not bound by an initial universal quantifier – it is not an 'all-statement'. The only candidate translation that looks even remotely feasible is '∀x(if x is salt, then ∃y(y dissolves x))'. But this too clearly will not do, because it could be true even if no lawlike sentence of the form 'φ dissolves salt' were true, where 'φ' is a sortal term. It would be true, for instance, if each individual piece of salt was indeed disposed to be dissolved by *some* individual body of liquid of some sort, but some pieces of salt were only disposed to be dissolved by bodies of liquid of *one* sort – *water*, say – while other pieces of salt were only disposed to be dissolved by bodies of liquid of *another* sort, such as *alcohol*. In this case, neither 'Water dissolves salt' nor 'Alcohol dissolves salt' nor any other lawlike sentence of the form 'φ dissolves salt' would be true – and, indeed, we would appear to have two different *kinds* of salt, one water-soluble and the other alcohol-soluble. Hence, in this case, the lawlike sentence

'Something dissolves salt' would *not* be true, whereas its proposed Popperian translation *would* be true.

A much better known objection to the Popperian analysis of laws is that it fails to account adequately for the distinction between nomic or lawlike generalizations and 'accidental' generalizations.[7] I think that this objection is valid, but not for the reason that is commonly advanced – namely, that laws entail or support counterfactual conditionals. The standard argument is that a Popperian all-statement, such as 'All ravens are black', is translated as a universally quantified *material* conditional and thus is interpreted as ascribing blackness only to each and every *actual* raven, having nothing to say concerning *merely possible* ravens: but a natural law, it is said, displays its nomic force precisely in its power to legislate for possible but *non*-actual cases, in addition to all actual ones.

However, I am doubtful about this objection and its associated counterfactual characterization of nomic force, for two reasons. First of all, there appears to be an internal difficulty for any theory which takes a lawlike sentence of the form 'φs are *F*' to support counterfactuals of the form 'If *a* were a φ, then *a* would be *F*', where 'φ' is a sortal term and '*a*' an individual term. This is because it seems that a good many such counterfactuals are simply *incoherent*. Consider again, thus, the lawlike sentence 'Ravens are black'. According to such a theory, this putative law should apparently be taken to support, for example, the counterfactual 'If *that white shoe* were a raven, then it would be black', the implication being that the law can hold only if that counterfactual is true. However, this counterfactual, far from being *true*, scarcely even seems to make sense. For, surely, nothing which is *in fact* a white shoe *could* have been a raven, in any metaphysically serious sense.[8] I should stress that my doubt here is not directed against counterfactuals in general – only those with an antecedent of the form 'If *a* were a φ', where 'φ' is a sortal term denoting a natural kind to which *a* does not actually belong. But it seems that these would have to be included amongst the counterfactuals supposedly supported by a law, according to the kind of theory now under consideration.

Observe that it will *not* do to try to overcome this problem by restricting the 'possible' ravens to which 'Ravens are black' is supposed to apply to *nomically* possible ravens, because the very question now at issue

---

[7] See, for example, Kneale, *Probability and Induction*, pp. 70ff. It has to be acknowledged, however, that Popper takes careful cognizance of Kneale's views in an appendix that he later added to *The Logic of Scientific Discovery*, pp. 420ff.

[8] Certainly, this verdict is supported by arguments of a kind for which Kripke is now justly famous: see Saul A. Kripke, *Naming and Necessity* (Oxford: Blackwell, 1980).

concerns *which* things, both actual and non-actual, come within the scope of this putative law: but since 'nomically possible raven' just *means* a raven to which the laws governing ravenkind apply, this attempted solution is blatantly circular and uninformative. An alternative response might be to point out that, at least according to some leading accounts of the semantics of counterfactuals, any counterfactual with a *metaphysically* impossible antecedent is just *vacuously true*, in which case such counterfactuals do not really create any difficulty for such a theory of laws.[9] But, even if this strategy technically succeeds in circumventing the problem, it is surely still a weakness in such a theory that it needs to rely in this fashion upon an account of the semantics of counterfactuals which is far from being uncontroversial.

Secondly and more importantly, it is far from clear that a lawlike sentence such as 'Ravens are black' even purports to describe all *actual* ravens, much less all *possible* ones, since we do not take it to be falsified by the existence of abnormal or 'freak' counterexamples, such as albino ravens. Thus, my criticism of Popper is not the usual one that he does not throw his net wide enough, when it comes to specifying the individual things that are covered by a law, but on the contrary that he throws it *too* wide. As I see it, the most that a putative law such as 'Ravens are black' purports to tell us *concerning individuals* is what we should expect any *normal* individual raven to be like in respect of its colour – and apart from this it appears to be concerned, rather, with characterizing the raven *species* or *kind*. Such a law is 'normative' or *regulative* in force with regard to individuals and it is precisely in this that its 'nomic' character resides. This, indeed, is why the title 'law' is so appropriate and no mere relic of a theocentric perspective on the natural world. For *laws*, whether of man, God or indeed nature precisely *are* normative: they set or register certain *standards*. I shall say more of this in a moment.

Incidentally, I should perhaps try to forestall at this point a criticism that might be levelled at me for concentrating on commonplace and 'unscientific' examples of lawlike sentences, such as 'Ravens are black'. One reason why I do so, at least at this early stage of my inquiry into laws, is that our intuitive judgements regarding the logical character of laws are likely to be much more reliable when we focus on such relatively uncomplicated examples. It is important here that I also believe that science is not *separated* from common sense by a linguistic and epistemic gulf but is really just a more methodical *extension* of it and consequently that 'scientific' laws are not fundamentally different in kind from everyday ones. And, indeed, that this is so seems clear enough from the list of examples of laws, both

---

[9]   For such an account, see David Lewis, *Counterfactuals* (Oxford: Blackwell, 1973), pp. 24–6.

everyday and scientific, that I presented earlier. In particular, the *normative* character of laws in the more advanced sciences certainly seems evident enough, because many of those laws are quite explicitly regarded as having an 'ideal' status – as is the case, for example, with the so-called *ideal Gas Laws*, such as Boyle's Law and Charles's Law.

Before saying more in defence of my own 'normative' account of nomic status, I should briefly mention some further difficulties which attend more orthodox and better-known accounts. First of all, then, not least amongst the problems of employing *modal* logic in an analysis of natural law are those connected with the ontological implications of its currently popular 'possible worlds' semantics. Certainly, a realism regarding possible worlds as robust as that of David Lewis will seem, to most nominalists, like the proverbial fire to the frying pan of realism regarding sorts or kinds.[10]

On the other hand, if a *non*-realist view of possible worlds is exploited in the analysis of laws, there would appear to be a danger of treating laws as being in some way *subjective*, contrary to the intuitions of most scientists that they are, in fact, amongst the most objective or mind-independent features of the natural world. Besides, a 'possible worlds' account of the truth-conditions of lawlike sentences will almost certainly require some means of distinguishing between *naturally* and merely *logically* or *metaphysically* possible worlds and it is hard to see how such an approach could achieve this without circularity – as indeed we noticed a little while ago. Obviously, it would not do, on such an account, simply to define a naturally possible world as being one in which all the natural laws of this, the actual world, obtain – plausible though such a definition might be, given an independent account of what a natural law *is*.[11]

In defence of my own account of nomic status, I would urge that a recognition of the 'normative' character of natural laws is quite crucial to an understanding of scientific methodology, particularly with regard to the empirical confirmation of such laws by experiment and observation.[12] For a feature of this methodology which the 'all-statement' analysis – and *a fortiori* any stronger, modal analysis – of laws completely fails to explain

---

[10]   See his *Counterfactuals*, pp. 84ff. and, more generally, David Lewis, *On the Plurality of Worlds* (Oxford: Blackwell, 1986).

[11]   For an attempt to tackle this problem within the possible worlds framework, see Nicholas Rescher, *A Theory of Possibility* (Oxford: Blackwell, 1975), pp. 144ff. I present an account of my own of the nature of 'natural' possibility in my 'Miracles and Laws of Nature', *Religious Studies* 23 (1987), pp. 263–78.

[12]   I discuss some of these matters more fully in my 'What *Is* the "Problem of Induction"?', *Philosophy* 62 (1987), pp. 325–40.

is the willingness of scientists sometimes to accept even just a *single* well-conducted experiment or observation as almost conclusive evidence in support of a law.[13] Popper himself is at least to be commended for acknowledging that the 'all-statement' analysis effectively rules out *any* account of the empirical confirmation of laws even by non-deductive methods, although his consequent endorsement of falsificationism seems like a counsel of despair.

Yet, of course, nothing could be more natural or reasonable than to take any arbitrarily chosen normal exemplar of a given sort or kind as its representative. If a normal sample of water is found to dissolve a normal sample of salt, it is eminently rational to conclude, without repeating the experiment, that *water dissolves salt* – and thus that a certain natural law obtains. I shall say more in a moment about the notion of 'normality' that is in play here. But the key point is that experiments are repeated only when there is some doubt either as to what *sorts* of objects are being tested or as to their *normality* as representatives of sorts to which they are known to belong. A *well-conducted* experiment or observation is precisely one in which the experimenter or observer has good reason to suppose that he *has* correctly identified what sorts of things he is dealing with and that his specimens or exemplars are indeed 'normal' representatives of those sorts. Thus, for example, in a chemical experiment this will be a matter of correctly identifying the chemical substances under investigation and establishing the 'purity' of the experimenter's samples of those substances.

Now, of course, we may *on occasion* – or perhaps even fairly often, in more difficult epistemic circumstances – *misidentify* an object's sortal character or *mistakenly* take something to be a 'normal' specimen of a given sort when really it is not. None of us can be infallible in these regards, however careful we may be. However, it is surely incoherent to suppose that we might be *consistently* and *systematically* mistaken in such matters,

---

[13]   It may, I acknowledge, be disputed whether this criticism does in fact automatically extend to a stronger, modal analysis of laws: see, in particular, John Foster, 'Induction, Explanation and Natural Necessity', *Proceedings of the Aristotelian Society* 83 (1982/3), pp. 87–101. However, Foster confesses that he has not provided, in this article, any substantive account of what natural necessity is supposed to *be* – and if, as I believe, it should ultimately be explicated in terms of laws themselves, then the modal analysis is in any case implicitly circular. More recently, Foster has advanced a *theistic* account of laws as being more satisfactory than any other alternative: see his *The Divine Lawmaker: Lectures on Induction, Laws of Nature, and the Existence of God* (Oxford: Clarendon Press, 2004). However, Foster does not include my own account of laws amongst the alternatives that he considers and none of the objections that he raises against those views tell against mine. In contrast, the theistic account is subject to many obvious difficulties.

always mistaking one sort of thing for another quite different sort and *always* unluckily encountering abnormal specimens which we are unable to detect as being such. It must be reasonable to suppose that our most carefully formed judgements in these matters are *on the whole* correct and hence that our knowledge of natural law is broadly well-founded as a system, although obviously not infallible in every respect.

To suppose otherwise – to suppose that, despite our best endeavours, we really might be consistently and systematically mischaracterizing the nature of the objects that we encounter in our experience of the natural world – is surely a form of global scepticism that is ultimately just incoherent. Here we should bear in mind once more that criteria of identity for individuals are sortal-relative, so that there can be no possibility of our successfully identifying *individuals* while systematically mistaking what *sorts* of individuals they are, nor any possibility of our succeeding in the former task while abandoning any recourse whatever to sortal concepts and distinctions. Furthermore, it is clear that any workable system of sortal concepts presupposes an ability on the part of its users to distinguish, more often than not, normal exemplars of a given sort from abnormal ones.

If this line of reasoning seems to have a 'Kantian' flavour, appealing to certain apparently necessary preconditions of our experience of the natural world, that is because it *does* – and it is, I think, none the worse on that account, for it doesn't commit me to any of the more extravagant aspects of Kant's philosophy, such as his transcendental idealism. Note, too, that the anti-sceptical line that I am taking here is not simply a version of one common response to Humean *inductive* scepticism: the response that it is somehow reasonable to believe in the 'uniformity of nature'. For, in the Humean context, the principle of the uniformity of nature concerns the existence of *universal regularities amongst individuals*, which is supposed to guarantee that at least some 'all-statements' are true. But, as I conceive of laws, they are *not* expressed by 'all-statements' and primarily concern *sorts* rather than individuals. Once one rejects, with Hume, the objective existence of sorts and posits a world of intrinsically unsorted individuals, all entirely 'loose and separate' (as Hume would put it), there really is no adequate response to inductive scepticism. The right response is not to appeal forlornly to some principle of the uniformity of nature, but to reject as incoherent the Humean conception of a world of intrinsically unsorted individuals.

It is incumbent upon any satisfactory analysis of natural law to explain how our knowledge of natural laws should be possible on the basis of experience. For that we actually possess such knowledge seems incontrovertible in view of the manifest progress of the natural sciences and that this knowledge is ultimately empirically founded seems equally clear from the practice of scientists, however much the role of theory in the interpretation of experimental results may very rightly be emphasized. I would claim that this is something that the normative account of laws can explain significantly more convincingly than can any of its rivals, while also presenting an historically more accurate picture of scientific method.

While on the topic of confirmation, it is worth pointing out that Hempel's famous paradox, popularly known as the paradox of the ravens, may be seen as constituting further evidence of the incorrectness of the 'all-statement' analysis of natural laws (and, indeed, of any stronger, modal analysis employing a sentential operator expressing natural necessity).[14] It will be recalled that the paradox plays upon the fact that the two sentences '$\forall x$(if x is a raven, then x is black)' and '$\forall x$(if x is non-black, then x is a non-raven)' are logically equivalent (as, of course, are the sentences obtained by prefixing each of these two sentences with a necessity operator). In my view, all that this shows, very graphically, is that the first of these two sentences is *not* an adequate translation of the law 'Ravens are black'. Here we should observe that whereas an 'all-statement' like 'All ravens are black' is contraposable as 'All non-black things are non-ravens', there is no corresponding transformation available in the case of a lawlike sentence like 'Ravens are black'. That is to say, there is no lawlike sentence which is logically equivalent to this, in which the terms of the original are negated and transposed. Certainly, 'Non-black things are non-ravens' is *not* a lawlike sentence, because there is no *sort* or *kind* which embraces just those things that are not black.[15] In fact, even 'black things' is not a genuine sortal term since, as Geach points out, it has no criterion of identity associated with it.[16] Still less so, then, could 'non-black things' qualify as a sortal term since, as Geach also points out, even the negation of a sortal term is never itself a sortal term.[17]

Now, it may be wondered whether the normative account of nomic force just outlined suggests a means of reformulating lawlike sentences containing sortal terms in subject position in terms of sentences committed only to the existence of *normal exemplars* of the sorts in question, in a way which might satisfy a nominalist. I think not. First of all, the problem of sortally

[14]   For the paradox, see C. G. Hempel, 'Studies in the Logic of Confirmation', in his *Aspects of Scientific Explanation* (New York: Free Press, 1965).

[15]   Compare George Schlesinger, 'Natural Kinds', in R. S. Cohen and M. W. Wartofsky (eds), *Boston Studies in the Philosophy of Science*, Volume III (Dordrecht: D. Reidel, 1967).

[16]   See P. T. Geach, *Reference and Generality*, 2nd edn (Ithaca: Cornell University Press, 1968), pp. 38ff. Nor, obviously, could it be argued with any plausibility that *black thing* is a 'basic' sort in my sense.

[17]   See Geach, *Reference and Generality*, 2nd edn, p. 40.

quantified laws, such as 'Something dissolves salt', would still remain. Secondly, even if it were the case – which I do not concede it is – that the law 'Ravens are black' is true if and only if the universally quantified conditional '$\forall x$(if x is a *normal* raven, then x is black)' is true, it is obvious that this equivalence could not be of any use to a nominalist if the notion of 'normality' cannot be explicated in a nominalistically satisfactory way. My own view is that to say of a given individual that it is a 'normal' raven is just to say that it is a raven which 'conforms to type', that is, which satisfies all the natural laws pertaining to the raven kind. Thus, an albino raven is 'abnormal' precisely insofar as it violates, or fails to conform with, the law 'Ravens are black' – assuming, for present purposes, that this lawlike sentence is indeed true and so expressive of a law concerning ravens.

Hence, I do not profess or even desire to offer an explication of normality that is *independent* of my account of natural law nor, for that reason, one which holds out any hope of our restating the truth-conditions of lawlike sentences without commitment to the existence of sorts or kinds. Furthermore, I do not consider that my explication of normality presents any threat to the account of scientific method that I sketched a little earlier. All that we may conclude – which in any case seems independently entirely plausible – is that scientific method is not exclusively *foundationalist* in spirit, but includes many elements of *coherentism*. As I see it, checking the 'normality' of an experimental specimen is a matter of establishing, as far as possible, that it conforms to *currently accepted* laws pertaining to things of its sort. The aim of an experiment is then to discover *new* laws by observing the behaviour of this putatively normal specimen in hitherto unexamined conditions. In the course of carrying out such procedures we may, of course, eventually come to revise our previous beliefs either regarding the normality of our specimens or regarding the accuracy of the putative laws that we had recourse to in checking their normality. This only goes to show that scientific results are always potentially revisable and are dependent upon one another in a host of ways – a point which, as I say, we ought to be happy to accept in any case.

The only rival analysis of 'normality' which could conceivably be exploited by a nominalist in this connection would be a purely *statistical* one, according to which a raven, say, is 'normal' just in case it shares the characteristics of most other members of its species. Such an analysis, however, is plainly unsatisfactory for present purposes, for a variety of reasons. For one thing, in order to avoid any apparent reference to a *species* or *kind* to which all these statistically relevant individuals belong, it seems that the nominalist will first have to define the predicate '— is a raven' in terms of some list or cluster *adjectival* expressions, all of which describe various more or less observable features of individuals. Such a project is unpromising, as we know from the work of Kripke and Putnam on natural kind terms:

a point to which I shall return later.[18] But even if it could succeed, it still seems clear that what is 'normal' is not *definable* merely as what is usually the case, even though it is always reasonable to assume – in the absence of evidence to the contrary – that what is normal is usually the case (which is why, on the normative account, laws have predictive utility). A sudden spate of albino ravens would not call into question the normality of black ones. Only if, through some evolutionary process of adaptation to changed circumstances, ravens became white – so that the lawlike statement correctly describing their plumage came to be 'Ravens are white' – would the occasion black 'throw-back' rightly come to be regarded as abnormal. The concept of normality is theory-relative – and thus law-dependent – and for this very reason it is futile to attempt to state the truth-conditions of laws in terms of the characteristics of normal specimens, if it is hoped thereby to satisfy nominalist desiderata by avoiding ontological commitment to anything but actual individuals.

In sum, everything that has been said so far tends to reinforce the idea that statements of natural law unavoidably carry reference to *sorts* or *kinds*, conceived as setting norms or standards to which actual individuals may conform in greater or lesser degrees. Such reference seems ineliminable, even if it is still not clear exactly what ontological implications this fact has. It has been confirmed, maybe, that we need to endorse 'reference to' or 'quantification over' sorts, in order to provide an adequate analysis of scientific theory and practice. But whether this means that we must regard sorts as being 'real', or part of the 'furniture' of the world – in the full-blooded sense in which individuals are ordinarily acknowledged to be – remains perhaps an open question, whose answer depends at least in part on how much truth there is in Quine's criterion of ontological commitment.

So let us turn, therefore, to the *second* strategy mentioned earlier as being available to the nominalist: that of querying Quine's criterion. Now, certainly, this criterion *has* frequently been queried, notably by Prior in the context of the debate over 'objectual' versus 'substitutional' interpretations of the quantifiers.[19] And, undoubtedly, a substitutional account of sortal quantification can be advanced. Indeed, I implicitly employed just such an account earlier, when I explained the use of sortal quantification in a lawlike sentence such as 'Something dissolves salt'. For there I took it that a necessary and sufficient condition of this sentence's being true is that

---

[18] See Kripke, *Naming and Necessity*, and Hilary Putnam, 'The Meaning of "Meaning"', in his *Mind, Language and Reality* (Cambridge: Cambridge University Press, 1975).

[19] See A. N. Prior, *Objects of Thought* (Oxford: Clarendon Press, 1971), pp. 33ff., and compare Geach, *Reference and Generality*, 2nd edn, p. 161.

there is – or at least *could* be, subject only to an extension of the limited stock of sortal terms presently to be found in English – some true sentence differing from it only in that 'something' is replaced by a sortal term. (We obviously need to insert this qualification regarding the limitations of existing English vocabulary, since no actual human language can be expected to contain already the lexical resources to express *every* law that might actually obtain.) And it was, indeed, precisely in order to avoid begging any ontological question as to the objective existence of sorts or kinds that I drew upon such an account of sortal quantification. All the same, we must break out of the circle of language at some point in explaining how words attach to the world and it is certainly not clear that a substitutional account of sortal quantification simply *obviates* commitment to the existence of sorts or kinds. Rather, it seems at best only to provide a temporary means of putting off the ontological question, pending the development of some satisfactory theory of the semantics of sortal terms.

The following line of argument, however, at least seems very plausible. First, the normal use of *proper names* certainly *does* carry with it ontological commitments, since the standard use of such a name presupposes the existence of an individual which is its bearer or referent.[20] Such ontological implications then naturally carry over to the use of individual *variables*, since these are proxies for proper names. And thus the ineliminability from our discourse of individual quantification may indeed be taken as indicative of our ontological commitment to the real existence of *individuals*. This is not to say that *every* use of a proper name or individual variable to make a particular assertion must be regarded as ontologically committing *on its own account*, only that the *general practice* of using such names and variables commits its users to the existence of a world including individual objects. After all, there is nothing incoherent about an assertion such as 'Vulcan does not exist' or 'Some of the kings mentioned in the Bible never existed'.

Similarly, then, whether or not the use of *sortal* variables carries with it ontological implications will depend, in like manner, upon whether or not sortal *terms* are *name-like*, in that the standard use of such a term presupposes the existence of something that is its bearer or referent. So, I suggest, if sufficiently close parallels can be drawn between the semantics of sortal terms and the semantics of proper names, then the ineliminability of sortal quantification may indeed justly be taken as committing us ontologically to the existence of sorts or kinds, quite as strongly as the ineliminability of individual quantification commits us ontologically to the existence of individuals. Thus, I can endorse the general spirit of Quine's

---

[20]   Compare Prior, *Objects of Thought*, p. 169, and Geach, *Reference and Generality*, 2nd edn, pp. 162ff.

criterion of ontological commitment, without accepting every aspect of his doctrine concerning it – and, in particular, without accepting that the quantifier '∃', or its English counterpart, 'some', expresses *existence* (on which point, see Chapter 4 above).

Now, that sortal terms – and above all simple natural kind terms – are indeed name-like in important respects has been argued by a number of philosophers: notably by Geach – who has drawn attention to the syntactical similarities[21] – and by Kripke and Putnam, who have emphasized the semantic similarities.[22] On the latter score, a point that I take to be of immense importance is that simple natural kind terms are no more *definable* in terms of lists or clusters of *adjectival* expressions describing observable features of individuals than proper names are equivalent to lists or clusters of identifying descriptions. Just as 'Aristotle' cannot be taken to be *synonymous* with anything like 'the most famous pupil of Plato and tutor of Alexander the Great, born in Stagira in 384 BC . . .', neither can 'gold' be taken to be synonymous with anything like 'ductile, malleable metal, with a melting point of 1062°C and a density of 19.3 gm/cc, soluble in aqua regia . . .'. That gold is, for example, soluble in aqua regia can in no sense be regarded as a 'defining characteristic' of that metal, because the term 'gold' is in fact *simple and indefinable*. Rather, 'Gold is soluble in aqua regia' is just a purely *a posteriori* statement of *natural law* – and the same applies to all of the other sentences that can be constructed by making 'gold' the grammatical subject of the descriptive predicates listed a moment ago, beginning with 'Gold is ductile'.

It is, of course, perfectly feasible to maintain this while acknowledging that investigation of a chemical specimen's empirically detectable properties *guides* us in classifying it as being an exemplar of this or that chemical kind and hence, say, as being a particular instance of the kind named 'gold'. In somewhat the same way, descriptive information about an individual can guide us in identifying it as the bearer of a certain proper name, even though the name is not synonymous with a description possessing that informational content. But if the meaning of a natural kind term like 'gold' is not analysable in terms of the meanings of any such set of descriptive predicates, so that '— is gold' is not just a condensed way of expressing a complex physical property, then there seems to be little alternative but to suppose that it gets its meaning in just the way that a proper name does: that is, simply by standing for or referring to some

---

[21] See Geach, *Reference and Generality*, 2nd edn, especially the closing remark on p. 191. See also his *Reference and Generality*, 3rd edn (Ithaca, NY: Cornell University Press, 1980), p. 216.

[22] See Kripke, *Naming and Necessity*, and Putnam, 'The Meaning of "Meaning"'.

thing or things – the obvious proposal being that it refers to a certain *kind of material stuff*.

My concurrence with the views of Kripke and Putnam does not, I should remark, extend to an acceptance of the suggestion that the predicate '— is gold' is in some sense *ostensibly* definable by means of the predicate '— is the same kind of stuff as *this*', where 'this' refers to some individual sample or exemplar picked out for the purpose.[23] There are, I believe, serious difficulties with this line of thought. First of all, this could not succeed as a general account of the semantics of sortal terms simply because, as I have emphasized in previous chapters, successful reference to individuals itself already presupposes an ability to individuate them as being individuals of this or that *sort* – so that the semantics of sortal terms cannot be, as the foregoing proposal seems to imply, logically posterior to that of individual terms. Rather, there must be an even-handed mutual dependence between the two.

Secondly, our possession of the notion of two or more individuals being exemplars of *the same kind of stuff* – as being 'consubstantial' – clearly stands in need of explanation and the only plausible one that I can envisage will appeal to our familiarity with *instances* of this relationship. We possess the notion, that is to say, precisely because we can at least sometimes make justified judgements of the form '*this* and *that* are both φ(s)', for some sortal term 'φ'. So our *general* capacity to judge that an individual instantiates a certain sort or kind is already *presupposed by*, and so cannot be explained in terms of, our capacity to judge that two or more individuals are individuals of the *same* sort or kind. This, indeed, should be evident inasmuch as any sentence of the form '*a* is the same kind of stuff/thing as *b*' is plausibly analysable as meaning, quite simply, 'For some kind of stuff/thing, φ, *a* is (a) φ and *b* is (a) φ'. Consequently, it seems, sentences of the form '*a* is the same kind of stuff/thing as *b*' cannot be invoked non-circularly in explicating the meaning of *instantiation sentences*, that is, sentences of the form '*a* is (a) φ' nor, hence, in explicating the meaning of predicates of the form '— is (a) φ', such as '— is gold'. Indeed, I take sentences of the form '*a* is (a) φ' to be semantically basic and irreducible. In sum, the notion of an individual's being an instance of a certain kind of substance is *logically prior* to the notion of two or more different individuals' being instances of the *same* kind of substance, or being 'consubstantial'.

Suppose it is conceded now, as I think it must be, that the ineliminability of sortal quantification *does*, as Quine's criterion would have us believe, commit us ontologically to the existence of a domain of entities over which

[23] See, for example, Putnam, 'The Meaning of "Meaning"', p. 225, and Kripke, *Naming and Necessity*, pp. 135–6.

the variables of such quantification range.[24] There still remains the *third* strategy adumbrated earlier as being open to the nominalist who denies the objective existence of sorts or kinds. According to this suggestion, sortal variables need only be supposed to range over *individuals*, not over entities of a quite different order.

What lies behind this suggestion is the idea that although sortal terms, like individual terms, have meaning simply in virtue of *standing for* or *referring to* certain entities – their 'bearers' or 'referents' – the semantic difference between them resides not in the *nature* of their respective referents but only in the 'mode' of reference that they involve. Thus, on this view, whereas the individual term 'Julius Caesar' refers to just one particular man, the sortal term 'man', or 'men', does not refer to the sort *mankind*, conceived as having an objective existence distinct from that of any or all particular men, but rather refers *collectively* or *plurally* to all such particular men. In short, according to this view, 'man' just refers to *men in general*, rather than to any *man in particular*. Such an approach still permits us to go on talking about 'sorts', but only on the understanding that this is merely a way of talking about their individual members 'collectively'. The old-fashioned grammatical description *common name* for terms like 'man' may even seem to accord well with this proposal, the suggestion being that 'man' differs from 'Julius Caesar' only in being a name for *more than one individual* – that is, not only for *Caesar*, but also for *Brutus*, *Cassius*, and so on.

The basic difficulty with this account of the semantics of sortal terms may perhaps be brought out most graphically by recalling that most proper names in common use are *not*, of course, tied to a single individual: there are any number of different Joneses and Smiths and even quite a few different Caesars. That is to say, proper names themselves seem to have the very semantic property which, on the account under examination, is supposed to be distinctive of sortal terms *as opposed to* proper names. To this it may be objected that when a speaker uses a token of a certain proper name, such as 'John Smith', he or she will be using it to refer only to some *one* John Smith, not 'collectively' to all the various John Smiths that there are. This is, of course, normally true, but it raises the following further point. As the sentence immediately preceding the last itself shows, we *can* and *do* speak of John Smiths plurally or collectively, in what appears

---

[24]   Quine himself, it is worth remarking, seems to think that reliance on reference to sorts or kinds can be dispensed with in 'mature' or 'advanced' sciences: see W. V. Quine, 'Natural Kinds', in his *Ontological Relativity and Other Essays* (New York: Columbia University Press, 1969), p. 138. I see no reason for such optimism, which fails to recognize how deep-seated the individual/sort distinction is.

to be, according to the nominalist proposal now under consideration, the very way in which we allegedly speak of *men* and *horses* and so forth: and yet, of course, the John Smiths do *not* constitute the members of a distinct sort or kind, classifiable together as they are merely in virtue of their common possession of the name 'John Smith'. Plainly, we *do* assert generalizations such as 'John Smiths are plentiful in this part of town', which may superficially seem akin to ones like 'Elephants are plentiful in Africa'. But it is manifestly incorrect to suppose that the grammatical subjects of these two assertions submit to the same semantic treatment.

Of course, what one may be tempted to say in response to this objection is that 'man' functions as a genuine sortal term in a way in which 'John Smith' cannot simply because, although both *can* be understood as referring 'collectively' to a number of individuals, the individuals so referred to by 'man' are classifiable together not merely in virtue of their common possession of the name 'man', but rather in virtue of their all being individuals of the same sort or kind, *man*kind. But, transparently, this is not a response available to the nominalist, however plausible it might be in itself. Nor, clearly, will it do for the nominalist to say instead that the individuals referred to by 'man' are classifiable together in virtue of their common possession of certain *empirically describable characteristics*: for we have already seen that natural kind terms like 'man' are not definable or analysable in the way that this proposal would seem to require.

A further problem for the nominalist strategy now under examination – that of attributing to sortal terms only a distinctive *mode of reference* to individuals – is that, as I have repeatedly emphasized in this study, reference to individuals, whether it be 'singular' reference or the species of 'collective' reference now being canvassed, only makes sense relative to a background classification of individuals into sorts or kinds, since individuals are only *individuable* at all *qua* individuals *of some sort or other*. Hence, sense cannot be made of affirming of an individual that it belongs to a certain sort, φ – for instance, that it is a *man* – if the only account available of the meaning of the sortal term 'φ' is just that it refers collectively to a certain *plurality of individuals*: for this either just ignores or takes for granted as unproblematic what still remains to be accounted for, namely, the fact that each of these individuals can only be individuated as an individual *of some sort*.

That what may be called 'plural' – as opposed to 'singular' – reference is a genuine feature of natural language cannot, I think, be in doubt, somewhat neglected though it has been by modern logicians.[25] It is clearly at

---

[25] But, for one very important exception, see George Boolos, 'To Be Is to Be a Value of a Variable (or to Be Some Values of Some Variables)', *Journal of Philosophy* 81 (1984), pp. 430–49.

work in *plural* definite descriptions and demonstrative noun phrases, such as 'the horses in Farmer Brown's field' and 'those men'. What I am now contending is that the distinction between *individual* and *sortal* reference and quantification is not to be confused with that between *singular* and *plural* reference and quantification, which in fact cut quite across each other. One can, for instance, have *plural* reference to *sorts*, as is exemplified by the plural definite descriptions 'the mammals of Europe' and 'the inert gases'.

I should, incidentally, make it clear that my opposition to the nominalist strategy now under discussion by no means obliges me to *deny* that a sortal term like 'man' can refer 'collectively' or 'plurally', in the way suggested, to individual men 'in general'. For one thing, I can allow that it may do so precisely in virtue of referring – *singularly* – to a sort or kind of which they are all individual instances. And indeed it is highly plausible to say that, when one affirms some such nomic generalization as 'Men are bipeds', one *is* in some sense speaking 'about' *individual men* and not just 'about' the sort mankind, as it were *in abstracto*.

However, that is really beside the point. For, firstly, the *semantic* notion of 'reference' with which we are now concerned is not to be confused with the pragmatic notion of a speaker's using an expression to speak 'about' – and in this sense 'refer to' – an object or objects. And, secondly and more obviously, the observation in question – that 'Men are bipeds' concerns *individual men* – is entirely accommodated by the fact that 'Men are bipeds' may be expanded, *without alteration of either sense or logical form*, as '*Individual* men are bipeds': after all, there can be no men other than *individual* men! The real issue, though, is whether an adequate account of the meaning of the sortal term 'man' – or indeed 'individual man', with its redundant adjective – can be provided solely in terms of its semantic relations to certain *individuals* or *particulars*, or whether such an account should instead or additionally invoke the existence of a distinct *sort* or *kind* to which these individuals must be presumed to belong. I consider the latter to be the case. And that is why I consider that the apparent ineliminability from our discourse of sortal reference and quantification does indeed commit us ontologically to the objective reality of sorts or kinds.

As for the *style* of realism regarding sorts or kinds that I favour, I lean very much towards the 'Aristotelian' or 'immanent' – as opposed to the 'Platonic' or 'transcendent' – position. According to this approach, the existence of sorts should be seen as *distinct* but not *separable* from that of their individual instances – and this is why I am loath to countenance the existence of sorts that are not individually instantiated. But I should stress that my 'Aristotelianism' does not involve the notion that individuals or particulars are in any sense 'more real' than sorts or kinds, or that they somehow enjoy a more fundamental species of existence – for 'exist', I believe, is perfectly univocal. Individuals may indeed be 'ontologically prior' to the sorts that they instantiate, in the sense that the existence of the individuals *grounds* the existence of their sorts, but not *vice versa*. But we can acknowledge such 'existential grounding' while at the same time insisting that individuals are no less essentially individuals *of some sort* than sorts are essentially sorts *of individuals*. The notion of ontological dependency is a complex and multifaceted one, capable of accommodating *both* the thought that sorts are, in *one* sense, asymmetrically dependent for their existence upon their individual instances, *and* the thought that, in *another* sense, there is a symmetrical essential dependency between individuals and sorts.[26]

---

[26]   For more about such matters, see my *The Possibility of Metaphysics: Substance, Identity, and Time* (Oxford: Clarendon Press, 1998), Chapter 6.

10

Plural Quantification and Sortal Reference

Towards the end of the preceding chapter, I argued in favour of a certain view concerning the semantics of sortal terms and quantifiers, according to which our use of such expressions commits us ontologically to *sorts* or *kinds*, conceived as *universals* rather than particulars, or pluralities of particulars. But I am acutely aware of the hostility to this view that will be felt in many philosophical and logical quarters. Consequently, I propose, in this chapter, to revisit the issue in more depth. I suspect that my view is one that would meet with little resistance from anyone not habituated to seeing the syntactic structures of natural language through the distorting lens of orthodox first-order quantificational logic. Unfortunately, however, almost all modern analytic philosophers are so habituated by their training.

My basic claim is just this: that we standardly use common nouns to refer to *sorts* or *kinds* of individuals. That is to say, common nouns really are *names*, quite on a par with proper names. But they do not – unlike proper names – name individuals: rather, they name *kinds* of individuals. It should be evident at once why this claim should appear alien to anyone brought up on the formalism of orthodox first-order predicate logic. For that formalism simply has no resources for distinguishing between adjectives and verbs on the one hand and common nouns on the other: all are lumped together as 'predicates'. And the referential apparatus of the formalism is restricted to *individual* constants and variables of quantification. So much the worse for the formalism, say I. Without more ado, let us see why.

One of the lessons that we are supposed to have learned from Frege and Russell is that many noun phrases in natural language actually function as quantifier expressions rather than as referring expressions, despite their syntactical similarities with proper names. Thus – to take a famous example of Russell's[1] – the indefinite noun phrase 'a man' in the sentence

(1)   I met a man

is properly to be understood as playing the role of an existential quantifier expression, rather than as referring to an individual. Thus, (1) is to be analysed as being equivalent to something like

(2)   For some x, x is a man and I met x.

Of course, (2) itself contains an open sentence which again features the indefinite noun phrase 'a man', namely,

(3) x is a man

and hence the move from (1) to (2) may not appear to advance matters much. However, such a criticism would be too swift, because it is open to us to maintain that the predicate '— is a man' is a simple semantic unit, which cannot plausibly be urged on behalf of the predicate '— met a man' in (1). To urge this on behalf of the latter would require us to do likewise for innumerable other predicates, such as '— saw a man', '— hit a man' and so forth, which would render unanalysable their mutual logico-semantic relations and also render inexplicable our ability to learn their meanings systematically.

This is not, of course, the only way in which the apparent difficulty can be circumvented. One could instead contend, for instance, that although '— is a man' is *not* a simple semantic unit – because, on this view, the 'is' featuring in it makes a distinctive and separable contribution to the meaning of the predicate – 'a man' does not function there in the same way as it functions in (1), in which it does indeed function as an existential quantifier expression. Such, in fact, is my own view, as I shall explain more fully in due course.

However, there is yet another way of approaching the issue which agrees with the spirit of the Frege–Russell analysis of (1) without generating the apparent difficulty raised by (2)'s incorporation of (3). On this approach, we may again say that 'a man' in (1) functions as an existential quantifier expression, but render this perspicuous by analysing (1) not as (2) but as

[1]   See Bertrand Russell, 'On Denoting', in his *Logic and Knowledge: Essays 1901–1950*, ed. R. C. Marsh (London: George Allen and Unwin, 1956), p. 43. The paper originally appeared in *Mind* 14 (1905), pp. 479–93.

(4)   For some man x, I met x

in which the indefinite noun phrase 'a man' no longer appears at all. Analogously, (3) itself may now be analysed as

(5)   For some man y, $x = y$.

A *prima facie* problem with this analysis, it should be said, is that if it were correct, then 'x is *not* a man' ought seemingly to exhibit *scope ambiguity* and be interpretable under one resolution of that ambiguity as meaning 'For some man y, $x \neq y$' – which is not the case.[2] This problem does not beset the view that '— is a man' in (3) is a simple semantic unit, nor does it beset the analysis of (3) that I myself shall eventually come to espouse below.

Of course, if this third approach – invoking so-called 'restricted' quantifiers – really is to avoid the apparent difficulty raised earlier, then it must be maintained that (4) is not just a stylistic variant of (2), with the latter constituting the logically prior form. And, indeed, it had better be argued not just that (4) has different truth-conditions from (2) but that (2) itself is in some way defective or improper, on account of its employment of an 'unrestricted' quantifier. I myself do not believe that a convincing argument to this conclusion exists. Sentences featuring restricted quantifiers should be seen as merely stylistic variants of ones featuring unrestricted quantifiers, rather than as having their own distinctive truth-conditions. However, neither of these opinions of mine is particularly crucial to what follows, since it will emerge that there are contexts in which certain types of noun phrase, while not functioning as individual referring expressions after the manner of proper names, cannot by *any* account be seen as functioning as quantifier expressions either – and this will be the chief burden of this chapter. Accordingly, in order to emphasize the irrelevance to my present purposes of the dispute over restricted versus unrestricted quantifiers, I shall in fact adopt henceforth the restricted style, which also has the advantages of clarity and brevity.

So far I have concentrated on the analysis of sentences containing *indefinite* noun phrases, that is, noun phrases of the form '*a* so-and-so'. But similar issues arise in the case of *plural* noun phrases, that is, noun phrases of the form 'so-and-so*s*'. Indeed, it is often assumed that this grammatical distinction in general reflects no logical distinction of any real importance,

---

[2]   Compare James Higgenbotham, 'Indefiniteness and Predication', in E. J. Reuland and A. G. B. ter Meulen (eds), *The Representation of Indefiniteness* (Cambridge, MA: MIT Press, 1987), p. 50.

so that many a logic textbook would suggest that not only (1) above but equally the sentence

(6) I met men

may be analysed as either (2) or (4) above. In fact, of course, this seems unacceptable as an observation about actual English usage, since (6) unlike (1) would normally be taken to imply that I met *more than one* man.

However, it may seem easy enough to accommodate this point by analysing (6) not as (4) but as something like

(7) For some man x, for some man y, $x \neq y$ and I met x and I met y.

Yet one might still feel less than entirely satisfied with (7) as an analysis of (6), at least on one interpretation of the latter – namely, on the interpretation which implies that I met some men *collectively* rather than *severally*. Observe here that the definite description 'the men that I met', as it might characteristically be invoked in such circumstances, very arguably needs to be treated as involving what is now called *plural reference*. Such reference is not to be confused with reference to the *set* or *group* whose members the objects referred to are. That is to say, 'the men that I met' does not refer *singularly* to the set or group of men that I met, but rather refers *plurally* or *collectively* to those very men.

Now, if plural reference to individuals is a semantic phenomenon which we cannot ignore or analyse away, then arguably we also need variables of quantification which take pluralities of individuals as their values. And this would suggest that (6), at least on one possible interpretation of that sentence, should in fact be analysed not as (7) but as

(8) For some men X, I met X

where the upper case 'X' is just such a variable.[3] In what follows I shall assume that plural quantification does indeed need to be invoked to

---

[3] For more on plural quantification and related issues, see Richard Sharvy, 'A More General Theory of Definite Descriptions', *Philosophical Review* 89 (1980), pp. 607–24, George Boolos, 'To Be Is to Be a Value of a Variable (or to Be Some Values of Some Variables)', *Journal of Philosophy* 81 (1984), pp. 430–49, George Boolos, 'Nominalist Platonism', *Philosophical Review* 94 (1985), pp. 327–44, and David Lewis, *Parts of Classes* (Oxford: Blackwell, 1991), pp. 62–71. Like Lewis, I have some doubts concerning Boolos's assimilation of plural quantification to second-order quantification, for further criticisms of which see Michael D. Resnik, 'Second-Order Logic Still Wild', *Journal of Philosophy* 85 (1988), pp. 75–87.

explain one semantic role which plural noun phrases can sometimes play in natural language.

I shall now turn to certain occurrences of plural noun phrases in which they *cannot*, I believe, be construed as functioning as quantifier expressions in any of the ways so far canvassed, nor even in other ways yet to be suggested. Consider, then, a sentence such as the following:

(9)   Fido chases cats.

On the most natural interpretation of what this sentence means, it seems clear that (9) is *not* analysable as involving an existential quantifier whose variable ranges over either individuals or pluralities of individuals. Thus, (9) is evidently not equivalent to

(10)   For some cat x, Fido chases x

since (10) could be true and yet (9) false. For instance, (10) could be true because Fido chases toothless old Tibbles and yet (9) still be false because Fido flees in terror from almost any other cat. In short, in such circumstances it is not relevant to the fact that Fido chases Tibbles that Tibbles is a *cat*: indeed, it is only because Tibbles is a pretty poor specimen of catkind that Fido chases her at all.

For the same reason, (9) is not – again on its most natural interpretation – analysable as

(11)   For some cat x, for some cat y, $x \neq y$ and Fido chases x and Fido chases y.

Merely multiplying the individual cats which Fido may be said to chase cannot as such suffice to make it true of him that he *chases cats*, in the sense that we are now trying to pin down.

Again, it will not do to suggest that (9) in our intended sense is analysable as

(12)   For some cats X, Fido chases X

where the variable of quantification ranges over pluralities of cats. I do not deny that there may be a reading of (9) on which it does have this sense, but that is not the reading which now concerns us. For what would entail (12)'s truth would be the truth of some such sentence as

(13)   Fido chases the cats in our alley

where the definite description 'the cats in our alley' refers collectively to a certain plurality of cats. But the truth of (13) does not suffice to render (9) true, in the sense of (9) that we now have in mind, since Fido might once again flee in terror from almost any other cat or cats.

Nor will it do to invoke a *universal* rather than an existential quantifier in the analysis of (9). Just as (10), (11) and (12) were all too weak to pose as equivalents of (9), so

(14)   For any cat x, Fido chases x

and indeed

(15)   For any cats X, Fido chases X

are both too strong. Clearly, (9) can be true even though there is *some cat* – or are *some cats* – from whom Fido flees in terror, such as the monstrous and fearsome *Tom*, the bane of all dogs in the neighbourhood. In any case, would we want to deny that *Fido chases cats* simply because there are cats in *Japan* which he does not chase, when Fido has lived all his life in suburban London? Surely not. (That he *would* chase them, given the opportunity, may indeed be significant for the truth of (9), but is perfectly compatible with a denial of (14) or (15). That he *would* chase them does not imply that he *does*.) For the same reason, it will not do to suggest that (9) is analysable as meaning something like

(16)   For *most* cats x, Fido chases x.

What, then, *is* required for the truth of (9), under the interpretation which we are trying to elucidate? Perhaps we can begin to get some grip on the problem by considering what *difference* to truth-conditions is made by exchanging the plural noun 'cats' in (9) by another plural noun, such as 'rats', as in

(17)   Fido chases rats.

Intuitively, the difference between (9) and (17) is solely a difference concerning *what*, according to each sentence, Fido chases. But how, exactly, are we to characterize the semantic status of the noun phrase 'what Fido chases', as one is inclined to use it here? On the face of it, it looks as though it is a *referring* expression of some kind. And, indeed, there are uses of this very expression in which it undoubtedly does have a referential role, namely, one of either singular or plural reference to one or more *individuals*. Thus, 'what Fido chases' could, in suitable circumstances, be taken to refer to

Tibbles, or to *the cats in our alley*. But, clearly, the context of use with which we are now concerned is not one such as these.

Another way of focusing on the same issue is to point out that there is a certain interpretation of the question

(18)   Does Fido chase anything?

on which (9) and (17) would both be taken as supporting the answer 'Yes', and correspondingly an interpretation of the sentence

(19)   Fido chases something

which might intuitively be seen as following from both (9) and (17) by the rule of existential generalization. Clearly, though, the domain of quantification which would need to be invoked in interpreting a sentence like (19), thus understood, would not be one whose elements were either individuals or pluralities of individuals.

If the noun phrase 'what Fido chases', as used above, *is* a referring expression and 'something', as used in (19), *does* involve a domain of quantification whose elements are not individuals, then *what* is referred to and *what* are those elements? The obvious – and I think the *right* – answers are that a *sort* or *kind* of individuals is referred to and that *sorts* or *kinds* of individuals are the elements of the domain. This view – to which, of course, I have already committed myself in previous chapters of this book – does, I concede, encounter some *prima facie* difficulties which need to be overcome. However, if it is correct, then it will supply us with the following answer to our original question of how we are to interpret the plural noun phrase 'cats', as it appears in (9): that plural noun functions there as what we may appropriately call a *singular sortal referring expression*.

One *prima facie* difficulty with treating 'cats' in (9) as a singular sortal referring expression, which has a certain sort or kind of animals as its reference, is that this may appear to be tantamount to holding that (9) is equivalent to something like

(20)   Fido chases the cat species

and this seems plainly mistaken. But this presupposes that I should have to regard the noun phrase 'the cat species' in (20) as involving *singular sortal reference*, as I propose that we understand the latter semantic phenomenon. In fact, however, it seems proper for me to hold that 'the cat species' involves singular *individual* reference: that is, that a species – in the biological sense, at least – should be regarded as an individual and that sorts should not be assimilated to species. (I concede that in earlier parts of this book I have not always respected this distinction, but that was because it only becomes pressing in cases such as the present one, where we are concerned with 'species' as these are understood by current biological science.)

The cat species, I suggest, is best understood as being a mereological sum of individual animals *all of the same sort or kind*, namely, *catkind*.[4] In defence of this suggestion I would point out that we happily regard the cat species as having a history and a geographical distribution – in short, as having a spatiotemporal distribution – whereas sorts or kinds, being universals, are very arguably not literally occupants of space and time at all.[5]

Another objection is that if 'cats' in (9) does, as I propose, involve singular reference to a sort and sorts are indeed universals rather than particulars (individuals), then it seems unclear how Fido could be said to *chase* such a thing. How can one chase something that is not even an occupant of space and time? Now, in the first place, it should be pointed out that (9), on the current proposal, is not being represented as differing in any way in its sense from

(21)   Fido chases individual cats

since, clearly, the qualification 'individual' in (21) is entirely redundant. (What other cats are there but *individual* ones?) Thus, although it is proposed that 'cats' in (9) *refers to a sort of animals*, it is not therefore being suggested that (9) somehow does not concern, or is not 'about', *individuals* of that sort: for 'individual cats' in (21) has the same reference, yet obviously does not lack that concern.

But, furthermore, it would in any case be wrong to presume that a transitive verb like 'chase' must have a perfectly univocal sense irrespective of whether its grammatical object refers to an individual or a sort – in short, that 'chases' in 'chases Tibbles' and 'chases cats' has precisely the same sense. Systematic ambiguity of this type is a common enough semantic phenomenon. For instance, we should be happy enough to allow that we do not *count numbers* in precisely the same sense that we may *count chairs*,

---

[4]   Observe that circularity in this proposal can be avoided only on the presumption that catkind is indeed *not* to be identified with the cat species – a presumption which is confirmed by the fact that we speak of individual cats being *members* of the cat species but *instances* of catkind. For another defence of the view that biological species are individuals, see D. L. Hull, 'Are Species Really Individuals?', *Systematic Zoology* 25 (1976), pp. 174–91.

[5]   That universals are not occupants of space and time is something that I argue for in my *The Possibility of Metaphysics: Substance, Identity, and Time* (Oxford: Clarendon Press, 1998), pp. 155–6.

although the two senses are obviously very closely related. (It is indeed a matter of indifference to us whether we are asked to count the *number* of chairs in the room or simply to count the *chairs*: but from the equivalence in meaning of these two requests we cannot, of course, infer an identity of meaning between the two uses of the verb 'count'.) Certainly, it will be incumbent upon someone adopting my proposal to offer some *account* of the systematic ambiguity of verbs like 'chase' which the proposal seems to entail: but it is not any *flaw* in the proposal that it should incur this obligation, provided that such an account can in fact be given. And, indeed, we shall see in Chapter 11 that it *can*.

Yet another objection is that, on the current proposal, it may appear obscure what sort of empirical evidence could be brought to bear upon the truth or falsehood of a sentence like (9). My answer is that we must be careful not to confuse epistemological with semantic and ontological issues. The sort of empirical evidence which *would* support or undermine the truth of (9) is something that is broadly familiar to us all, although it is by no means a *simple* matter. If Fido is found to chase a good many different cats, of varying sizes, colours, ages and temperaments, then, *ceteris paribus*, we shall consider (9) to be empirically well supported – and if not, then not. But we should not, of course, confuse evidence with what it is evidence for. We should not assume, just because the evidence concerns Fido's behaviour towards a number of different individual cats, that therefore the proposition which this evidence confirms must likewise relate to those individual cats rather than to catkind.

So far I have attempted to rebut some likely objections to the thesis that the plural noun 'cats' in (9) functions as a singular sortal referring expression – that it has there the status of what, in the remainder of this chapter, I shall call a *generic name*. But more needs to be done now by way of providing positive evidence in favour of the thesis. The fact that the plural noun in question cannot, as we have seen, plausibly be regarded as functioning as an individual quantifier expression of any kind certainly rules out the most likely rivals to my thesis, but does not in itself constitute positive evidence in favour of it. Unfortunately, my task is hampered somewhat by the apparent absence of any generally agreed criteria for the acceptance of a thesis like mine – a thesis to the effect that expressions of a certain class function as names or referring expressions.

One criterion which we could perhaps invoke – calling to mind the Quinean dictum that 'to be is to be the value of a variable'[6] – is that an

---

[6]   See W. V. Quine, 'A Logistical Approach to the Ontological Problem', in his *The Ways of Paradox and Other Essays* (Cambridge, MA: Harvard University Press, 1976), p. 199.

occurrence of an expression is name-like if its position in a sentence is open to government by a quantifier, on the grounds that it must then be taken to name some element in the domain of quantification. On this criterion it is significant that, as we saw earlier, (9) is taken to entail

(19)   Fido chases something.

For 'something' here cannot be taken to be functioning as an *individual* existential quantifier expression and so, if 'cats' in (9) must, in accordance the suggested criterion, be taken to name some element in the domain of quantification appropriate to an interpretation of this quantified sentence, then the element in question must be something other than an individual (or plurality of individuals) – so why not, indeed, a *sort* or *kind* of individuals? My own feeling is that this line of argument should be fairly persuasive, but I realize that not everyone will share my views about the ontological implications of the semantics of quantificational sentences, particularly those who favour a 'substitutional' interpretation of the quantifiers over an 'objectual' one. (See again, here, my extended discussion of such matters in Chapter 9 above.)

However, a quite different consideration which might be adduced in favour of my thesis is the following. It should be noticed that just as (9) differs from

(22)   Fido chases Tibbles

in containing the plural noun 'cats' in place of the proper name 'Tibbles', so there are sentences which differ from (9) in containing yet other plural nouns in place of the proper name 'Fido' – for example:

(23)   Dogs chase cats.

Moreover, all the arguments deployed earlier against the possibility of 'cats' in (9) functioning as an individual quantifier expression may be adapted to show equally that neither 'dogs' nor 'cats' has such a function in (23). And in this case we can appeal to another supplementary argument to this effect, which also lends support of a positive nature to the contention that both of these plural nouns in fact function as generic names here.

The argument in question is one based on the widely – albeit not universally – accepted view that quantifier expressions *are*, while names are *not*, subject to distinctions of *scope*.[7] Thus, to take a familiar example, the sentence

---

[7]   See, for example, P. T. Geach, 'Quine's Syntactical Insights', in his *Logic Matters* (Oxford: Blackwell, 1972), pp. 116ff.

(24)   Every boy loves some girl

is open to interpretation in two different ways, depending on whether or not 'every' is taken to have wider scope than 'some'. Now, it seems clear that (23) – as it would normally be construed – does *not* exhibit this phenomenon, any more than does a sentence like (22) which contains two proper names. And this suggests that (23) likewise contains two *names*, but this time 'generic' ones.

Of course, an isolated example like (23) cannot provide conclusive evidence of the absence of scope distinctions where plural nouns are used in the way that they are here, since there *are* sentences containing pairs of quantifier expressions which are unambiguous not because scope distinctions are *absent* but simply because it makes no difference to truth-conditions *which* expression is taken to have wider scope – for example:

(25)   Some boy loves some girl.

But now it should be added that, where quantifier expressions are concerned, scope ambiguity can of course arise not only in cases in which two or more such expressions interact with each other in a sentence, but also in cases in which a single such expression interacts with a logical expression of another kind, such as a negative particle. Thus

(26)   John does not love some girl

exhibits scope ambiguity, arising from the fact that either 'not' or 'some' may be taken as having the wider scope. But it is apparent that

(27)   Fido does not chase cats

is not ambiguous in this way, any more than is

(28)   John does not love Mary

which again tends to confirm that the occurrence of 'cats' in (27), as that sentence would normally be construed, is scopeless and hence name-like.

The same seems to apply to the sentence

(29)   Dogs do not chase cats

in respect of the occurrences of both plural nouns. This consideration may appear to be particularly telling in favour of the thesis that I am now trying to defend. (However, matters may not be quite as simple as they presently seem to be, as will emerge in Chapter 11, where we shall see that sentences like (29) appear to call for a distinction to be drawn between two different types of negation: *sentence* negation and *predicate* negation.)

One final piece of evidence which may be construed as supporting the view that plural noun phrases sometimes function as generic names is the fact, which I am by no means the first to have noticed, that plural nouns have certain close affinities with *mass* nouns. Thus, (9) and (23) may usefully be compared with, respectively,

(30)   Fido eats meat

and

(31)   Water dissolves sugar.

The affinities of which I speak include, strikingly, the admissibility of both plural and mass nouns in certain grammatical constructions expressive of *quantity*: thus, we may talk of 'lots of cats' and 'more cats' in what appears to be much the same way in which we talk of 'lots of water' and 'more water' and, indeed – deplored by grammatical purists though it may be – it is increasingly common now to hear people say 'less cats' (rather than 'fewer cats'), just as they say 'less water'. The relevance of these affinities is simply that it will not, I suspect, seem particularly novel or controversial to suggest that the mass nouns in sentences like (30) and (31) do not function as quantifier expressions, are not subject to scope distinctions, and do in fact have the status of *names*.

Now, some philosophers, it is true, take the view that the mass nouns involved in such sentences as (30) and (31) function in effect as *proper* names, that is, as singular individual referring expressions which have as their references certain 'scattered' particulars. On this view, 'water' as it appears in (31) may be taken to name the mereological sum of all the various portions or bodies or quantities of water that are scattered about the world.[8] This would be to treat the reference of the mass noun 'water' much as I earlier suggested that we treat the reference of the singular term 'the cat species'. But for precisely the same reasons that I would *not* wish to assimilate use of the plural noun 'cats' to use of the latter singular term, I would also wish to resist the current suggestion that the mass noun 'water' in (31) functions as an *individual* referring expression. I would again wish to urge that it functions as a *sortal* referring expression, or generic name, having as its reference *waterkind* – a *universal* rather than a *particular*. If

[8]   See, for example, W. V. Quine, *Word and Object* (Cambridge, MA: MIT Press, 1960), p. 98.

we seek a term which *does* function in the way that the mass noun 'water' has – wrongly, as I believe – just been said to function, then we have one ready to hand in such a term as 'the world's water' or 'all the water in the world'.

However, despite this disagreement over the question of whether mass nouns function as *individual* or as *sortal* referring expressions, it is still significant that there is not undue resistance to the view that they do at least have the status of *names*, for this I think provides reassurance for those who, like myself, wish to extend this status also to plural noun phrases in certain of their uses.

I shall conclude by returning briefly to the concerns with which this chapter opened. We saw at the outset that there are two different approaches which may be adopted in making explicit the idea that the indefinite noun phrase 'a man' in

(1)   I met a man

functions as an individual quantifier expression. Using *unrestricted* quantification, we may analyse (1) as

(2)   For some x, x is a man and I met x

whereas, using *restricted* quantification, we may analyse it as

(4)   For some man x, I met x.

The latter approach has the seeming advantage of eliminating altogether any occurrence of the indefinite noun phrase 'a man', whereas on the former approach this recurs in the *analysans* in the context of the predicate '— is a man'. I remarked, however, that it was open to an adherent of this approach to urge that in the latter context 'a man' does not make an independent contribution to the meaning of the predicate, as it clearly must in the case of a predicate like '— met a man': the claim being that '— is a man' is a *simple semantic unit*, which is just to say that it is not further analysable.

However, I must now point out that neither this proposal on behalf of the unrestricted quantifier approach, nor the proposal of the alternative restricted quantifier approach, can be regarded as entirely satisfactory, in the light of the conclusions that I have reached concerning generic names. Either proposal might have been defensible if I had not succeeded in showing – as I think I have – that a plural noun like 'men' may sometimes function as a singular sortal referring expression. But now that I have, as

I take it, established this point, the question arises as to how *this* use of the *plural* form of the common noun 'man' is semantically and logically related to the use of its *singular* form, as it appears either in the context of the supposedly unanalysable predicate '— is a *man*' or in the context of the restricted quantifier expression 'for some *man x*'.

The solution to this problem that I favour is to adopt the unrestricted quantifier approach by analysing (1) in terms of (2), but to regard the predicate '— is a man' *not* as a simple semantic unit but rather as semantically complex, with the indefinite noun phrase 'a man' functioning here once more as a *generic name*, taking *mankind* (a universal) as its reference, while the 'is' functions as what, in Chapter 3, I called the 'is' of *instantiation*. This 'is' simply expresses the relation that obtains between a particular and a sortal universal when the former is an *instance* of the latter. By adopting this position it is possible for me to maintain that, while 'a man' and 'men' may function at the level of 'surface grammar' sometimes as quantifier expressions and sometimes as referring expressions, in a perspicuous representation of the logical form of sentences containing these noun phrases they will *always* appear in a referential role, functioning as generic names.

Observe that this claim is perfectly consistent with what I said earlier concerning plural individual quantifier expressions. For instance, we can now analyse

(6)   I met men

as

(32)   For some X, X are men and I met X

where the variable 'X' ranges over pluralities of individuals and the 'are' in 'X are men' is just the plural form of the 'is' of instantiation. The plural noun 'men' in the latter context is, thus, once again to be seen as functioning as a generic name.

Note, incidentally, that we do not have to regard the plural form of the 'is' of instantiation, 'are' in (32), as being logically irreducible, because we can take 'X are men' simply to mean 'For all x, if x is one of X, then x is a man'. We need the 'is one of' construction in any case, in sentences such as 'Tom is one of the Brown brothers', though it seems clear that this construction is *not* further reducible.[9] Thus we see, for instance, that 'The Brown brothers *are* men' just means, in effect, 'Each of the Brown brothers *is* a man'.

---

[9]   See further my *The Possibility of Metaphysics*, pp. 221–2.

The conclusion, therefore, of this chapter is not only that indefinite and plural noun phrases such as 'a man' and 'men', or 'a cat', and 'cats', *may* function as generic names, but that in a perspicuous representation of the logical form of the sentences in which they appear they will *only* function as generic names. In short, common nouns exist purely in order to name what is common to individuals of the same sort, namely, the *sort* of individuals that they are.

11

Laws, Dispositions, and Sortal Logic

The view to which the arguments of the preceding two chapters lead is the following. Dispositional predications with sortal terms in subject position – that is, nomic generalizations – form a fundamental and semantically irreducible category of elementary sentence, just as do occurrent predications with individual terms in subject position. We shall see in due course, however, that dispositional predications with *individual* terms in subject position and occurrent predications with *sortal* terms in subject position are *not* irreducible.[1] All this being so, however, the categories and symbolism of currently favoured systems of formal logic – in particular, standard first-order predicate logic with identity and modal extensions of it – are quite obviously inadequate for some of our most important scientific and philosophical purposes, so they need to be revised accordingly. I shall now briefly indicate the key revisions that I have in mind.

I shall begin by describing a simple formalized sortal language, which I shall call 'FSL'. The *vocabulary* of FSL consists of these symbols:

---

[1] In point of fact, if we endorse the *four-category* ontology described in the Introduction and further developed in my *The Four-Category Ontology: A Metaphysical Foundation for Natural Science* (Oxford: Clarendon Press, 2006), then it becomes apparent that the dispositional/occurrent distinction is *never* irreducible. For example, we can say that an individual, *a*, is *occurrently F* just in case *a* is characterized by a mode, *m*, of the attribute *F*ness. However, for the purposes of the present chapter I am explicitly invoking only *two* of the four ontological categories of this system – the category of *individuals* (that is, individual objects) and the category of *sorts* or *kinds*, of which such individuals are particular instances.

Non-logical vocabulary

Objectual symbols

individual constants: a, b, c, . . .
individual variables: x, y, z, . . .
sortal constants: α, β, γ, . . .
sortal variables: φ, χ, ψ, . . .

Predicate symbols

n-ary predicate letters: F^n, G^n, H^n, . . .

Logical vocabulary

identity sign: $=$
instantiation sign: $/$
truth-functional operators: $\sim$, $\&$, $\vee$, $\rightarrow$, $\leftrightarrow$
quantifiers: $\exists$, $\forall$
brackets: $($, $)$

The *syntax* of FSL may be described as follows. *Atomic* formulas of FSL consist of either (1) an n-ary predicate letter either *preceded* or *followed* by a string of n objectual symbols or (2) either the identity sign or the instantiation sign flanked in each case by a pair of objectual symbols. Complex formulas are constructed from atomic ones and the logical vocabulary of FSL in the usual manner – that is to say, truth-functional operators may be used to construct compound formulas from simpler ones and quantifiers may be used to bind free variables. Thus, in its syntactical appearance, FSL differs from a standard formal language of first-order predicate logic with identity only in containing (1) instantiation formulas, (2) two styles of predication and (3) two types of constants and variables.

Now I need to say something about the *semantics* of FSL. By the 'informal semantics' of a formalized language I mean its intended interpretation in terms of natural language. I contrast *informal* semantics in this sense with *formal* semantics, or so-called model theory, with which I shall not be concerned at present. Inevitably, informal semantics is, to a degree, an imprecise device for attaching meaning to symbols, simply because the semantic and syntactic distinctions of natural language are themselves imprecise. Nonetheless, I would contend, it is ultimately only in virtue of its informal semantics that a formalized language can be regarded as having any substantive philosophical interest. This is, firstly, because natural language is the primary vehicle of human thought and, secondly, because the construction of a formal semantics, while it may be indispensable for certain metalogical purposes, is an exercise which need pay scant regard to any practical application of the formalized language in question. This accepted, briefly what we may say concerning the informal semantics of FSL is as follows, beginning with the interpretation of atomic formulas.

Individual constants of FSL serve to translate proper names in natural language, while sortal constants serve to translate semantically simple sortal terms (although, more cautiously, we should perhaps say only that they serve to translate simple *natural kind* terms). Next, *n*-ary predicate letters serve to translate *n*-adic *dispositional* or *occurrent* predicates. They *never*, thus, serve to translate predicates to which the dispositional/occurrent distinction simply does not apply, such as '— is a horse' or '— is identical with . . .'. When an *n*-ary predicate letter is *preceded* by a string of *n* objectual symbols, *dispositional* predication is thereby expressed. When an *n*-ary predicate letter is *followed* by a string of *n* objectual symbols, *occurrent* predication is thereby expressed. The identity sign serves to translate the 'is' of identity, while the instantiation sign serves to translate the 'is' of instantiation, so that we may use the instantiation formula 'a/β' to translate a sentence such as 'Fido is (a) dog' and the instantiation formula 'β/γ' to translate a sentence such as 'Dogs are mammals'.

Incidentally, the syntax of FSL permits the instantiation sign to be flanked on *both* sides by individual symbols, but we can stipulate that any such instantiation formula is to be regarded as equivalent to the corresponding *identity* formula, so that 'Cicero is Tully' may be represented indifferently either by the formula '$a = b$' or by the formula 'a/b'. We may also stipulate that any sentential formula in which the instantiation sign is flanked by a *sortal* symbol on its *left* and an *individual* symbol on its *right* is false, because no *sort* can be an instance of an *individual*.

The truth-functional operators of FSL may be translated in the customary ways as meaning 'not', 'and', 'or', 'if, . . . then', and 'if and only if', with all the usual precautions and provisos about the limitations of some of these translations, especially those involving 'if'. Quantifiers are used with individual variables to provide a means of translating of individual quantifier expressions, such as 'some (particular) horse', and with sortal variables to provide a means of translating sortal quantifier expressions, such as 'every (sort of) mammal'. For example, 'Some horse is eating grass' may be represented by '$\exists x(x/\alpha \ \& \ F^1 x)$', where '$\alpha$' translates '(a) horse' and 'F^1' (taking its argument on the *right* to express *occurrent* predication) translates '— is eating grass'. By contrast, 'Some mammals eat grass' may be represented by '$\exists \varphi(\varphi/\beta \ \& \ \varphi F^1)$', where '$\beta$' translates 'mammal(s)' and 'F^1' (taking its argument of the *left* to express *dispositional* predication) translates '— eats grass'. (Of course, we could if wished break these sentences down still further, translating the mass noun 'grass' by a sortal symbol and the dyadic predicate(s) '— is eating/eats . . .' by a binary predicate letter,

'G^2'.) By these means, thus, we are able to represent both of the following entailments as being, quite equally, consequences of existential generalization: the entailment of 'Some horse is eating grass' by 'Dobbin is a horse and Dobbin is eating grass' and the entailment of 'Some mammals eat grass' by 'Horses are mammals and horses eat grass'.

It is important to point out that, although FSL clearly differs in its expressive power from a standard first-order formal language, there is still a perfectly good sense in which it is only a 'first-order' language, because it involves no quantification into *predicate* positions. Of course, a *standard* first-order formal language would be compelled to translate a sortal term in natural language by means of a predicate letter, representing 'Fido is (a) dog', say, by an atomic predicative formula such as 'F^1a', whereas FSL would represent it by an *instantiation* formula, such as 'a/β'. However, the mere fact that, in FSL, quantification into the position occupied by 'β' in such a formula *is* allowed, whereas in a standard first-order formal language quantification into the position occupied by the predicate letter 'F^1' in 'F^1a' is *not* allowed, does not imply that FSL is somehow covertly a 'second-order' language. It just reveals that the domain of 'objects' over which quantification is permitted in FSL is wider than that of standard first-order formal languages, inasmuch as it includes *sorts* as well as individuals. It should also be pointed out that FSL is, of course, a purely *extensional* language.

It can be seen that, in FSL, atomic monadic predicative formulas fall into four categories, depending on whether the predication is dispositional or occurrent and on whether the objectual symbol is an individual or a sortal one. I have already indicated that, of the four corresponding basic types of sentence in natural language, I am now taking two to be primitive and irreducible: dispositional predications with sortal terms in subject position and occurrent predications with individual terms in subject position. However, that *occurrent* predications with *sortal* terms in subject position are very arguably *not* irreducible was recognized in Chapter 9, where it was observed that a sentence such as 'A horse is eating grass' is plausibly analysable in terms of an existentially quantified conjunction, '$\exists x(x$ is a horse and x is eating grass)'. Notice that one of the conjuncts here, 'x is a horse', has the form of an instantiation sentence while the other, 'x is eating grass', is an occurrent predication with an individual variable in subject position.

Formally, we may represent the principle involved in such a reduction by means of the following biconditional, whose universal closure we may correspondingly take to be a *theorem of sortal logic*:

SL1. $F^1\varphi \leftrightarrow \exists x(x/\varphi \ \& \ F^1x)$

Before we proceed, some comments on this proposed reduction are in order.

First of all, it should be recalled, from the discussion of this matter in Chapter 9, that the indefinite article preceding the sortal term 'horse' in the sentence '*A* horse is eating grass' is to be regarded as *logically redundant* when that sentence is interpreted, as it is now, as being merely a stylistic variant of the sentence 'Horse*s* are eating grass'. That there *is* such an interpretation, according to which the difference between the singular and plural forms of the sortal term in question is logically irrelevant, I take to be uncontroversial. In fact, I take it that this is the standard interpretation, even if others are admissible. On this interpretation, both of these sentences convey a proposition which could alternatively, if less idiomatically, be expressed by the sentence 'Grass is being horse-eaten', in which no distinctions of *number* are associated with the sortal term 'horse'. That is why it is appropriate to use the existential quantifier '∃' in SL1, for this is standardly read as meaning 'there is *at least one* . . .', which is consistent with both 'there is *exactly* one' and 'there is *more than* one'. Where only *mass* nouns rather than *count* nouns are in play, of course, this issue does not even arise at all. Thus, for example, 'Water is dissolving salt' – used, perhaps, to describe what is going on in some test-tube – quite unproblematically submits to the reduction represented by SL1, being equivalent to '∃x(x is water and x is dissolving salt)'.

Another point deserving a brief mention here concerns the status of a sentence obtained by *negating* one such as 'A horse is eating grass' – in this case, 'A horse is *not* eating grass'. It needs to be remarked at once that, for reasons which will be examined thoroughly in Chapter 12, when the logical distinction between dispositional and occurrent predication is properly recognized, a distinction must also be recognized between *sentence* negation and *predicate* negation. It should, indeed, be obvious that 'A horse is not eating grass' is ambiguous between '*It is not the case that a horse is eating grass*' and 'A horse *is-not-eating-grass*'. (This is not properly described as a *scope* ambiguity, however, as it does not turn on whether a *single* negation operator has wide or narrow scope, but rather on which of two *different* negation operators is in play.) The *first* of these two sentences can be represented in our formalized sortal language FSL by the formula '$\sim(F^1\alpha)$', which is equivalent, in accordance with SL1, to '$\sim\exists x(x/\alpha \ \& \ F^1x)$', but the *second* cannot be expressed in FSL, because FSL lacks the resources for representing predicate negation. This deficiency will be overcome by the expressively richer formalized sortal language which will be introduced in Chapter 12. However, for the purposes of the present chapter the temporary deficiency creates no difficulty.

Now, it would be pleasing if, paralleling SL1, we could find an analogous reduction of *dispositional* predications with *individual* terms in subject position, such as 'Dobbin eats grass'. And I think that we plainly can. For it is very plausible to propose that this sentence, too, is reducible to an existentially quantified conjunction – but to one involving *sortal* quantification, namely, '∃φ(Dobbin is (a) φ and (a) φ eats grass)'. Here, the first conjunct, 'Dobbin is (a) φ', again has the form of an instantiation sentence while the second, '(a) φ eats grass', is a dispositional predication with a sortal variable in subject position and thus has *law-like* form. Generalizing, the following accordingly seems plausible as a theorem of sortal logic paralleling SL1:

SL2. $xF^1 \leftrightarrow \exists\varphi(x/\varphi \ \& \ \varphi F^1)$

Why do I consider this plausible? Because it seems very reasonable to suppose that whenever a disposition is predicated of an individual, it is thereby implied that the individual in question conforms, in respect of its possession of that disposition, to some *natural law* governing the *kind* of individual that it is. Thus, for example, when I point towards a particular grain of white, crystalline substance and assert that it is *water-soluble*, it is plausible to suppose that I thereby imply that this piece of matter is an instance or exemplar of some *sort* or *kind* of substance that is water-soluble – in other words that, for some *sort* of substance, φ, of which this piece of matter is an instance, 'Water dissolves φ' is a true nomic generalization.[2] That this is plausible is indicated by the fact that, very often, my grounds for ascribing such a disposition to an individual are precisely that I *do* have such further beliefs concerning it. Thus, one very good reason for supposing that this grain of white, crystalline substance is water-soluble is that I believe it to be a piece of *salt* and believe 'Water dissolves salt' to be a true nomic generalization. Similarly, a good reason for supposing that Dobbin eats grass is that Dobbin is a *horse* and 'Horses eat grass' is a true nomic generalization.

If the reductions represented by theorems SL1 and SL2 are correct – and I shall have more to say on the issue shortly – then ultimately we need recognize in the 'deep structure' of natural language only *two* types of elementary predicative sentence: dispositional predications involving only sortal terms and occurrent predications involving only individual terms. This

---

[2]   This suggestion is quite close to one made by W. V. Quine about dispositions, when he writes that 'Intuitively, what qualifies a thing as [water-]soluble though it never gets into water is that it is of the same kind as the things that actually did or will dissolve': 'Natural Kinds', in his *Ontological Relativity and Other Essays* (New York: Columbia University Press, 1969), p. 130. But there are also important differences between Quine's view and mine.

naturally suggests that the dispositional/occurrent distinction, fundamental though it is, is itself ultimately grounded in the very distinction between sorts and individuals. That is to say, dispositional predication on this view just *is*, ultimately, predication with regard to sorts and occurrent predication just *is*, ultimately, predication with regard to individuals. Thus, we could extend our formalized sortal language FSL by introducing symbolism for what we could call 'basic' predication, as follows. An *atomic basic predicative formula* consists of an *n*-ary predicate letter followed, in square brackets, by a string of *n* objectual symbols, *all* of which are individual symbols or else *all* of which are sortal symbols. Then we may posit the following definitional equivalences:

D1. $F^n[x_1 x_2 \ldots x_n] =_{df} F^n x_1 x_2 \ldots x_n$
D2. $F^n[\varphi_1 \varphi_2 \ldots \varphi_n] =_{df} \varphi_1 \varphi_2 \ldots \varphi_n F^n$

So we are left with just one univocal mode of predication, *basic* predication, and all formulas involving dispositional or occurrent predication may be reduced, by means of these definitional equivalences and generalized versions of SL1 and SL2, to formulas involving only basic predication. (The generalized versions of SL1 and SL2 will simply extend them to embrace *n*-place predicates, for any finite number *n*. See further the axiomatized system of sortal logic presented in the appendix at the end of this chapter.)

Might it now be fairly objected that FSL is effectively just a syntactic variant of a standard first-order predicate language with identity, because FSL's distinction between *individual* and *sortal* constants and variables is redundant, these being replaceable by a uniform set of *objectual* constants and variables together with two monadic predicate constants, '*I*' and '*S*', meaning '— is an individual' and '— is a sort' respectively? According to this proposal, for instance, the formulas '$F^1[x]$' and $F^1[\varphi]$', which differ only in that the first contains an *individual* variable where the second contains a *sortal* variable, could be rewritten using the 'objectual' variable '*A*' as follows: '$I[A]$ & $F^1[A]$' and '$S[A]$ & $F^1[A]$'.

My answer is that this objection is *not* a fair one. First of all, it ignores the fact that FSL contains a new *logical* constant which is not to be found in standard first-order languages, the instantiation sign, '/'. Secondly and even more importantly, the objection is comparable to the manifestly absurd suggestion that ordinary *English* is susceptible to such 'rewriting' in respect of pairs of sentences such as 'Fido is barking' and 'Dogs bark', with these being 'rewritten' as something like 'Fido is an individual and Fido is a barker' and 'Dog is a sort and Dog is a barker' respectively – where 'Fido' and 'Dog' are now supposedly terms belonging to a single grammatical category of *names*, which does not discriminate between *proper* names and *common* names.

This suggestion is absurd because it fails to take seriously the point, constantly emphasized throughout this study, that the individual/sort distinction is conceptually and metaphysically absolutely fundamental. No coherent sense can be attached to the notion that the names of a language might refer to, or its variables of quantification range over, certain 'objects' concerning any one of which it was simply an *additional fact* that it was an 'individual' rather than a 'sort', or *vice versa*.[3] The idea that there could be a domain of such neutral 'objects' is incoherent, because the very *identity* of an individual turns on which *sorts* it belongs to and the very *identity* of a sort turns on which *individuals* belong to it. An item cannot *first* be singled out as a mere 'object' and *then* assigned to the class of individuals or to the class of sorts, as the case may be, in the way in which one might assign a piece of fruit either to the class of apples or to the class of pears. Individuals are *essentially* particulars and sorts *essentially* universals and this is why the domain of quantification of FSL is *essentially* divided into entities of two distinct types, each requiring its own set of constants and variables. For the same reason, English could not be 'revised' so as to obliterate the distinction between proper names and common names, as we would then be left with no intelligible account of how the new 'neutral' names referred to their supposed bearers or, indeed, what these supposed bearers could really *be*.

Now, what we might seem to have achieved with the introduction of the definitional equivalences D1 and D2 is nothing less than a reductive analysis of dispositionality. But that is not really the case. All that we have really achieved is a way of eliminating dispositional predication *with respect to individuals* and, paralleling this, occurrent predication *with respect to sorts*. Certainly, we have not achieved a reduction of *the dispositional to the occurrent* or – to use Aristotelian terminology – of the 'potential' to the 'actual', nor indeed *vice versa*.

By contrast, the more familiar and currently still fairly popular attempts to provide *conditional* analyses of dispositionality do indeed seek to reduce the dispositional to the occurrent. Thus, one common suggestion is that a disposition statement such as 'This grain of salt is water-soluble' is analysable in terms of some such counterfactual or subjunctive conditional

---

[3]   This observation may appear to be in tension with remarks made in Chapter 3 above regarding the putative *definitions* of 'individual' and 'sort' offered there, which were expressed using supposedly 'neutral' variables. But the lesson, I think, is that while we may hope to render more perspicuous the distinction between individuals and sorts in the way proposed in that chapter, it would be facile to imagine that we could achieve a *reductive analysis* of the distinction by that or indeed any other means.

as 'If this grain of salt were currently immersed in water, then it would be dissolving'. Now, I do not want to dispute that the truth of this disposition statement would at least provide strong *prima facie* support for the truth of such a conditional, but it does nonetheless seem clear that no general *reduction* of dispositional sentences to conditional ones along any such lines can be correct, for a number of reasons.

The main reason for this is that the *manifestation* of any disposition – which is what one expects to find mentioned in the consequent of any conditional purportedly analysing it – can be *prevented* by indefinitely many *interfering factors*, including factors which may forever remain unknown to us.[4] For instance, one such known factor, in the case of solubility, is the *saturation* of the solvent. Thus, the conditional suggested above as a putative analysis of '*a* is water-soluble' – 'If *a* were currently immersed in water, then *a* would be dissolving' – already needs to be modified, in the light of this factor, to something like 'If *a* were currently immersed in water *not already saturated with the substance of which a is a sample*, then *a* would be dissolving'. However, we simply have no guarantee that we shall ever be able to identify *every* such factor and make the all corresponding modifications required for a satisfactory conditional analysis.

The only alternative strategy available, it seems, is to include in the antecedent of the original conditional some catch-all *ceteris paribus* qualification, along the lines of 'If *a* were currently immersed in water *and nothing interfered*, then *a* would be dissolving'. But this just appears to trivialize the analysis, since 'and nothing interfered' can surely only be understood to mean 'and nothing succeeded in preventing the water from dissolving *a*': but if nothing succeeded in *preventing* the water from dissolving *a*, then *of course a* would be dissolving. That is to say, the consequent of this conditional simply follows trivially from its antecedent, so the conditional cannot really be providing a substantive and informative analysis. Bear in mind here also that *one* thing that would clearly succeed in preventing the water from dissolving *a* would be *a*'s *not being water-soluble*. So by implicitly excluding *this* 'interfering factor' we are implicitly interpreting the antecedent of the foregoing conditional in such a way that this antecedent actually entails the very disposition statement purportedly being analysed, '*a* is water-soluble'. This surely makes the proposed analysis implicitly *circular*, as well as being vacuous.

Another reason, however, for doubting the possibility of a quite general reduction of dispositional sentences to conditional ones is that the truth-conditions of counterfactuals cannot apparently be adequately specified

---

[4] Compare C. B. Martin, 'Dispositions and Conditionals', *Philosophical Quarterly* 44 (1994), pp. 1–8. See also W. V. Quine, *The Roots of Reference* (La Salle, IL: Open Court, 1974), pp. 12ff.

without at least implicit reference to *natural laws*. Thus, if they are specified, as is currently fashionable, in terms of what is the case in 'nearby'
naturally possible worlds, then since the notion of natural possibility seems
to rest upon that of natural law, it seems that the latter notion is at least
implicitly being relied upon in such an approach. But we have already seen
that laws themselves are characteristically expressed in natural language by
means of *dispositional predication*, using sentences which are certainly not
reducible to conditional sentences involving only occurrent predication.
Hence, a counterfactual analysis of dispositionality seems to hold out no
hope for a thoroughgoing reduction of that notion to non-dispositional ones.
Moreover, if the notion of a natural law has to be relied upon in specifying
the truth-conditions of counterfactuals, then there can be little point in
appealing to the latter for the purpose of analysing dispositional sentences
with *individual* terms in subject position – such as '*a* is water-soluble' –
since we might as well appeal *directly* to natural laws themselves instead.
And this, of course, is precisely what my own account of such sentences
proposes, by way of theorem SL2 above (and its generalization to *n*-place
predicates).

I now have to introduce a complication into the account developed over
the last few pages. This is that theorem SL2 is unsatisfactory as it stands
and requires amendment. The reason for this is connected with the fact
that natural laws, according to the view of them defended in Chapter 9,
are *normative* in character. For example, the law-statement 'Ravens are black'
may be true even though *some* individual ravens – 'abnormal' ravens, such
as albinos – are *not* black by disposition (are not *dispositionally black*). Suppose
that Nipper is an albino raven. Then the following two sentences, we may
assume, are *both* true: 'Nipper is a raven' and 'Ravens are black'. However, by the rule of existential generalization, the conjunction of these two
sentences entails '∃φ(Nipper is (a) φ and φs are black)' – and this, according to SL2, entails 'Nipper is (dispositionally) black'. But the latter is *ex
hypothesi* false, since Nipper is an albino and so *white*, not black, by disposition. Hence SL2 cannot be correct as it stands.

As we shall see more fully in Chapter 12, this difficulty is in fact only
a relatively superficial one, although our formalized sortal language FSL
currently lacks the syntactic resources to deal with it. The solution will lie
in adding to it a capacity to accommodate *complex sortal terms*. I shall briefly
indicate now the line of thought behind this solution, leaving its full development until the next chapter.

Suppose again, then, that Nipper is an albino raven and thus white by
disposition. Although 'Nipper is a *raven* and *ravens* are white' is plainly
not true, it is still plausible to suppose that there is some *complex* sortal
term, 'α', such that 'Nipper is (an) α' is a true instantiation sentence and

'αs are white' is a true nomic generalization or law. Indeed, the complex sortal term 'albino raven' will itself perhaps serve this purpose well enough. But so too, no doubt, will some rather more informative complex sortal term involving microbiological genetic descriptors. For we very reasonably assume that Nipper's abnormal coloration is ultimately *explicable* in terms of some law covering his and similar birds' plumage condition. Hence, it may appear that SL2 is satisfactory in the *left-to-right* direction and only problematic in the *right-to-left* direction, implying that a further clause is needed on its right-hand side. But then we need to recall that FSL as it stands doesn't include the resources for representing complex sortal terms, so that we can't really even say that SL2 is satisfactory in the left-to-right direction. As I say, a complete resolution of the difficulty must wait until Chapter 12, where a thoroughgoing analysis of sentences containing complex sortal terms will be presented. But at least it should be clear already that a law-based account of dispositionality is not fatally undermined by the kind of example that we have just been looking at.

Meanwhile, it is interesting and important to note that SL2 plausibly *is* valid if we restrict our attention to individuals belonging to a certain special class of sorts or kinds, which are denoted by what I propose to call 'perfect' sortals. These are, or at least include, the *theoretical* sortal terms of the more advanced sciences, which are distinguished by the fact that the sorts that they denote admit of *no* 'abnormal' individual exemplars.

Consider, for instance, the true nomic generalization 'Protons carry unit positive charge'. Now, 'proton' would certainly appear to be a perfect sortal. For it seems clear that *every* individual proton without exception *must*, according to current physical science, conform perfectly to *all* of the natural laws concerning the proton kind – and so must, amongst other things, carry positive unit charge. But this is just tantamount to saying that there can be no 'abnormal' protons since, as I explained in Chapter 9, a *normal* exemplar of any sort φ – in the sense of 'normality' now at issue – is precisely one that satisfies all the natural laws governing φ. However, I think that it is no mere coincidence that perfect sortals are, typically, *theoretical* terms. For tidiness of the kind that they demand is simply not to be found amongst the objects of everyday experience (things such as ravens). Indeed, it would seem that the price that advanced scientific theorizing pays in return for the elimination of abnormal individuals from its ontological purview is that the entities whose existence it postulates take on a *semi-ideal* status: they are just too uniformly perfect to be regarded as fully real. Or, to put the point less picturesquely, the exceptionless laws of the advanced sciences relate only indirectly to the real world, via simplified 'models' of it.

However, the idealizing tendency of scientific theory-construction, while reflecting a perfectionist urge to exclude all mention of abnormality from the most fundamental description of reality, at the same time reinforces the idea that it is the *normative* character of nomic generalizations that makes them distinctive. Advanced theoretical laws, no less than everyday 'empirical' laws, dictate only to the *normal* exemplars of their respective sorts or kinds. It is just that the theorist will not countenance the existence of *any but* normal exemplars and as a consequence incorporates a degree of fiction into his picture of reality.[5]

I might point out here that what I have just been saying, in terms of my own normative account of laws, about the distinction between 'theoretical' and 'empirical' laws and its relation to the idealizing tendency of advanced scientific theory could perhaps also be made – in a manner more familiar to most contemporary philosophers of science – in terms of the presence or absence of '*ceteris paribus* clauses' in sentences expressing laws. However, it is an advantage of the normative account that it has no need to invoke such clauses, since from its perspective these are merely devices to defeat the falsification of putatively nomic 'all-statements' by abnormal counterexamples and thus simply reflect the inherent inadequacy of the 'all-statement' approach to laws.

Sortal logic can, I believe, throw considerable light on the rationale of scientific method, particularly with regard to the empirical confirmation of natural laws by means of controlled experimentation and observation. As was briefly mentioned in Chapter 9, one point especially worth emphasizing is that the normative account of laws can explain why it is that scientists can sometimes take just a *single* well-conducted experiment to provide virtually conclusive evidence in support of a law – something that orthodox 'inductivist' accounts of scientific method struggle to make intelligible. A 'well-conducted' experiment, it should at once be said, is one in which the experimenter at least has reason to suppose that he has correctly identified what *sorts* of objects his experimental specimens are and that they are *normal* exemplars of those sorts. Given such knowledge, he may then apparently fairly safely infer that any disposition displayed by these specimens reflects a law governing the sorts to which they belong.

Thus, if a normal sample of water is found to dissolve a normal sample of salt, it is eminently reasonable to conclude that 'Water dissolves salt' is a true nomic generalization. However, while reasonable, it must certainly be acknowledged that this inference is not *deductively valid*, even according to the normative account of laws. This is because there may be more than one *kind* of salt, say salt$_1$ and salt$_2$, such that water dissolves salt$_1$ but

5   Compare Nancy Cartwright, *How the Laws of Physics Lie* (Oxford: Oxford University Press, 1983) and *The Dappled World: A Study of the Boundaries of Science* (Cambridge: Cambridge University Press, 1999).

not salt$_2$ – and, likewise, there may be more than one kind of water. What *does* appear to be deductively valid, though, is an inference from the fact that a normal sample of water is found to dissolve a normal sample of salt to the truth of the following *disjunction* of nomic generalizations: '*Either* water dissolves salt *or* some kind of water dissolves salt *or* water dissolves some kind of salt *or* some kind of water dissolves some kind of salt'. It is, however, reasonable to assume, in the absence of evidence to the contrary, that water and salt have no distinctive sub-kinds: such sub-kinds would have to be postulated only if various putatively normal samples of water and salt were found to behave in distinctive ways. So, in the absence of such contrary evidence, the truth of the nomic generalization 'Water dissolves salt' – that is, the disjunct of widest scope – may reasonably be assumed on the basis of experimental data of the type just described.

Here it may be asked precisely *how* we are to ascertain empirically that an individual possesses a given disposition, which is the type of experimental 'datum' with which we are now concerned. The answer is not quite as straightforward as might be supposed, since it would appear that '— is *F*ing' does not always entail '— *can F*', at least where the 'can' is the 'can' of *dispositionality* or *capacity*. For instance, 'John is hitting the bull's eye' – said truly on a certain occasion of a mediocre darts-player – does not appear to entail 'John *can* hit the bull's eye', other than in the relatively weak sense of 'can' in which this expresses mere physical possibility rather than signifying a robust capacity or ability. John might just be very lucky on this occasion. Nonetheless, in the case of most predicates substitutable for '*F*' which are applicable to ordinary natural objects – including 'dissolve' – the inference in question seems quite unproblematic, even if it falls short of a deductively valid one. Thus, that x is *actually being dissolved by* y leaves little scope for denying that y *can dissolve x*, in the dispositional sense of 'can'. For it apparently makes no sense to suppose that *luck* might be involved in such a case. The complications that arise in cases like that of the darts-player are consequently ones which I feel warranted in ignoring for present purposes, interesting and important though they may be in other contexts.

It is not difficult to see why the inference to the disjunction of nomic generalizations stated earlier should appear to be deductively valid, for it *is* so, at least under the simplifying assumption that theorem SL2 is correct. When sortal logic is made subject to this simplification, I propose to call it *perfect* sortal logic. Such a system of sortal logic, while it is inadequate to accommodate completely the imperfect sortals of everyday language, is nonetheless useful as a first approximation to a fully adequate system of sortal logic – and it is with that object chiefly in mind that I shall continue to explore and deploy it. For our immediate purposes, however, an important point to recognize is that if a certain inference can be shown to be valid in *perfect* sortal logic, then even in regard to *imperfect* sortals it may be expected to hold with respect to *normal* exemplars of the sorts in question. And, of course, we are precisely supposing our samples of water and salt to *be* normal ones in the illustrative example now under discussion.

Here is a proof of the validity of the inference now in question. Suppose, as hypothesis, that a is a (normal) sample of water and b is a (normal) sample of salt and that a is found to dissolve b, with the implication that the singular dispositional sentence 'a dissolves b' is true. Now, applying theorem SL2 – or, more exactly, its generalization to n-place predicates – we may deduce from this true dispositional sentence the truth of an existentially quantified conjunction of the following form: '$\exists\varphi\exists\chi(a$ is φ and b is χ and φ dissolves $\chi)$'. So, by existential instantiation, we are already assured that *some* nomic generalization of the form 'α dissolves β' is true, where α and β are sorts instantiated by a and b respectively. However, we have the additional information that 'a is water' and 'b is salt' are true instantiation sentences. So we know that a instantiates both the water kind and the α kind, while b instantiates both the salt kind and the β kind. Now, it would appear to be a correct principle of sortal logic that if an individual, x, instantiates both of two kinds, φ and χ, then *either* φ and χ are identical, *or* one is a sub-kind of the other, *or else* x also instantiates some third kind, ψ, which is a sub-kind of both φ and χ.[6] Formally, then, we appear to have as another theorem of sortal logic the following principle (in which '$\rightarrow$' is the connective of widest scope and from which I omit initial universal quantifiers and superfluous brackets to avoid unnecessary clutter):

SL3. x/φ & $x/\chi \rightarrow \varphi = \chi \vee \varphi/\chi \vee \chi/\varphi \vee \exists\psi(x/\psi$ & ψ/φ & $\psi/\chi)$

Thus, in the example now under discussion, *sixteen possible cases* arise by taking in turn, for each of the four possible relationships that SL3 allows between α and water, each of the four possible relationships that it allows between β and salt. Upon examination of these sixteen possible cases, however, we see that in each case *one or other* of the disjuncts in the disjunction of nomic generalizations stated earlier turns out to be true. I omit the proof because it is elementary but fairly lengthy. However, I should mention that it involves appeal to one further important principle of sortal logic, which may be expressed formally (for the case of dyadic predicates like 'dissolve') as follows:

---

[6]   It may be recalled that precisely this principle was invoked, in another context, in Chapter 5 above.

SL4. $\varphi\chi F^2$ & $\psi/\varphi \to \psi\chi F^2$

It is this principle which sanctions the inference from, for instance, 'Mammals breathe air' and 'Dolphins are mammals' to 'Dolphins breathe air'.

Hence we see that SL2, SL3 and SL4 together sanction the inference from the singular dispositional sentence 'a dissolves b', in conjunction with the instantiation sentences 'a is water' and 'b is salt', to the disjunction of nomic generalizations stated earlier, '*Either* water dissolves salt *or* some kind of water dissolves salt *or* water dissolves some kind of salt *or* some kind of water dissolves some kind of salt'. More generally, we may conclude that the following principle is yet another theorem of 'perfect' sortal logic:

SL5. xyF^2 & x/φ & $y/\chi \to \varphi\chi F^2 \vee \exists\psi(\psi/\varphi$ & $\psi\chi F^2)$
       $\vee \exists\zeta(\zeta/\chi$ & $\varphi\zeta F^2) \vee \exists\psi\exists\zeta(\psi/\varphi$ & ζ/χ & $\psi\zeta F^2)$

Now, of course, the preceding result rested upon a presupposition that our experimental exemplars – of water and salt, in the example used for purposes of illustration – were *normal*. But here it might be protested that, in view of my own definition of 'normality', we can simply never *determine* whether an individual, x, is a normal specimen of a given kind, φ, since to establish conclusively that x is 'normal' in my sense we must establish that x conforms with all the true nomic generalizations concerning the kind φ, that is, with all the natural laws governing φs. And yet it seems that, according to my preferred account of scientific method, our only available empirical evidence for believing such nomic generalizations to be *true* precisely involves appeal to the appearance or behaviour of putatively normal specimens of φ, such as x itself. So are we not trapped in a vicious circle?

I don't think so. The correct lesson to draw here – as I urged before, in Chapter 9 – is just that we should adopt a view of scientific method which is at least partly *coherentist* in character, as opposed to a naïve *foundationalist* one. There is, I suggest, no intelligible sense in which there can be a *beginning* to the process of acquiring scientific knowledge of natural laws. Rather, the growth of scientific knowledge always presupposes an existing framework of accepted nomic truths. So we cannot intelligibly conceive of an epoch in which *no* nomic generalizations were accepted as true by the human community, unless perhaps we retreat to a period prior to the inception of language altogether. For reasons that I have stressed before in this study, coherent thought about the natural world necessarily presupposes *some* framework of nomically related sortal concepts and cannot be restricted merely, say, to occurrent predications concerning individuals. The key reason, once again, is that the very *criteria of identity* of individuals – and with them their very principles of individuation – presuppose some such framework. For individuals are only conceivable as individuals of some conceivable *sort* or *kind*, while sorts or kinds themselves – at least, *natural* sorts or kinds – are themselves only distinguishable, in large measure, by means of differences in the laws governing them.

The growth of natural knowledge consists, then, in a process of revision and refinement of such a framework *from within*, calling to mind Neurath's famous metaphor of the raft which we rebuild as we float in it. Thus, for a great many sortal concepts at any given time we shall inevitably have available an accepted body of natural law to which we may appeal for the purposes of testing the normality of experimental specimens exemplifying the sorts in question. *New* laws governing these sorts may then be discovered by subjecting putatively normal specimens to hitherto untried experiments – although in the process of doing this we may, of course, find that we need to revise the existing system of sortal concepts and some of our currently accepted laws. Testing the normality of an experimental specimen as an exemplar of a given sort or kind is, thus, essentially a matter of determining whether it satisfies various presently well-entrenched laws pertaining to that sort or kind. For instance, in the case of a sample of water, its normality – or 'purity' – may currently be ascertained by checking that it is colour-less, tasteless and odourless, that it is neither acidic nor alkaline, that it boils at 100°C and freezes at 0°C, that it expands upon freezing, and so forth. Obviously, no such test, even if it involves advanced techniques of chemical analysis, can be completely decisive in the sense that its verdict is immune to subsequent reversal in the light of new evidence. New evid-ence can always, in principle, lead one to reclassify as 'abnormal' a specimen hitherto justifiably regarded as 'normal' or even, more radically, to reclas-sify it as belonging to another sort or species altogether.

In sum, the claim of sortal logic to constitute at least one vital element in a logic of scientific method is not in any way impugned by the fact that empirical evidence must always be interpreted in the light of currently accepted law. On the contrary, it reinforces the objections to any form of inductivist foundationalism concerning the growth of scientific knowledge.

Appendix: An Axiomatic System of Sortal Logic

The axiomatic system of sortal logic presented below is system of 'perfect' sortal logic in the sense explained earlier in this chapter. It is, however, stronger in a few minor respects than is strictly required for the purposes of this chapter, as will be pointed out later.

The *symbols* and *rules for well-formed formulas* of the system are simply provided by the vocabulary and syntax of the formalized sortal language FSL described at the beginning of the chapter. The *axioms* and *rules of inference* of the system are then specified as follows. First of all, we appropriate any suitable set of axioms for standard first-order predicate logic with identity which utilizes *modus ponens* and definitional interchange as the only rules of inference.[7] We do this, however, while at the same time making certain necessary adjustments to allow for the presence in FSL of *dual-sorted* variables and constants and *dual-mode* predication (that is, both *dispositional* and *occurrent* predication). What these adjustments require is (1) that the axioms governing quantifiers and identity be specified separately but in parallel fashion for *individual* and for *sortal* variables and constants and (2) that formulas differing only in respect of the *mode of predication* of some predicate letter be thus far handled as though they involved different predicate letters uniformly predicated. So far, then, we have a system which differs only stylistically from a standard system of first-order predicate logic with identity. Now we need to add to this the following axiom-schemata:

Axiom-schemata of instantiation

Where o_1, o_2, o_3 are objectual symbols:

A1. o_1/o_1
A2. $(o_1/o_2 \;\&\; o_2/o_3) \rightarrow o_1/o_3$
A3. $(o_1/o_2 \;\&\; o_1/o_3) \rightarrow (o_2/o_3 \lor o_3/o_2)$

Axiom-schemata of occurrent and dispositional predication

Where o_1, o_2, ... o_n are objectual symbols and P^n is an *n*-ary predicate letter:

A4. $P^n o_1 o_2 \ldots o_n \rightarrow o_1 o_2 \ldots o_n P^n$
      where o_1, o_2, ... o_n are all *individual* symbols.
A5. $P^n o_1 o_2 \ldots o_i \ldots o_n \leftrightarrow \exists v(v/o_i \;\&\; P^n o_1 o_2 \ldots v \ldots o_n)$
      where o_i is a *sortal* symbol and v is an *individual* variable not occurring amongst o_1, o_2, ... o_n.
A6. $o_1 o_2 \ldots o_i \ldots o_n P^n \leftrightarrow \exists v(o_i/v \;\&\; o_1 o_2 \ldots v \ldots o_n P^n)$
      where o_i is an *individual* symbol and v is a *sortal* variable not occurring amongst o_1, o_2, ... o_n.

---

[7]   See, for example, Benson Mates, *Elementary Logic*, 2nd edn (New York: Oxford University Press, 1972), pp. 165ff.

A7. $(o_1o_2 \ldots o_i \ldots o_nP^n \ \& \ o_j/o_i) \rightarrow o_1o_2 \ldots o_j \ldots o_nP^n$
       where o_i and o_j are both *sortal* symbols.

A8. $(P^no_1o_2 \ldots o_i \ldots o_n \ \& \ o_j/o_i) \rightarrow P^no_1o_2 \ldots o_j \ldots o_n$
       where o_i and o_j are both *individual* symbols.

The *axioms* of instantiation and of occurrent and dispositional predication consist of the universal closures of all formulas exemplifying the foregoing axiom-schemata.

Consistency

That the foregoing system is *consistent* is easy enough to demonstrate. We merely have to reinterpret formulas of the system in such a way that (1) the distinction between individual and sortal symbols is discounted, (2) the instantiation sign is equated with the identity sign and (3) the distinction between dispositional and occurrent predication is discounted, thus equating an atomic formula consisting of a predicate letter *preceded* by a string of objectual symbols with the formula consisting of the same predicate letter *followed* by that string of symbols. It is easily seen that, under this reinterpretation, axiom-schemata A1 to A8 all reduce to theorem-schemata of standard first-order predicate logic with identity, while the rules of inference of the system remain those of the previously adopted axiomatization of standard first-order predicate logic with identity. Hence, granted the consistency of standard first-order predicate logic with identity, sortal logic as axiomatized above must likewise be consistent. That this is only a *relative* consistency proof obviously does not diminish its value in any way. And here it is perhaps worth emphasizing again that sortal logic thus axiomatized is *not* just a syntactic variant of standard first-order predicate logic with identity, not least because it includes an additional logical constant, the instantiation sign. Moreover, that the system can be *reinterpreted* in the foregoing fashion does not, of course, in any way support the suggestion that it is merely a syntactic variant of standard first-order logic with identity.

Some remarks on the axioms

It may be noted that axiom-schema A5 supplies us with the generalized version of principle SL1 presented earlier in this chapter, while A6 supplies us with the generalized version of SL2 and A7 with the generalized version of SL4. A8 becomes redundant once it is stipulated that a formula in which the instantiation sign is flanked on both sides by individual symbols is equivalent to an identity formula. A3 is stronger than is required for the truth of principle SL3. And A4 ignores our previous *caveat* about the inference from '— is *F*ing' to '— *can F* '.

The definition of identity

It should be observed that if the definition of identity in terms of mutual instantiation – mooted earlier in Chapter 3 – is adopted, namely:

D3. $o_1 = o_2 =_{df} o_1/o_2 \ \& \ o_2/o_1$

where o_1 and o_2 are objectual symbols, then all the standard *laws of identity* – those of the reflexivity, symmetry and transitivity of identity, together with the principle of the substitutivity of identicals – may be recovered from the remainder of the system.

12

What Sorts of Things Are There?

In this final chapter, I want to complete two so far unfinished but closely related tasks. One is to analyse sentences containing semantically complex sortal terms and extend the formalized sortal language FSL of Chapter 11 to enable it to represent sentences containing such terms. The second is to inquire into the identity conditions of sorts or kinds, with a view to understanding how they should be distinguished from one another and consequently how we can hope to identify *which* sorts or kinds of things there really are. These two tasks are related inasmuch as we have reason to believe that semantically *simple* sortal terms denote genuine sorts or kinds, whereas semantically *complex* ones do not – the latter being, in Geach's words, 'a sort of logical mirage'. Intimately connected with the first task is some other important unfinished business carried over from Chapter 11, that of finding a way to overcome the limitations of what I there called a system of 'perfect' sortal logic, which is unable to handle sorts or kinds possessing *abnormal* instances or exemplars.

The Syntax and Semantics of Complex Sortal Terms

I begin now with the first of these tasks that I have so far had to postpone, that of analysing semantically complex sortal terms – or, more accurately, that of analysing sentences containing such terms, since it will emerge that such terms do not really constitute genuine logico-semantic units in their own right.

Complex sortal terms, as we have already seen, may be formed syntactically from simple ones by the adjunction of adjectives or adjectival phrases as in, for example, 'wild horses', 'boiling water', '(an) animal which lactates' and '(a) tree which sheds its leaves in winter'. A little regimentation will provide all such terms with a common form, namely, 'α which is F', where 'α' is a simple sortal term and '— is F' is a predicate.[1] Thus, '(a) wild horse' may be rewritten as '(a) horse which is wild' and 'boiling water' as 'water which is boiling'. This observation, however, properly only applies to syntactically complex sortal terms which are also genuinely *semantically* complex. So, for instance, 'heavy water' is plainly *not* synonymous with 'water which is heavy'. And indeed this supplies us with a test for semantic complexity, albeit one that is directly applicable only to syntactically complex sortal terms. In the case of a syntactically *simple* sortal term which is suspected of being semantically complex, such as 'ice', one must first establish its synonymy with a syntactically complex sortal term – in this case, plausibly, 'frozen water' – to which the test may then be applied. In this case, the test has a positive result, since 'frozen water' *is* synonymous with 'water which is frozen'.

However, applying now the distinction between *dispositional* and *occurrent* predication, we can see that, even if we rewrite all complex sortal terms in the form 'α which is F', they will still fall into two grammatically distinct classes, depending on whether the predicate '— is F' is to be understood dispositionally or occurrently. And we shall in fact discover that this grammatical distinction reflects logical ones of considerable importance. Thus, for example, two sentences which differ only in that one contains the *dispositionally* qualified complex sortal term '(an) animal which *lactates*' where the other contains the *occurrently* qualified complex sortal term '(an) animal which *is lactating*' will in general turn out to have quite different underlying logical forms.

In the formalized sortal language FSL described in Chapter 11, the distinction between dispositional and occurrent predication is marked by writing objectual constants and variables – whether these be individual or sortal symbols – to the *left* of predicate letters to signify *dispositional* predication and to the *right* of them to signify *occurrent* predication. So we are now in a position to extend our formalized language so as to permit the symbolization of our two classes of complex sortal terms. Thus, a complex sortal term involving *dispositional* predication, such as '(an) animal which lactates',

---

[1] English prose stylists often maintain that 'that' should be used in preference to 'which' in restrictive relative clauses, while acknowledging that colloquial usage is more flexible. I have no particular quarrel with this claim as an observation concerning literary style. Even so, for my present purposes, which are logical rather than literary, I prefer the regimentation 'α which is F' to the alternative, 'α that is F', because 'that' has so many more and diverse uses than 'which' and in that sense lacks the latter's precision. It should be clear, from the absence of a comma, that 'α which is F', as I use it, is never to be confused with 'α, which is F', in which the relative clause is not restrictive.

may be symbolized as '$\langle\alpha{:}\alpha F^1\rangle$', while one involving *occurrent* predication, such as '(an) animal which is lactating', may be symbolized as '$\langle\alpha{:}F^1\alpha\rangle$', where '$\alpha$' translates the simple sortal term '(an) animal' and 'F^1' translates the monadic predicate '— is lactating/lactates'. Complex sortal symbols like these may now be permitted to occupy all the positions in atomic formulas of FSL available to its simple sortal symbols.

The task of analysis which consequently lies before us is one of providing transformation rules which will enable us, if possible, to *eliminate* complex sortal symbols from all such positions by replacing the formulas in which they occur by equivalent formulas utilizing only the original vocabulary and syntax of FSL. The task may usefully be compared to the one that Russell and Whitehead set themselves of eliminating *definite description* symbols, of the form '$(\iota x)Fx$', representing singular definite descriptions of the form 'the F'.[2] For we shall analogously want to say that complex sortal symbols are 'incomplete symbols' – that they do not constitute genuine semantic units and that they cannot be properly interpreted independently of the complete sentential formulas to which they belong. However, we shall also see that, in fact, the original vocabulary and syntax of FSL are *not* fully adequate for us to complete the task of elimination, but require extension in important new ways.

For present purposes, I am going to concentrate on two important types of sentence featuring complex sortal terms: (1) dispositional predications with complex sortal terms in subject position and (2) instantiation sentences featuring proper names and complex sortal terms. Examples of the former type of sentence would be 'An animal which lactates is warm-blooded' and 'Water which is boiling emits steam'. Examples of the latter type of sentence would be 'Daisy is an animal which chews the cud' and 'Dobbin is a horse which is eating grass'. I shall begin with the second type of sentence, whose analysis is relatively straightforward.

Sentences of this second type have either the form '$a/\langle\alpha{:}\alpha F^1\rangle$' or the form '$a/\langle\alpha{:}F^1\alpha\rangle$' in our new notation. (To simplify matters, I am for the time being treating all the predicates involved as being *monadic*, even if they are really susceptible to further analysis, as in the case of '— is eating/eats grass'.) Now, it should be clear enough that with sentences of this type our two classes of complex sortal terms call for quite different logical treatments. In fact, the following two definitional equivalences seem to be required:

D4. $a/\langle\alpha{:}\alpha F^1\rangle =_{df} \exists\varphi(\varphi/\alpha\ \&\ a/\varphi\ \&\ \varphi F^1)$
D5. $a/\langle\alpha{:}F^1\alpha\rangle =_{df} a/\alpha\ \&\ F^1 a$

---

[2]   See A. N. Whitehead and B. Russell, *Principia Mathematica*, 2nd edn (Cambridge: Cambridge University Press, 1927), Volume I, pp. 66ff.

Observe here, incidentally, that the right-hand side of D5 is equivalent to '$\exists x(x/\alpha \;\&\; a/x \;\&\; F^1x)$', so that there is more symmetry between D4 and D5 than at first meets the eye.

As an illustration of the plausibility of D4, 'Daisy is an animal which chews the cud' is very naturally taken to mean 'For some kind of animal, φ, Daisy is a φ and φs chew the cud'. This will be true if, say, Daisy is a *cow* – since cows are animals and cows chew the cud. And recall here that this may be true even if, owing to some aberration of anatomy, Daisy herself does *not* chew the cud and thus is not a *normal* cow. As an illustration of the plausibility of D5, 'Dobbin is a horse which is eating grass' is very naturally taken to mean 'Dobbin is a horse and Dobbin is eating grass'.

The essential point which emerges, then, is the following. In the analysis of the *first* class of instantiation sentences a dispositional predication is made with respect to some *sort* or *kind* to which the individual in question belongs, whereas in the analysis of the *second* class of instantiation sentences an occurrent predication is made with respect to *that individual* itself. I do not dispute, incidentally, that the English sentence 'Daisy is an animal which chews the cud' *might*, in a suitable context, be taken to mean 'Daisy is an animal and Daisy chews the cud', along the lines of D5 rather than D4, although this is certainly not its most natural reading. But, in any case, my present task is to provide an *unambiguous* analysis of formulas of the form '$a/\langle\alpha{:}\alpha F^1\rangle$' in our extended version of FSL and for that purpose it is only sensible to adopt one which corresponds to the most natural reading of corresponding English sentences.

It may be observed next that, in the case of formulas of the form '$a/\langle\alpha{:}\alpha F^1\rangle$', we may replace the individual constant 'a' by a sortal constant 'β' and the resulting formula will admit of an analysis paralleling that provided in D4, namely:

D6. $\beta/\langle\alpha{:}\alpha F^1\rangle =_{\mathrm{df}} \exists\varphi(\varphi/\alpha \;\&\; \beta/\varphi \;\&\; \varphi F^1)$

The plausibility of D6 may be illustrated by the following example: 'A cow is an animal which chews the cud' is very naturally taken to mean 'For some kind of animal, φ, a cow is a φ and φs chew the cud'. To this it might be objected that the first of these sentences is even more naturally interpreted as meaning, quite simply, 'A cow is an animal and a cow chews the cud'. But this objection would, I think, be misconceived because the two interpretations are in fact equivalent. They are so, at least, provided that we accept that '$\beta/\varphi \;\&\; \varphi F^1$' entails '$\beta F^1$', as is implied by axiom-schema A7 in the Appendix to Chapter 11. For, given this, it is easy to show that the right-hand side of D6 is equivalent to '$\beta/\alpha \;\&\; \beta F^1$'. Notice, however, that we do *not* correspondingly have any very natural use for sentences corresponding to the formula which results from replacing the individual constant 'a' in a formula of the form '$a/\langle\alpha:F^1\alpha\rangle$' by a sortal constant '$\beta$'. Thus, for instance, 'A cow is an animal which *is chewing* the cud' makes very doubtful sense, in contrast with both '*Daisy* is an animal which is chewing the cud' and 'A cow is an animal which *chews* the cud'.

I turn now to the case of *predicative* formulas containing complex sortal symbols and, more specifically, those that represent *dispositional* predications. These are particularly important because they are required for the formal representation of many nomic generalizations. They again fall into two classes, depending on whether the complex sortal symbols involved themselves involve dispositional or occurrent predication. I shall deal first with the easier class to analyse, which is the former. These, then, are formulas of the form '$\langle\alpha:\alpha F^1\rangle G^1$'. (Again I restrict myself for the time being to monadic predicates.) Such a formula could be used to represent, for example, the nomic generalization 'An animal which chews the cud lactates'. And here I propose the following definitional equivalence:

D7. $\langle\alpha:\alpha F^1\rangle G^1 =_{df} \forall\varphi((\varphi/\alpha \ \& \ \varphi F^1) \to \varphi G^1)$

By this account, 'An animal which chews the cud lactates' may be taken to mean 'For any sort of animal, φ, if φs chew the cud, then φs lactate' – from which one might validly infer, for instance 'If cows chew the cud, then cows lactate'. One very important implication of this analysis is that, in a sentence like 'An animal which chews the cud lactates', the complex sortal term which is its *grammatical* subject does not play the role of a *logical* subject. From '$\langle\alpha:\alpha F^1\rangle G^1$' one cannot validly infer '$\exists\varphi(\varphi G^1)$', if D7 is correct. Thus, 'an animal which chews the cud' is not, in such a context, to be seen as denoting any *sort* or *kind* of thing, such as the zoological suborder of *ruminants*. Analogously, 'an animal which lactates' should not be regarded as denoting the sort or kind *mammal*. Obviously, this immediately casts serious doubt on the ancient notion of 'defining' a species *per genus et differentiam*, at least if such a 'definition' is regarded as establishing *synonymy* between terms.[3] However, this is a notion to which I am

---

[3]   Compare P. T. Geach's remarks on the terms 'rhombus' and 'parallelogram that has equal sides', in his *Reference and Generality*, 3rd edn (Ithaca, NY: Cornell University Press, 1980), pp. 147ff. Geach, indeed, maintains quite generally that complex sortal terms are 'a sort of logical mirage' (p. 145) and I agree with him, at least in spirit. I disagree, thus, with the contrary view of Anil Gupta: see his *The Logic of Common Nouns* (New Haven, CT: Yale University Press, 1980), pp. 10ff. Geach's arguments for his position have received incisive criticism from Gareth Evans: see his 'Pronouns, Quantifiers and Relative Clauses (II)', in his *Collected Papers* (Oxford: Clarendon Press, 1985). However,

opposed in any case, because I do not consider that natural kind terms are *definable* at all and hold that generalizations such as 'Mammals lactate' and 'Ruminants chew the cud' are not analytic truths but, rather, *a posteriori* statements of natural law (see again Chapter 9 above).

The second class of dispositional predicative formulas that I have to deal with are those involving complex sortal symbols which themselves involve *occurrent* predication – that is, formulas of the form '⟨α:F¹α⟩G¹', which could be used to represent a nomic generalization such as 'Water *which is boiling* emits steam' or, in other words, '*Boiling* water emits steam'. Clearly, this generalization must be distinguished from 'Water *which boils* emits steam' – in other words, '*Boilable* water emits steam' – where the complex sortal term involves *dispositional* predication. And, indeed, the undeniable oddness of the latter sentence can readily be explained by our previous analysis of such generalizations, as arising from the fact that we assume that *every* sort of water boils or, in other words, is 'boilable'. Other everyday examples of sentences representable by formulas of the form '⟨α:F¹α⟩G¹' would be 'An animal which is lactating defends its young' and 'A dog which sees a cat barks'.

Now, of course, according to a Popperian 'all-statement' analysis of laws, a formula of this form would be taken to be analysable as having the following underlying logical form: '$\forall x((x/\alpha \,\&\, F^1 x) \to G^1 x)$'. And this proposal even reflects a nice symmetry with D7 above. It implies, for instance, that 'Water which is boiling emits steam' may be taken to mean 'For any individual body of water, x, if x is boiling, then x is emitting steam'. However, this is not a proposal that I can accept, for reasons which I have already made plain in earlier chapters. Natural laws, by my account, do not primarily concern individuals but rather the *sorts* or *kinds* to which they belong. Thus, the nomic generalization 'Water which is boiling emits steam' is, I would urge, a sentence primarily concerning the sort or kind *water* and only derivatively its individual exemplars or instances.

At the same time, however, it is also sufficiently clear that, in this nomic generalization, the complex sortal term 'water which is boiling' cannot seriously be taken to denote a certain distinctive *sub*-sort or *sub*-kind of water. My suggestion, consequently, is that the logical subject of this sentence is in fact the *simple* sortal term 'water' and that the adjectival clause 'which is boiling' should properly be seen as contributing to the sentence's *predicate*. This could be made more explicit by paraphrasing the generalization in question in the following way: 'Water *emits steam if it is boiling*'.

whatever may be the merits of Evans's criticisms of Geach's arguments, they do not touch on the considerations which make me sympathetic with Geach's position.

Similarly, our other two examples of nomic generalizations in this class could be paraphrased, respectively, as 'An animal *defends its young if it is lactating*' and 'A dog *barks if it sees a cat*'.

At a formal level, what we evidently now require are the means to represent *complex predicates*, by allowing the sentential connectives of FSL to serve also as *predicate connectives*. Thus, taking the two monadic predicate letters 'F^1' and 'G^1' and the conditional connective '$\rightarrow$', we want to be able to form the complex predicative expression '$(F^1 \rightarrow G^1)$' which, we assume, can be either *preceded* or *followed* by an objectual symbol of FSL, depending on whether we wish to represent a *dispositional* or an *occurrent* predication by these means. This understood, I propose the following further definitional equivalence to deal with the class of dispositional predicative formulas presently under consideration:

D8. $\langle \alpha{:}F^1\alpha \rangle G^1 =_{df} \alpha(F^1 \rightarrow G^1)$

At first blush, there may seem to be little parallel between definitional equivalences D7 and D8. But, in fact, they may be rewritten in forms which bring out both a striking resemblance and an important difference between them, as follows:

D7*. $\langle \alpha{:}\alpha F^1 \rangle G^1 =_{df} \forall \varphi(\varphi/\alpha \rightarrow (\varphi F^1 \rightarrow \varphi G^1))$
D8*. $\langle \alpha{:}F^1\alpha \rangle G^1 =_{df} \forall \varphi(\varphi/\alpha \rightarrow \varphi(F^1 \rightarrow G^1))$

These reformulations make it clear that the logical differences between the two *definienda* turn entirely on the distinction between complex *sentences* and complex *predicates*.

What now requires special emphasis is that a formula which has the form of the one appearing on the right-hand side of D8 is *not* equivalent to any formula that can be constructed from atomic formulas FSL employing only *non-complex* predicative expressions of FSL. Thus, in particular, '$\alpha(F^1 \rightarrow G^1)$' is *not* equivalent to '$\alpha F^1 \rightarrow \alpha G^1$'. And so, for example, 'Water emits steam if it is boiling' is not equivalent to 'If water boils, then water emits steam', nor is 'A dog barks if it sees a cat' equivalent to 'If a dog sees a cat, then a dog barks'.

These non-equivalences may be made still more manifest by considering sentences in which *individual* terms feature as the subjects of the same complex dispositional predicates: for example, 'Fido barks if he sees a cat', which by my account is of the form '$a(F^1 \rightarrow G^1)$'. This, I say, is *not* equivalent to 'If Fido sees a cat, then Fido barks' – not, at least, if the latter sentence is regarded as genuinely being of the form '$aF^1 \rightarrow aG^1$', that is, as being constructed from the sentences 'Fido sees a cat' and 'Fido

barks' by means of a *sentential* conditional connective, 'if —, then . . .'.[4]
Nor will it do to suggest that '$a(F^1 \rightarrow G^1)$' is equivalent to '$F^1a \rightarrow G^1a$',
in which only *occurrent* predication is deployed. 'Fido barks if he sees a
cat' clearly does *not* mean 'If Fido is seeing a cat, then Fido is barking'.
The latter sentence, in conjunction with 'Fido is seeing a cat', entails 'Fido
is barking'. But this is not true of 'Fido barks if he sees a cat', which predicates of Fido only a general conditional *disposition* to *bark-if-he-sees-a-cat*.
Fido's failure to bark upon seeing a *particular* cat, Tom, on some particular occasion, would not defeat an ascription of this general conditional
disposition to him, provided that a suitable explanation of his failure to
do so on that occasion was forthcoming. The explanation might be, for
instance, that Fido was muzzled on that occasion, or that Fido grew up
with Tom since he was a puppy.[5]

So far, I have restricted my examples to ones that I have analysed as involving only *monadic* predicates, even if some of these examples in fact submit to a more complex analysis. But further complications arise when we
have take into consideration cases unavoidably involving polyadicity. For
instance, we need to be able to extend our approach in order to deal with
a sentence such as 'A dog which smells a rat chases it', which I would
wish to paraphrase as 'A dog chases a rat if it smells it'. It is worth remarking at once here the similarity between the former sentence and Geach's
well-known problem sentence, 'Any man who owns a donkey beats it',
sentences like the latter now being known, indeed, as 'donkey sentences'.[6]
Geach himself holds, as one would expect, that 'man who owns a donkey'
in this case should not be regarded as a genuine semantic unit, synonymous with 'donkey-owner' – a claim with which I have much sympathy.[7]

[4] In point of fact, though, it would appear that many ostensibly 'conditional'
sentences in natural language should really be seen as involving a complex
conditional *predicate* and hence *not* as being of the form 'If *P*, then *Q*', where
'*P*' and '*Q*' are whole sentences. Compare V. H. Dudman, 'Parsing "If"-
Sentences', *Analysis* 44 (1984), pp. 145–53.
[5] For the same reason, we may dismiss the suggestion that 'Fido barks if he
sees a cat' is analysable as meaning something like 'For all times, *t*, if Fido sees
a cat at *t*, then Fido barks at *t*', where 'sees' and 'barks' are *tenseless*. Such
a proposal is implicit in Ivor Alexander, ' "If" and Quantification', *Analysis*
45 (1985), pp. 186–90.
[6] See P. T. Geach, *Reference and Generality*, 3rd edn, pp. 143ff.
[7] I say this despite the well-known criticisms of Geach voiced in Evans's
'Pronouns, Quantifiers and Relative Clauses (II)'. As I see it, what superficial
credibility Evans's view may have in opposition to Geach's rests upon an
assumption that 'man' in Geach's donkey sentence designates – or has as its

However, I should emphasize that my own example sentence – 'A dog which smells a rat chases it' – differs crucially from Geach's in that, whereas his involves an *individual quantifier expression*, 'any man', I see mine as involving no quantification over individuals at all. For, of course, I see '(a) dog' in this case as functioning simply as a sortal or 'generic' *name*.

Now, 'A dog which smells a rat chases it' can, in line with our preceding practice, be represented symbolically by a formula of the form '$\langle\alpha{:}F^2\alpha\beta\rangle\beta G^{2\prime}$', where '$\alpha$' and '$\beta$' translate '(a) dog' and '(a) rat' respectively, while 'F^2' and '$G^{2\prime}$' translate '— smells . . .' and '— chases . . .' respectively. And, as I have just remarked, I would wish to paraphrase this sentence as 'A dog chases a rat if it smells it', which indeed seems intuitively correct. However, we now seem to be faced with a technical difficulty if we attempt to represent the latter sentence simply by some such formula as '$\alpha\beta(F^2 \rightarrow G^2)$'. For this formula fails to allow for the fact that the sentence in question is, at least in principle, subject to *two non-equivalent readings*, namely, 'A dog chases a rat if it (the dog) smells it (the rat)' and 'A dog chases a rat if it (the rat) smells it (the dog)'. The second of these is equivalent, on my analysis, to 'A dog *which a rat smells* chases it', this being representable by the formula '$\langle\alpha{:}F^2\beta\alpha\rangle\beta G^2$'.

Of course, natural language can tolerate such syntactical ambiguity, because context will normally render the relevant order of the terms obvious – but a formal logical language cannot. What we could do, however, to overcome this technical difficulty is simply to replace the numerical superscripts attached to the predicate letters in a formula such as '$\alpha\beta(F^2 \rightarrow G^2)$' by a suitably ordered string of sortal symbols of the corresponding length, thus representing the above two different readings of our ambiguous sentence by the formulas '$\alpha\beta(F^{\alpha\beta} \rightarrow G^{\alpha\beta})$' and '$\alpha\beta(F^{\beta\alpha} \rightarrow G^{\alpha\beta})$' respectively. This device was obviously unnecessary when only *monadic* predicate letters were in use, but could be applied also in their case to preserve uniformity. Note, incidentally, that 'A dog chases a rat if it smells it', on its more obvious reading, can readily be reformulated as 'If a dog smells a rat, it chases it', which is thus again representable by the first of the above two formulas, whereas 'If a dog is smelt by a rat, it chases it' is representable by the second of them.

To sum up, the proposal is to extend definitional equivalence D8 to such dyadic cases as follows:

D8(2/2). $\langle\alpha{:}F^2\alpha\beta\rangle\beta G^2 =_{\mathrm{df}} \alpha\beta(F^{\alpha\beta} \rightarrow G^{\alpha\beta})$
$\langle\alpha{:}F^2\beta\alpha\rangle\beta G^2 =_{\mathrm{df}} \alpha\beta(F^{\beta\alpha} \rightarrow G^{\alpha\beta})$

'semantic value' – the set of all individual men, a sub-set of which is supposedly designated by 'man who owns a donkey'. But this, I believe, is an assumption which, for reasons made plain in earlier chapters, has no place in an adequate semantics for sortal terms.

D8 itself can now correspondingly be reformulated, using the new super-script notation, as follows:

D8(1/1). $\langle \alpha{:}F^1\alpha \rangle G^1 =_{df} \alpha(F^\alpha \rightarrow G^\alpha)$

The labels '(1/1)' and '(2/2)' here are used to represent the fact that in D8(1/1) both predicates, 'F' and 'G', are monadic, while in D8(2/2) both are dyadic.

Clearly, there are also *mixed* cases to deal with, such as '$\langle \alpha{:}F^1\alpha \rangle \beta G^2$', which can now be regarded as equivalent to '$\alpha\beta(F^\alpha \rightarrow G^{\alpha\beta})$'. This formula could be used, for example, to translate 'Water scalds human skin if it is boiling' or, equivalently, 'If water is boiling, it scalds human skin', which I take to be a paraphrase of 'Boiling water scalds human skin'. Obviously, there are other even more complex cases than any so far dealt with, but enough has been said already to indicate how these could be handled. It should also be remarked that the superscript notation used here is just one means of overcoming the technical difficulty identified earlier and no doubt other devices could be used instead. The important thing is that the difficulty can easily be overcome. With that fact in mind, I shall hence-forth return to simpler examples in which only monadic predicate letters are involved, thus rendering the superscript notation unnecessary.

A question which I have so far not addressed is that of how we can account satisfactorily for the dual role now being proposed for logical connectives such as '$\rightarrow$', whereby they can serve as both sentential and predicate con-nectives. I think we have to acknowledge here an irreducible systematic ambiguity. The ambiguity is systematic in that the connectives are *inter-definable* in the same ways in each of their roles – and, indeed, it is this fact above all that entitles us to speak of them as being the *same* connectives playing two different logical roles. Thus, just as the complex *sentential* for-mula '$P \rightarrow Q$' is definitionally equivalent to '$\sim(P \& \sim Q)$', so the complex *predicate* expression '$F \rightarrow G$' is definitionally equivalent to '$\sim(F \& \sim G)$'. This is borne out by examples in natural language. For instance, 'Fido barks if he sees a cat' is indeed plausibly equivalent to 'Fido doesn't see a cat and not bark' or, more colloquially, 'Fido doesn't see a cat without bark-ing'. We are at liberty, then, to take predicate negation and conjunction as our primitives, just as we are at liberty to take their sentential counter-parts as primitive, defining the other connectives in terms of these.

The reason, it would seem, why the irreducibly dual role of the logical connectives has not hitherto attracted much attention is just that logicians have tended to ignore *sorts* as genuine subjects of predication and have not been even-handed in their treatment of dispositional and occurrent pre-dication, according the latter primary status. If we restrict our attention to *occurrent* predications concerning *individuals*, the distinction between sentential and predicate connectives may indeed appear to be more a matter of style than of substance. For example, '*It is not the case that* this coin is landing heads up' is surely equivalent to 'This coin is *not landing heads up*', as is 'John is eating *and* John is reading' to 'John is *eating and reading*'. But once *dispositional* predication is taken into consideration, such equivalences begin to look like special cases. Thus, it is reasonably clear that '*It is not the case that* this coin lands heads up' is *not* equivalent to 'This coin *doesn't land heads up*', since the former but not the latter is consistent with the coin being an unbiased one. The former, after all, denies that the coin is disposed to land heads up while the latter affirms that it is disposed *not* to land heads up. Equally, 'John eats *and* John reads' is *not* equivalent to 'John *eats and reads*', since the latter but not the former implies that John is disposed to engage in these activities *jointly*.

Now, one possible response here would be to regard these non-equivalences as providing *prima facie* evidence that dispositional predication always involves hidden operators or quantifiers in the 'deep structure' of the sentences involving it. And in the case of sentences involving dispositional predication concerning *individuals*, as in the foregoing examples, I can even agree that this is so, since I see these as implicitly involving *sortal* quantification. However, if earlier arguments of mine are correct, this diagnosis cannot apply to dispositional predication quite generally. For non-equivalences of the type in which we are presently interested arise also in the case of *nomic generalizations*, which I hold to constitute a logically basic and irreducible class of sentences. Thus, 'Horses *don't eat meat*' is clearly stronger than – entails but is not entailed by – '*It is not the case that* horses eat meat'. For the former affirms that horses are disposed *not* to eat meat whereas the latter only denies that they *are* disposed to eat it. And yet, by my account, 'Horses eat meat' is an *atomic* sentence, which accordingly harbours no hidden operator or quantifier in its 'deep structure'. Consequently, we need two different ways of introducing negation into this sentence in order to generate the two preceding non-equivalent sentences. Altogether, then, it seems that an adequate formalized sortal language will *have* to contain both sentential connectives and predicate connectives, so that my introduction of the latter for the purpose of analysing formulas containing complex sortal symbols cannot be regarded as being merely an *ad hoc* device.

I am now in a position to return to the other unfinished business carried over from Chapter 11. We saw there that the following important principle

SL2. $xF^1 \leftrightarrow \exists\varphi(x/\varphi \ \& \ \varphi F^1)$

is not valid unless attention is restricted to sorts or kinds which have no *abnormal* instances or to individuals which are *normal* instances of their sorts or kinds. Nonetheless, we also saw that, even where x is an abnormal instance of its kind, it is still reasonable to suppose that, if a sentence of the form 'xF^1' is true, so too will be a sentence *apparently* of the form 'x/α & αF^1', providing we allow that 'α' may need to represent a *complex* sortal term.

Now, in such a case, we are not guaranteed that a sentence of the form '$\exists\phi(x/\phi$ & $\phi F^1)$' is true, because – as we have just seen – complex sortal terms do not denote sorts or kinds, in the way that simple sortal terms plausibly do. Thus, where 'α' represents a complex sortal term, we cannot legitimately invoke the rule of existential generalization to infer '$\exists\phi(x/\phi$ & $\phi F^1)$' from 'x/α & αF^1'. At least, we cannot do this if, as I have been presupposing, we adopt an 'objectual' – as opposed to a 'substitutional' – interpretation of the quantifiers. Even so, we now know enough about the semantics of complex sortal terms to see that, if a sentence of the form 'xF^1' is true, so too will be one of the form '$\exists\phi(x/\phi$ & G^1x & $\phi(G^1 \rightarrow F^1))$'. This will be true precisely *because* there will be some possibly complex sortal term, 'α', such that a sentence of the form 'x/α & αF^1' is true. For 'α', if complex, will have the form '$\langle\beta:G^1\beta\rangle$', and we already know that '$x/\langle\beta:G^1\beta\rangle$ & $\langle\beta:G^1\beta\rangle$ F^1' entails 'x/β & G^1x & $\beta(G^1 \rightarrow F^1)$', in virtue of definitional equivalences D5 and D8. Moreover, 'β' here represents a *simple* sortal term, with respect to which the rule of existential generalization may legitimately be applied, thus allowing us to infer '$\exists\phi(x/\phi$ & G^1x & $\phi(G^1 \rightarrow F^1))$' from '$x/\beta$ & G^1x & $\beta(G^1 \rightarrow F^1)$'.

The key point being made here may be illustrated by means of our previous example – discussed in Chapter 11 – of an albino raven, Nipper, which is white rather than black by disposition, unlike normal ravens. As I indicated then, we have every reason to suppose that there either is, or could be introduced, some complex sortal term, of the form '(a) raven which is G' – where 'G' may, for example, express some special genetic condition – such that 'Nipper is a raven which is G' is a true instantiation sentence and 'Ravens which are G are white' is a true nomic generalization: one which, moreover, may be recast in the form 'Ravens are white if they are G'. Hence, we may be confident that there is some true sentence of the form 'For some sort, ϕ, Nipper is (a) ϕ and Nipper is G and ϕs are white if they are G'. Formally, then, we are in a position to endorse the following general principle, where 'P^1' is a variable ranging over monadic *properties*:[8]

---

[8] Of course, since SL6 involves quantification into *predicate* position, we have now transcended the confines of a system of first-order logic. But that is not something that should be regretted by any realist concerning universals, such as I am. See further my *The Four-Category Ontology: A Metaphysical Foundation for Natural Science* (Oxford: Clarendon Press, 2006).

SL6. $xF^1 \rightarrow \exists\varphi\exists P^1(x/\varphi \ \& \ P^1x \ \& \ \varphi(P^1 \rightarrow F^1))$

However, SL6 is not a *biconditional*, unlike SL2, so the question arises as to whether it is also valid in the right-to-left direction. The answer is clearly negative, as may again be seen with the help of our raven example. For, even given that a certain individual raven, x, is G and that ravens which are G are white, it does not necessarily follow that x *itself* is white by disposition since, once more, x might be an *abnormal* example of a raven which is G. A particular raven might possess the genetic mechanism which, in albino ravens, is responsible for their whiteness and yet *not* be white by disposition, owing to some abnormality in the functioning of that genetic mechanism in this particular case. Now, rather than attempt to modify the right-hand side of SL6 so as to turn it into a valid biconditional, which would involve us in undue formal complexity, I shall address this issue by reverting to the use of complex sortal symbols, safe in the knowledge now that these are in principle always eliminable.

What I therefore propose to do is to add to our formalized sortal language FSL a new style of sortal constants and variables, distinguished from the existing ones by being printed in *boldface type*, thus: **α**, **β**, **γ**, . . . (constants) and **φ**, **χ**, **ψ**, . . . (variables). These are to be deployed on the understanding that they may be used to represent *either* simple *or* complex sortal terms and quantifier expressions in natural language and that the boldface quantifiers used with them are to be given a *substitutional* interpretation. According to such an interpretation, for example, a formula of the form '$\exists\boldsymbol{\varphi}(\boldsymbol{\varphi}F^1)$' may be taken to be true just in case some formula of the form '$\boldsymbol{\alpha}F^1$' is true. Now, the reasons which led us, a moment ago, to endorse principle SL6 evidently lead us correspondingly to endorse the following principle, expressed in the new notation:

SL7. $xF^1 \rightarrow \exists\boldsymbol{\varphi}(x/\boldsymbol{\varphi} \ \& \ \boldsymbol{\varphi}F^1)$

Thus, if we let 'xF^1' represent 'x is (dispositionally) white' and suppose this to be true, the right-hand side of SL7 represents a truth in virtue of the truth of some sentence of the form '$x/\boldsymbol{\alpha} \ \& \ \boldsymbol{\alpha}F^1$'. The latter sentence, as we have just seen, could be one such as 'x is a raven which is G and ravens which are G are white', where 'G' expresses some genetic condition explaining albinism in ravens. SL7, then, is the equivalent of SL6, but expressed more compactly with the aid of the new-style sortal symbols and quantifiers. And, of course, SL7 – apart from the fact that it is not a biconditional – differs *formally* from SL2 only in its deployment of these new-style symbols. What we are now looking for, then, is a way of modifying the right-hand side of SL7 so as to turn it into a valid *biconditional*.

The biconditional principle that we are looking for is, I suggest, the following:

SL8. $xF^1 \leftrightarrow \exists\varphi(x/\varphi \, \& \, \varphi F^1 \, \& \, \forall\chi((x/\chi \, \& \, \chi/\varphi) \rightarrow \chi F^1))$

The rationale behind this principle can be illustrated, once more, using our raven example. Suppose that Nipper is a raven which is G and that ravens which are G are white, where 'G' again expresses some genetic condition explaining albinism in ravens. As we saw earlier, it doesn't necessarily follow that *Nipper* is white by disposition, because Nipper might be an *abnormal* example of a raven which is G, being one that possesses the genetic condition in question and yet, on account of some abnormality in the functioning of the genetic mechanism involved, has plumage that is *not* white. What the additional conjunct on the right-hand side of SL8 serves to do, in effect, is to exclude this kind of possibility, by implying – in terms of our illustrative example – that Nipper belongs to *no* non-white 'sub-sort' of ravens which are G.[9] According to SL8, if this further requirement is satisfied in the case of Nipper, then Nipper is white by disposition.

It is hard to see how this proposal could meet with any serious objection. For if *every* 'sub-sort' of ravens which are G to which Nipper belongs is one that is white and yet Nipper itself is *not* white but, say, green by disposition, then the implication must be that Nipper's greenness is a *purely* idiosyncratic disposition which has no explanation in terms of the truth of any nomic generalization applying to Nipper. But, I suggest, the notion that there could be such purely idiosyncratic dispositions is scarcely intelligible. It would imply that two distinct individuals could belong to exactly the same 'sub-sorts' of a certain natural kind and yet differ in respect of their possession of a certain disposition.

I am by no means denying, of course, that two different individuals of the same natural kind – two individual *ravens*, for instance – may indeed differ in respect of some of their dispositions. After all, Nipper, we suppose, is *white* by disposition whereas 'normal' ravens are *black*. But this difference, I claim, is still to be explained in terms of natural laws governing the raven kind. Amongst the laws in question is the law that ravens which are G are white. *All* ravens are governed by this law, but *normal* ravens are not white because they are *not* ravens which are G. A raven with a *purely idiosyncratic* disposition to be white would be one belonging to *no* 'sub-sort' of ravens which are white, unlike an albino raven. Thus there

---

[9]   I place 'sub-sort' in scare quotes here as a reminder that we are not talking about an individual's belonging to a genuine *sort* or *kind* of ravens, but rather about the applicability to an individual of a *complex sortal term* of the form '(a) raven which is G and H'.

could not, even in principle, be a lawlike explanation of this raven's sup-posed disposition, which would accordingly have to be a kind of miracle. It is preferable to conclude, I suggest, that SL8 is indeed a correct principle connecting an individual's dispositions with laws governing the natural kind to which it belongs.[10]

On the Identity of Sorts

One remaining question that I have not yet properly addressed is this: how are we to ascertain that given sortal term in a natural language really is semantically simple rather than complex? There is no point here, I believe, in simply appealing to 'linguistic intuition', whatever exactly that might be. This is the drawback of the test for semantic complexity described at the outset of the first section of the present chapter. We could no doubt find some people who, on the basis of such 'intuition', would urge that 'ice' *is* synonymous with 'frozen water' and for that reason is semantically com-plex, but we are equally likely to find other people who would just as strongly deny this. In any case, I am not really interested in the question of whether a given sortal term in a natural language is *regarded by speakers of that language* as semantically simple or complex – a matter on which their 'linguistic intuitions' might indeed have some bearing. Rather, I am inter-ested in the question of whether a given sortal term *ought* to be regarded as semantically simple or complex.

As I see it, the answer to this question ultimately turns on whether there *exists*, in fact, a distinct *sort* or *kind* of things or stuff which this sortal term may appropriately be taken to designate or denote – that is, of which it may be held to be a *name*. Thus, I would claim that 'ice' should *not* be regarded as designating a distinct kind of stuff and hence cannot be semantically simple, whereas 'heavy water' *should* be so regarded and there-fore *is* semantically simple. What motivates such claims on my part is not mere linguistic intuition but, at least in part, *scientific evidence*. Thus, for example, in scientific ignorance one might have supposed that 'tadpole' denotes a distinct kind of living creature. It is biological science, however, not linguistic intuition, which tells us that tadpoles are just *young frogs*.

[10]   To set the record straight, it is worth mentioning here that certain published criticisms of the treatment of dispositions in my *The Four-Category Ontology* fail to take into account the considerations that I have just discussed, although they were also discussed in the final chapter of *Kinds of Being*, the predecessor of the present book. I mentioned in *The Four-Category Ontology* (p. 127) that I was ignoring these complications for the purposes of my treatment of dispositions there, but in retrospect I now think that I should have included some discus-sion of them, if only to deflect these misconceived criticisms.

Equally, it is chemical science which tells us that ice is just *frozen water*. It is to the philosophy of science, then, that we must look for any credible account of the principles capable of warranting our judgements concerning the existence of and distinctions between sorts or kinds of things, at least within the natural world.

By appeal to what criteria, then, does science – in the broadest sense of that term – distinguish between sorts or kinds of things? Why, for instance, are tadpoles and caterpillars *not* thought to be distinct kinds of creatures, nor ice a distinct kind of material stuff? Part of the answer, no doubt, lies in the fact that science (or *modern* science, at least) embodies a general antipathy towards the general notion of *transubstantiation* – to the notion, that is, that one sort or kind of substance can be transformed or transmuted into another, in the way that alchemists thought that base metals could be turned into gold. Ice regularly changes into liquid water and tadpoles into adult frogs, which creates a *prima facie* presumption, in each case, in favour of these being things of the *same* kind, differing from each other merely in *phase*.

Here it might be objected that a quantity of heavy water will – let us suppose – *eventually* turn into ordinary water through the gradual decay of its deuterium atoms: and yet we should not on that account be persuaded to regard 'heavy water' as being, in Wiggins's terminology, a *phased* sortal.[11] Nor will it do to reply simply by pointing out that the change from ice to liquid water is a *naturally reversible* one, whereas the one from heavy water to ordinary water would not be. For natural irreversibility is not held to count against the change from tadpole to adult frog being merely one of phase.

At this point, it may be tempting to appeal to a theory of 'scientific essence'. Thus, it may be urged that it is part of the *essence* of ordinary water to be constituted by hydrogen and oxygen atoms in a ratio of two to one and, similarly, part of the *essence* of frogs to possess a certain genetic 'blueprint'. And this, it may be supposed, is ultimately why heavy water is *not* just a phase of ordinary water, in the way that ordinary ice is, and equally why a tadpole *is* just a phase of a frog. It is so precisely because tadpoles and adult frogs have the same genetic blueprint, whereas heavy water and ordinary water do not have the same atomic constitution. However, saying this has more the air of re-labelling the problem than genuinely solving it. For, of course, it immediately prompts the further question of what warrants the selection of this or that 'scientific' feature as belonging to the 'essence' of a given sort or kind of things or stuff. Far

[11] In point of fact, deuterium is a stable isotope of hydrogen, although its heavier isotope tritium is not. So called *tritiated* water is, consequently, unstable, unlike heavy water. However, this complication need not detain us for the purpose of the argument that is being developed in the main text.

from its being the case that the sameness of their genetic blueprint explains why tadpoles and frogs should be regarded as 'consubstantial' – that is, as belonging to the same substantial sort or kind – it would appear, on the contrary, that it is only *because* they are deemed to be consubstantial that their sameness of genetic blueprint can at all plausibly be regarded as 'essential' to them. If we were to discover that tadpoles undergo extensive genetic changes upon turning into adult frogs, this would not, I think, persuade us that tadpoles and frogs are *not* after all creatures of the same kind. It would only persuade us that possessing a certain genetic structure is not in fact essential to a creature of this kind.

I am not implying here that *all* talk of 'scientific essences' in the manner made famous by Kripke and Putnam is perfectly idle. I am merely saying that I doubt whether talk in these terms can have any very fundamental role to play in an account of how we can or should identify and distinguish between sorts or kinds of natural 'substances'.[12] In this respect, I am to some extent in sympathy with Locke, who likewise thought that we cannot be supposed to rank things into sorts or kinds primarily on the basis of what he called their 'real essences'.[13] Where I am in disagreement with Locke is in believing, unlike him, that our distinctions between sorts of substances are not purely the workmanship of the understanding, but often reflect real boundaries in nature. Having said this, I can still concede that reference to a thing's scientific or 'real' essence may have a role to play in explaining *why* a thing of its kind undergoes a change from one phase to another. For example, it is to the frog's genetic blueprint that we look for an explanation of its development from the larval to the adult phase. All that I am denying is that reference to such an 'essence' can explain our original decision to interpret a given transformation as being one between phases of the same substance, since it is only subject to such a decision *being made* that the feature in question can be regarded as 'essential' in the first place. The criteria of sortal identity and distinctness that we seek must, I believe, be ones which principally find their application at the *macroscopic, observable* level, at least in the case of familiar, non-theoretical objects such as whole organisms and quantities of gross material stuffs, such as water and gold.

---

[12]   I say more about this in my 'Two Notions of Being: Entity and Essence', in Robin Le Poidevin (ed.), *Being: Developments in Contemporary Metaphysics* (Cambridge: Cambridge University Press, 2008). As will be clear from that paper, I certainly not an anti-essentialist, but favour a very different kind of essentialism from that associated with the work of Kripke and Putnam – one whose ultimate roots are Aristotelian rather than Lockean.

[13]   See John Locke, *An Enquiry Concerning Human Understanding*, ed. P. H. Nidditch (Oxford: Clarendon Press, 1975), III, VI, 13.

Earlier I remarked that it would not suffice to explain why we regard the change from ice to liquid water as being merely one of *phase* simply by pointing out that it is *naturally reversible*, since we deem this irrelevant to the case of tadpoles and adult frogs. However, the lesson, I believe, is not to dismiss the point about reversibility as a red herring, but rather to recognize that criteria of sortal identity and distinctness are *category-relative*. That is to say, the types of consideration which bear upon questions of 'consubstantiation' in the case, say, of *kinds of material stuff*, such as water and gold, may be quite different from those that are relevant in the case of *kinds of living creature*. This should hardly surprise us, since we are already familiar with the idea that different criteria of identity govern *individuals* of these very different kinds.

That reversibility of phase changes *is* generally demanded in the case of kinds belonging to the first of these two categories – kinds of material stuff – seems to be quite well attested. This partly explains, for instance, why we regard the change of paper into ash through combustion as a genuine substantial change rather than a mere phase change. Another example of a criterion of sortal distinctness which is quite evidently category-relative is the principle of *interbreedability* for conspecific animals, which indeed applies only to those kinds of animal which reproduce sexually.

Now, in view of this category-relativity of criteria of sortal identity and distinctness, it would, I think, be fruitless for me to attempt to draw up a complete inventory of such criteria. What is important, however, is that we should acknowledge the subtle interplay of empirical scientific considerations and *a priori* metaphysical considerations in the genesis of these criteria. We have already noted some of the scientific considerations that are operative in this regard, so it worth saying a little more now about some of the metaphysical ones.

It seems clear that our criteria of sortal identity and distinctness are not shaped *purely* by empirical scientific evidence, since such evidence can only be brought to bear appropriately on questions of sortal identity and distinctness in the light of general methodological and metaphysical principles which regulate and guide scientific investigation and theory-construction. One such principle already mentioned earlier is the presumption against transubstantiation, which is effectively a principle of ontological parsimony. We should not multiply *kinds* of substance beyond necessity and hence we should prefer, other things being equal, to explain a physical transformation as being a change of phase rather than of substance. But, of course, other things are *not* always equal. This is why we should reject any hyper-rationalistic vision of physical substance as being essentially *one*, with the transformation of paper into ash, say, being conceived as the change of 'prime matter' from one of its phases into another. The point is that considerations of ontological parsimony have to be weighed against – amongst other things – considerations of *nomological explicability*.

Different sorts or kinds of substance are governed by different *laws* – and such differences help us, indeed, to distinguish between them. But, of course, they cannot do this independently of other criteria of sortal distinctness. After all, solely on the basis of the laws ostensibly governing their appearance and behaviour, one might have supposed tadpoles and frogs to be as specifically different as we now take dolphins and horses to be. Prior to the identification of tadpoles with frogs in their larval phase, one would have accepted as true the simple nomic generalizations 'Tadpoles possess tails' and 'Frogs lack tails', which jointly entail the *non*-identity of tadpoles with frogs. Their subsequent identification requires us to replace these simple laws with more complex ones – 'Frogs in their larval phase possess tails' and 'Adult frogs lack tails' – but what is lost in terms of greater nomological complexity is more than compensated for by ontological economy and nomological integration.

However, there is a limit to how far this process of nomological integration can reasonably be expected to go. There certainly appear to be laws of biology, for instance, which are not reducible to any laws of chemistry or physics and so for this reason alone, even if for no other, it seems that we must recognize the reality of biological sorts or kinds in addition to that of chemical and physical ones. The answer, then, which begins to emerge to the question 'What *sorts* of things are there?' is one that is broadly realist without being naïvely so. Science *can* help us to 'carve nature at the joints', in the sense that it can motivate the recognition of sortal distinctions which are plainly not just the offspring of linguistic or cultural convention, nor merely the tools of pragmatic convenience. But we should never lose sight of the fact that science itself is guided by architectonic and methodological principles whose application often involves weighing different theoretical demands against one another. In *some* cases, the consequence may be that there is no clearly preferred solution to a boundary dispute between species. But it would be a mistake to magnify the importance and frequency of such cases, making them an excuse for a more general scepticism concerning the mind-independent reality of sortal distinctions. There really *are* different sorts or kinds of things in the natural world, quite independently of our classificatory schemes, and it is reasonable to suppose that *sometimes* – perhaps even *very often* – we succeed in identifying those sorts or kinds correctly.[14] That, I believe, is enough to vindicate the approach to laws of nature which is taken in this study.

---

[14]   I say more about these and related matters in my *The Possibility of Metaphysics: Substance, Identity, and Time* (Oxford: Clarendon Press, 1998), Chapter 8.

Bibliography

Alexander, I., ' "If" and Quantification', *Analysis* 45 (1985), pp. 186–90.

Angelelli, I., *Studies on Frege and Traditional Philosophy* (Dordrecht: Kluwer, 1967).

Aristotle, *Categories and De Interpretatione*, trans. J. L. Ackrill (Oxford: Clarendon Press, 1963).

Aristotle, *Metaphysics*, in W. D. Ross (ed.), *The Works of Aristotle Translated into English, Volume VIII: Metaphysica*, 2nd edn (Oxford: Clarendon Press, 1928).

Ayer, A. J., *Probability and Evidence* (London: Macmillan, 1972).

Baker, L. R., *Persons and Bodies: A Constitution View* (Cambridge: Cambridge University Press, 2000).

Barnes, J., *The Presocratic Philosophers*, 2nd edn (London: Routledge and Kegan Paul, 1982).

Bennett, J. and Alston, W., 'Identity and Cardinality: Geach and Frege', *Philosophical Review* 93 (1984), pp. 553–67.

Berkeley, G., *Philosophical Works*, ed. M. R. Ayers (London: Dent, 1975).

Boolos, G., 'Nominalist Platonism', *Philosophical Review* 94 (1985), pp. 327–44.

Boolos, G., 'To Be Is to Be a Value of a Variable (or to Be Some Values of Some Variables)', *Journal of Philosophy* 81 (1984), pp. 430–49.

Bower, T., *The Perceptual World of the Child* (London: Fontana, 1977).

Brody, B. A., *Identity and Essence* (Princeton, NJ: Princeton University Press, 1980).

Butler, J., 'Of Personal Identity', in John Perry (ed.), *Personal Identity* (Berkeley, CA: University of California Press, 1975).

Campbell, K., *Abstract Particulars* (Oxford: Blackwell, 1990).

Cartwright, H. M., 'Quantities', *Philosophical Review* 79 (1970), pp. 25–42.

Cartwright, N., *How the Laws of Physics Lie* (Oxford: Oxford University Press, 1983).

Cartwright, N., *The Dappled World: A Study of the Boundaries of Science* (Cambridge: Cambridge University Press, 1999).

Davidson, D., 'Mental Events', in his *Essays on Actions and Events* (Oxford: Clarendon Press, 1980).

Davidson, D., 'The Individuation of Events', in his *Essays on Actions and Events* (Oxford: Clarendon Press, 1980).

Doepke, F. C., 'Spatially Coinciding Objects', *Ratio* 24 (1982), pp. 45–60.

Dudman, V. H., 'Parsing "If"-Sentences', *Analysis* 44 (1984), pp. 145–53.

Dummett, M., *Frege: Philosophy of Language*, 2nd edn (London: Duckworth, 1981).

Dummett, M., *The Interpretation of Frege's Philosophy* (London: Duckworth, 1981).

Evans, G., 'Pronouns, Quantifiers and Relative Clauses (II)', in his *Collected Papers* (Oxford: Clarendon Press, 1985).

Fine, K., 'Mixing Matters', in David S. Oderberg (ed.), *Form and Matter: Themes in Contemporary Metaphysics* (Oxford: Blackwell, 1999).

Foster, J., 'Induction, Explanation and Natural Necessity', *Proceedings of the Aristotelian Society* 83 (1982/3), pp. 87–101.

Foster, J., *The Divine Lawmaker: Lectures on Induction, Laws of Nature, and the Existence of God* (Oxford: Clarendon Press, 2004).

Frege, G., *The Foundations of Arithmetic*, trans. J. L. Austin (Oxford: Blackwell, 1953).

Frege, G., *Translations from the Philosophical Writings of Gottlob Frege*, 2nd edn, ed. P. T. Geach and M. Black (Oxford: Blackwell, 1960).

Geach, P. T., 'Existential or Particular Quantifier', in P. Weingartner and E. Morscher (eds), *Ontology and Logic* (Berlin: Duncker & Humblot, 1979).

Geach, P. T., 'Quine's Syntactical Insights', in his *Logic Matters* (Oxford: Blackwell, 1972).

Geach, P. T., *Reference and Generality*, 2nd edn (Ithaca, NY: Cornell University Press, 1968).

Geach, P. T., *Reference and Generality*, 3rd edn (Ithaca, NY: Cornell University Press, 1980).

Geach, P. T., 'Reply to Lowe's Reply', *Analysis* 42 (1982), p. 32.

Goodman, N., *The Structure of Appearance*, 3rd edn (Dordrecht: D. Reidel, 1977).

Griffin, N., *Relative Identity* (Oxford: Clarendon Press, 1977).

Gupta, A., *The Logic of Common Nouns* (New Haven, CT: Yale University Press, 1980).

Hanson, N. R., *Patterns of Discovery* (Cambridge: Cambridge University Press, 1958).

Heil, J., *From an Ontological Point of View* (Oxford: Clarendon Press, 2003).

Hempel, C. G., 'Studies in the Logic of Confirmation', in his *Aspects of Scientific Explanation* (New York: Free Press, 1965).

Higgenbotham, J., 'Indefiniteness and Predication', in E. J. Reuland and A. G. B. ter Meulen (eds), *The Representation of Indefiniteness* (Cambridge, MA: MIT Press, 1987).

Hirsch, E., *The Concept of Identity* (Oxford: Oxford University Press, 1982).

Hull, D. L., 'Are Species Really Individuals?', *Systematic Zoology* 25 (1976), pp. 174–91.

Hume, D., *A Treatise of Human Nature*, ed. L. A. Selby-Bigge and P. H. Nidditch (Oxford: Clarendon Press, 1978).

Johnson, W. E., *Logic, Part I* (Cambridge: Cambridge University Press, 1921).

Kirk, G. S. and Raven, J. E., *The Presocratic Philosophers* (Cambridge: Cambridge University Press, 1957).

Kirk, R., 'From Physical Explicability to Full-Blooded Materialism', *Philosophical Quarterly* 29 (1979), pp. 229–37.

Kneale, W., *Probability and Induction* (Oxford: Clarendon Press, 1949).

Kripke, S. A., *Naming and Necessity* (Oxford: Blackwell, 1980).

Leibniz, G. W., *Discourse on Metaphysics*, trans. P. G. Lucas and L. Grant (Manchester: Manchester University Press, 1961).

Leonard, H. S. and Goodman, N., 'The Calculus of Individuals and its Uses', *Journal of Symbolic Logic* 5 (1940), pp. 45–55.

Lewis, D., *Counterfactuals* (Oxford: Blackwell, 1973).

Lewis, D., 'Many, but Almost One', in John Bacon, Keith Campbell and Lloyd Reinhardt (eds), *Ontology, Causality and Mind: Essays in Honour of D. M. Armstrong* (Cambridge: Cambridge University Press, 1993).

Lewis, D., *On the Plurality of Worlds* (Oxford: Blackwell, 1986).

Lewis, D., *Parts of Classes* (Oxford: Blackwell, 1991).

Lewis, D., 'Survival and Identity', in his *Philosophical Papers, Volume I* (Oxford: Oxford University Press, 1983).

Locke, J., *An Essay Concerning Human Understanding*, ed. P. H. Nidditch (Oxford: Clarendon Press, 1975).

Lowe, E. J., 'A Problem for A Posteriori Essentialism Concerning Natural Kinds', *Analysis* 67 (2007), pp. 286–92.

Lowe, E. J., *A Survey of Metaphysics* (Oxford: Oxford University Press, 2002).

Lowe, E. J., 'Against an Argument for Token Identity', *Mind* 90 (1981), pp. 120–1.

Lowe, E. J., *An Introduction to the Philosophy of Mind* (Cambridge: Cambridge University Press, 2000).

Lowe, E. J., 'Can the Self Disintegrate? Personal Identity, Psychopathology, and Disunities of Consciousness', in J. Hughes, S. Louw, and S. Sabat (eds), *Dementia: Mind, Meaning, and the Person* (Oxford: Oxford University Press, 2006).

Lowe, E. J., 'Coinciding Objects: In Defence of the "Standard Account"', *Analysis* 55 (1995), pp. 171–8.

Lowe, E. J., 'Identity, Composition, and the Simplicity of the Self', in Kevin Corcoran (ed.), *Soul, Body, and Survival: Essays on the Metaphysics of Human Persons* (Ithaca, NY: Cornell University Press, 2001).

Lowe, E. J., 'Identity, Vagueness, and Modality', in José L. Bermúdez (ed.), *Thought, Reference, and Experience: Themes from the Philosophy of Gareth Evans* (Oxford: Oxford University Press, 2005).

Lowe, E. J., 'Impredicative Identity Criteria and Davidson's Criterion of Event Identity', *Analysis* 49 (1989), pp. 178–81.

Lowe, E. J., 'Is Conceptualist Realism a Stable Position?', *Philosophy and Phenomenological Research* 71 (2006), pp. 456–61.

Lowe, E. J., *Kinds of Being* (Oxford: Blackwell, Aristotelian Society monograph series, 1989).

Lowe, E. J., 'Locke, Martin, and Substance', *Philosophical Quarterly* 50 (2000), pp. 499–514.

Lowe, E. J., 'Miracles and Laws of Nature', *Religious Studies* 23 (1987), pp. 263–78.

Lowe, E. J., 'Objects and Criteria of Identity', in Bob Hale and Crispin Wright (eds), *A Companion to the Philosophy of Language* (Oxford: Blackwell, 1997).

Lowe, E. J., 'On the Alleged Necessity of True Identity Statements', *Mind* 91 (1982), pp. 579–84.

Lowe, E. J., 'On the Identity of Artifacts', *Journal of Philosophy* 80 (1983), pp. 220–32.

Lowe, E. J., *Personal Agency: The Metaphysics of Mind and Action* (Oxford: Oxford University Press, 2008).

Lowe, E. J., 'Primitive Substances', *Philosophy and Phenomenological Research* 54 (1994), pp. 531–52.

Lowe, E. J., Review of David Wiggins's *Sameness and Substance Renewed*, *Mind* 112 (2003), pp. 816–20.

Lowe, E. J., 'Sortals and the Individuation of Objects', *Mind and Language* 22 (2007), 514–33.

Lowe, E. J., *Subjects of Experience* (Cambridge: Cambridge University Press, 1996).

Lowe, E. J., 'Substance', in G. H. R. Parkinson (ed.), *An Encyclopaedia of Philosophy* (London: Routledge, 1988).

Lowe, E. J., 'Substantial Change and Spatiotemporal Coincidence', *Ratio* 16 (2003), pp. 140–60.

Lowe, E. J., *The Four-Category Ontology: A Metaphysical Foundation for Natural Science* (Oxford: Clarendon Press, 2006).

Lowe, E. J., 'The Metaphysics of Abstract Objects', *Journal of Philosophy* 92 (1995), pp. 509–24.

Lowe, E. J., *The Possibility of Metaphysics: Substance, Identity, and Time* (Oxford: Clarendon Press, 1998).

Lowe, E. J., 'The Problem of the Many and the Vagueness of Constitution', *Analysis* 55 (1995), pp. 179–82.

Lowe, E. J., 'Two Notions of Being: Entity and Essence', in Robin Le Poidevin (ed.), *Being: Developments in Contemporary Metaphysics* (Cambridge: Cambridge University Press, 2008).

Lowe, E. J., 'What Is a Criterion of Identity?', *Philosophical Quarterly* 39 (1989), pp. 1–21.

Lowe, E. J., 'What *Is* the "Problem of Induction"?', *Philosophy* 62 (1987), pp. 325–40.

Maddy, P., *Realism in Mathematics* (Oxford: Clarendon Press, 1990).

Madell, G., *The Identity of the Self* (Edinburgh: Edinburgh University Press, 1981).

Martin, C. B., 'Dispositions and Conditionals', *Philosophical Quarterly* 44 (1994), pp. 1–8.

Mates, B., *Elementary Logic*, 2nd edn (New York: Oxford University Press, 1972).

McGinn, C., 'Anomalous Monism and Kripke's Cartesian Intuitions', *Analysis* 37 (1977), pp. 78–80.

McGinn, C., Review of Sydney Shoemaker's *Identity, Cause, and Mind*, *Journal of Philosophy* 84 (1987), pp. 227–32.

McGinn, C., *The Character of Mind* (Oxford: Oxford University Press, 1982).

Mellor, D. H., *Real Time* (Cambridge: Cambridge University Press, 1981).

Mellor, D. H., *Real Time II* (London: Routledge, 1998).

Nagel, T., 'Brain Bisection and the Unity of Consciousness', in his *Mortal Questions* (Cambridge: Cambridge University Press, 1979).

Noonan, H. W., *Objects and Identity* (The Hague: Martinus Nijhoff, 1980).

Olson, E. T., *The Human Animal: Personal Identity without Psychology* (New York: Oxford University Press, 1997).

Parfit, D., *Reasons and Persons* (Oxford: Clarendon Press, 1984).

Peacocke, C., *Holistic Explanation* (Oxford: Clarendon Press, 1979).

Penelhum, T., *Survival and Disembodied Existence* (London: Routledge and Kegan Paul, 1970).

Perry, J., 'Personal Identity, Memory, and the Problem of Circularity', in J. Perry (ed.), *Personal Identity* (Berkeley, CA: University of California Press, 1975).

Perry, J. (ed.), *Personal Identity* (Berkeley, CA: University of California Press, 1975).

Popper, K. R., *The Logic of Scientific Discovery* (London: Hutchinson, 1968).

Popper, K. R. and Eccles, J. C., *The Self and its Brain* (London: Springer Verlag, 1977).

Prior, A. N., *Objects of Thought* (Oxford: Clarendon Press, 1971).

Putnam, H., 'The Meaning of "Meaning"', in his *Mind, Language and Reality* (Cambridge: Cambridge University Press, 1975).

Quine, W. V., 'A Logistical Approach to the Ontological Problem', in his *The Ways of Paradox and Other Essays* (Cambridge, MA: Harvard University Press, 1976).

Quine, W. V., 'Identity, Ostension and Hypostasis', in his *From a Logical Point of View*, 2nd edn (Cambridge, MA: Harvard University Press, 1961).

Quine, W. V., 'Natural Kinds', in his *Ontological Relativity and Other Essays* (New York: Columbia University Press, 1969).

Quine, W. V., 'On What There Is', in his *From a Logical Point of View*, 2nd edn (Cambridge, MA: Harvard University Press, 1961).

Quine, W. V., *The Roots of Reference* (La Salle, IL: Open Court, 1974).

Quine, W. V., *Word and Object* (Cambridge, MA: MIT Press, 1960).

Reid, T., 'Of Mr. Locke's Account of Our Personal Identity', in J. Perry (ed.), *Personal Identity* (Berkeley, CA: University of California Press, 1975).

Rescher, N., *A Theory of Possibility* (Oxford: Blackwell, 1975).

Resnik, M. D., 'Second-Order Logic Still Wild', *Journal of Philosophy* 85 (1988), pp. 75–87.

Russell, B., 'On Denoting', in his *Logic and Knowledge: Essays 1901–1950*, ed. R. C. Marsh (London: George Allen and Unwin, 1956).

Schlesinger, G., 'Natural Kinds', in R. S. Cohen and M. W. Wartofsky (eds), *Boston Studies in the Philosophy of Science*, Volume III (Dordrecht: D. Reidel, 1967).

Searle, J. R., 'Proper Names', *Mind* 67 (1958), pp. 166–73.

Sharvy, R., 'A More General Theory of Definite Descriptions', *Philosophical Review* 89 (1980), pp. 607–24.

Sharvy, R., 'Aristotle on Mixtures', *Journal of Philosophy* 80 (1983), pp. 439–57.

Shoemaker, S., 'Identity, Properties, and Causality', in his *Identity, Cause and Mind* (Cambridge: Cambridge University Press, 1984).

Sider, T., *Four-Dimensionalism: An Ontology of Persistence and Time* (Oxford: Clarendon Press, 2001).

Simons, P., *Parts: A Study in Ontology* (Oxford: Clarendon Press, 1987).

Stevenson, L., 'The Absoluteness of Identity', *Philosophical Books* 23 (1982), pp. 1–7.

Strawson, P. F., 'Entity and Identity', in his *Entity and Identity and Other Essays* (Oxford: Clarendon Press, 1997).

Strawson, P. F., *Individuals: An Essay in Descriptive Metaphysics* (London: Methuen, 1959).

Suppes, P., *Axiomatic Set Theory* (New York: Dover, 1972).

Tarski, A., *Logic, Semantics and Metamathematics*, 2nd edn (Indianapolis, IN: Hackett Publishing Company, 1983).

Tiles, J. E., 'Davidson's Criterion of Event Identity', *Analysis* 36 (1976), pp. 185–7.

van Inwagen, P., 'Can Mereological Sums Change Their Parts?', *Journal of Philosophy* 103 (2006), pp. 614–30.

van Inwagen, P., *Material Beings* (Ithaca, NY: Cornell University Press, 1990).

van Inwagen, P., 'The Doctrine of Arbitrary Undetached Parts', *Pacific Philosophical Quarterly* 62 (1981), pp. 123–37.

van Inwagen, P., 'The Number of Things', *Philosophical Issues* 12 (2002), pp. 176–96.

Whitehead, A. N., and Russell, B., *Principia Mathematica*, 2nd edn (Cambridge: Cambridge University Press, 1927).

Wiggins, D., 'Mereological Essentialism: Asymmetrical Essential Dependence and the Nature of Continuants', in Ernest Sosa (ed.), *Essays on the Philosophy of Roderick M. Chisholm* (Amsterdam: Rodopi, 1979).

Wiggins, D., *Sameness and Substance* (Oxford: Blackwell, 1980).

Wiggins, D., *Sameness and Substance Renewed* (Cambridge: Cambridge University Press, 2001).

Wilkes, K. V., 'Multiple Personality and Personal Identity', *British Journal for the Philosophy of Science* 32 (1981), pp. 331–48.

Williams, B., *Ethics and the Limits of Philosophy* (London: Fontana, 1985).

Wright, C., *Frege's Conception of Numbers as Objects* (Aberdeen: Aberdeen University Press, 1983).

Zemach, E. M., 'Schematic Objects and Relative Identity', *Noûs* 16 (1982), pp. 295–305.

Index